D0877779

The Politics of Child Support in America

Political observers have long struggled to understand how new ideas are placed on the public agenda. Oftentimes, their accounts have focused on the pivotal group and/or individuals who manage to emerge from the public at large and "get things done." In their studies, most social scientists have relied on biographical sketches and intensive case studies to explore the intricacies of innovation. Researchers have had much more difficulty, however, in moving from these individual success stories to more generalizable theories of entrepreneurship.

This book builds such a theory by focusing on the critical issue of child support enforcement in the United States. Beginning in the nineteenth century, this book tracks the evolution of multiple sets of political entrepreneurs as they grapple with the child support problem: charity workers and local law enforcement in the nineteenth and early twentieth centuries, social workers from the early twentieth century through the 1960s, conservatives during the 1970s, women's groups and women legislators in the 1980s, and fathers' rights groups in the 1990s and beyond. In detailing their efforts, this book borrows methodological tools from both political science and economics in order to highlight the pivotal stages in the innovation process.

Jocelyn Elise Crowley is Assistant Professor of Public Policy at the Edward J. Bloustein School of Planning and Public Policy at Rutgers, The State University of New Jersey. She has been previously published in such prestigious journals as the *American Journal of Political Science*, *Legislative Studies Quarterly*, the *Justice System Journal*, the *Eastern Economic Journal*, *Publius: The Journal of Federalism*, and *Social Science Quarterly*.

The Politics of Child Support in America

JOCELYN ELISE CROWLEY

Rutgers, The State University of New Jersey

CAMBRIDGE
UNIVERSITY PRESS

University Printing House, Cambridge CB2 8BS, United Kingdom

One Liberty Plaza, 20th Floor, New York, NY 10006, USA

477 Williamstown Road, Port Melbourne, VIC 3207, Australia

314-321, 3rd Floor, Plot 3, Splendor Forum, Jasola District Centre, New Delhi - 110025, India

79 Anson Road, #06-04/06, Singapore 079906

Cambridge University Press is part of the University of Cambridge.

It furthers the University's mission by disseminating knowledge in the pursuit of education, learning and research at the highest international levels of excellence.

www.cambridge.org
Information on this title: www.cambridge.org/9780521535113

First published 2003

A catalogue record for this publication is available from the British Library

Library of Congress Cataloging in Publication data
Crowley, Jocelyn Elise, 1970–
The politics of child support in America / Jocelyn Elise Crowley.
    p. cm.
Includes bibliographical references and index.
ISBN 0-521-82460-5 (hc.) – ISBN 0-521-53511-5 (pbk.)
1. Child support – United States.   2. Child support – Government policy – United States.   I. Title.
HV741.C76 2003
346.01′72′0973–dc21   2002045513

ISBN 978-0-521-53511-3 Paperback

For Alan

Contents

Foreword

The "feminization" of poverty continues to grow at a rapid pace in America, and one of the main drivers of this growth is the lack of adequate child support and child support enforcement. Any American who buys a car on credit and moves across the state line knows he or she will still have to make the payments. We have made national enforcement of commercial credit laws very efficient. Not so with family credit. The federal government has worked to streamline the process, but there are still many glitches. There is also the issue that child support ordered by the court is often totally inadequate. Going back to my car payments comparison, many people's child support payments are less than their car payments. Do we care more about our cars than our children?

This book identifies the leaders in the child support issue arena. We should all be leaders in the cause, because children are our future. Even if a perfect child support system were in place, single parents would face serious difficulties supporting their families. It is easier to work on making the child support system fairer, more equitable, and more efficient than it is to tackle all the other imbalances a single parent faces.

So launch into this book and figure out as you read what all of us can do to solve the remaining problems. We thank all of those who have been working out there, and we know no one can do it alone. We are much smarter and more effective when we work together. Too many people say parents shouldn't be divorced and walk away. Well, if they are divorced, where does that leave the children? The public doesn't want to support them, so we should at least insist that the parents of a failed marriage do what they can to support their children economically. This is not totally adequate, but it may be the best result we can achieve.

Patricia Schroeder (former U.S. representative from Colorado)
President and CEO, Association of American Publishers

Acknowledgments

They say people write most passionately and honestly about the issues that they have faced in their own lives. I know all about parents breaking up, and I know all about how divorce impacts children. I also know all about child support enforcement. I know about its strengths, its weaknesses, and its potential for making a difference. Indeed, I am not alone. Many people have personal tales to tell. This book fills these personal spaces and sometimes personal tragedies with historical meaning.

Throughout the years, I have had three academic homes in which the ideas behind this book have happily percolated. At Georgetown University, where I earned my master's degree in public policy in 1994, I began thinking about child support enforcement as an important public policy issue for the first time. At this critical juncture, I was lucky enough to have R. Kent Weaver as a professor. He nurtured my interest in social policy in more ways than I can name. He was most influential, however, when he uttered seven key words that would shape my professional development – "Jocelyn, you should go get your Ph.D."

I then moved on to the Massachusetts Institute of Technology to earn my Ph.D. in political science. While in Cambridge, my ideas on child support would receive further nourishment through my interaction with both stellar faculty members and insightful colleagues. I would especially like to thank my dissertation committee, who pushed me in novel directions on this research. Charles Stewart III and Stephen Ansolabehere of MIT, as well as Theda Skocpol of Harvard University, provided enormous intellectual guidance when this project was in its early stages. Amy Black, Maryann Barakso, Miriam Murase, Anne Cammisa, Kira Sanbonmatsu,

Rachael Cobb, and Sue Crawford – all part of the Cambridge crew – deserve special thanks.

At long last, I am now teaching at Rutgers, The State University of New Jersey. Here once again I have cherished the intellectual environment I have needed to transform my ideas on the topic of child support enforcement, now fully formed, into a book. Spending the 2000–01 academic year attending weekly seminars at Rutgers' Institute for Women's Leadership focused my thinking on the book's remaining missing pieces. Outside of these seminars, Sue Carroll, Cynthia Daniels, Cliff Zukin, John Spry, and David Guston were particularly helpful in offering their encouragement to the project. In addition, I would like to thank Keri-Ann Eglentowicz, Amanda Smith, Molly Baab, and Devin Lush for their excellent research assistance. After spending far too many hours in the library hunting down materials, they still managed to maintain cheery dispositions. I would also like to thank the Rutgers University Research Council and the Edward J. Bloustein School of Planning and Public Policy at Rutgers University for their financial support of this project. Mary Jean Lush, Dee Bailey, and Ellen Oates provided me with excellent secretarial assistance.

There were also other critical people from a wide variety of academic and professional backgrounds who helped with the preparation of this book. The Gerald R. Ford Library, and especially Geir Gundersen, was most useful to me as I gathered materials for certain sections of the book. Paula Roberts at the Center for Law and Social Policy shared her expertise on the ever-changing face of child support law. Frank Baumgartner, Michael Mintrom, Irwin Garfinkel, Bill Gormley, and Jeff Milyo provided comments on this project at various stages and helped to clarify my thinking.

Several friends provided much-appreciated assistance at various stages of the project. My dear friend Theresa Luhm read through the entire manuscript and was brave enough to tell me when a section was not clear. Amy Schapiro and I exchanged "war stories" as we struggled to finish our respective manuscripts. All members of my family – including my mother, my grandparents, and M. B. Crowley – deserve special thanks for their patience and kindness. I also want to single out my sister, Dr. Monica Crowley, for her close reading of the final manuscript.

I would like to thank Lewis Bateman at Cambridge University Press for his excellent editorial assistance. Lauren Levin, also at Cambridge, amazed me with her consistently pleasant replies to my constant barrage of questions. Thanks also go to Russell Hahn for his meticulous copyediting. Two anonymous reviewers also provided insightful suggestions to improve the manuscript.

Finally, and most importantly, I would like to thank my husband, Alan Colmes, for his unwavering encouragement throughout the duration of this project. The manuscript is much stronger because of his unfailing support. This book is therefore dedicated to him with love.

The Limits of Studying Entrepreneurial Episodes

Americans love individual success stories, especially ones that have a major impact on public policy. The plot lines tend to be very similar. Insightful individuals perceive a problem that they believe the government can help to solve. They wage a long, many times painful campaign to bring about change. Usually there are clearly defined enemies: large corporations, loathsome criminals, corrupt politicians, and so forth. Yet, despite these formidable opponents, the champions of reform manage against all odds to defeat their opponents. When the issue is finally resolved, historians record how the domain of public policy was transformed forever because of their enterprising initiatives.

The emphasis on the crusade of the individual has also seeped into our attempt to map out entrepreneurial behavior in politics in a more formal sense. Social scientists have long struggled to understand how policies are placed on the public agenda. Oftentimes, their accounts have echoed those found in the popular media by focusing on the pivotal group or the unique individual who manages to emerge from the pack and "get things done." Much of this work has involved intensive case studies and biographical analyses, from which scholars have gleaned insight into the strategies of those individuals who rise above everyone else to solve a critical public problem. In sum, we know a lot about isolated actors and isolated incidents of change.[1]

---

[1] See, for example, Jameson Doig and Erwin C. Hargrove, eds. 1987. *Leadership and Innovation: A Biographic Perspective on Entrepreneurs in Government.* Baltimore: Johns Hopkins University Press; Richard F. Fenno. 1989. *The Making of a Senator: Dan Quayle.* Washington, DC: Congressional Quarterly; David E. Price. 1971. "Professionals and

But we need to know much more. The premise of this book is that we can more effectively increase our knowledge of the entrepreneurial process by focusing on the evolution of a single societal problem over time rather than on the individual or groups of individuals who seek to attack bits and pieces of the problem at any particular point in time. The reasoning is simple. When we focus on the individual, our scholarly interest remains parochial. Our research questions center on exploring how a particular group captures the public's attention, the methods used in translating their ideas into policy, and the ultimate impact of the ideas upon implementation.

Most importantly, by restricting our analysis to the actions of policy entrepreneurs at one particular point in time, we lose sight of the most important function of leaders in the public arena: *that of resource allocation in the long run.* A theory of innovation must be able to highlight the dynamism of this transformative process and can best be developed by examining a long-standing public problem. By definition, long-standing public problems do not respond to quick fixes, easy answers, or magical solutions. Rather than a single individual or group of policy entrepreneurs addressing the issue and then exiting the policy scene, then, a series of entrepreneurs is constantly involved in the process. Under one set of political circumstances, advocates from a certain political party, professional affiliation, or other type of advantageous position, evolve into powerful spokespeople for the specific cause under consideration. With all eyes focused on them, these entrepreneurs influence public policy by shaping the public discourse to match their view of the problem at hand. They are, in essence, successful at reallocating governmental resources away from traditional ways of conducting business and toward their own most preferred policy outcome.

With the passage of political time, new philosophies engage the public debate, different ideologies seize the attention of voters, and innovative perspectives come to define contemporary political culture. This changing environment provides the opportunity for *other* policy entrepreneurs to ascend in importance, overtake their opponents, and present *their* views of the problem at hand. In the end, if they are convincing, they can reallocate resources toward their preferred policy outcome. And, since most policy

'Entrepreneurs': Staff Orientations and Policy Making on Three Senate Committees." *Journal of Politics* 33(2): 548–574; Julian E. Zelizer. 1998. *Taxing America: Wilbur D. Mills, Congress, and the State, 1945–1975*. Cambridge: Cambridge University Press.

problems fail to achieve definitive resolution, this cycle is repeated time and time again.

Understanding the goal of resource allocation as *the* fundamental task of political entrepreneurs allows us to shift our attention away from the personal characteristics and tasks of the entrepreneur and to focus instead on the processes under which these cycles of change take place. We thus can reorient our research questions away from exploring the personal motivations of specific innovators and toward the entrepreneurial activity that occurs before they emerge on the scene of a particular problem and after they have disappeared. From this new, long-run perspective, the internal drive of the particular entrepreneur is less important than the challenges that all entrepreneurs must face in the political arena.[2]

This book examines this new view of entrepreneurship using the case of child support enforcement, one of the most fundamental social problems facing American society today. Scholars have consistently reported that the likelihood of a child growing up in poverty increases dramatically when the family unit is headed by a single parent, usually the mother.[3] In early American history, local charities and churches provided services to these fatherless families. Localized mothers' pension programs at the turn of the century also provided assistance. However, when community groups failed to respond to the massive economic dislocation created by the Great Depression, the federal government stepped in with the Aid to Dependent Children program (ADC) (later renamed the Aid to Families with Dependent Children program [AFDC], and in 1996 transformed once again into the Temporary Assistance for Needy Families program [TANF]). Begun in 1935, ADC provided welfare benefits to single-parent families – primarily widows – in economic need and represented a

---

[2] Recent work on the American presidency has moved in this direction as well. Compare Stephen Skowronek's 1993 work on patterns of historical change that influence presidential positioning (*The Politics Presidents Make: Leadership from John Adams to George Bush*. Cambridge: Belknap Press) to Benjamin Barber's 1972 psychological perspective on the presidency (*The Presidential Character: Predicting Performance in the White House*. Englewood Cliffs, NJ: Prentice Hall).

[3] Throughout this book, we will be considering the custodial parent to be the mother, usually the recipient of child support collections. The noncustodial parent will be the father, usually the payer of child support. The statistics warrant these generalizations. In the spring of 2000, 85 percent of all custodial parents were mothers, and only approximately 15 percent were fathers. In 1999, taking all families with an agreed-upon child support order in place, 90 percent of the recipients were custodial mothers. See Timothy Grall. 2002. "Custodial Mothers and Fathers and Their Child Support." Current Population Reports, series P60–217, United States Bureau of the Census.

monumental break with past, more localized types of assistance. When the client base began to tip away from widows toward divorced and never-married mothers, the Federal Child Support Enforcement Program was begun in 1975 in order to find and compel fathers to provide for their offspring.

Despite the introduction of a variety of new tools designed to improve support outcomes, program statistics demonstrate the problems inherent in ensuring that all nonmarital children have paternity established and that all noncustodial parents provide financial support for their children. Locating fathers of different socioeconomic backgrounds and then mandating that they pay has proved to be a difficult challenge. At the end of 2000, approximately 17 million families were enrolled in the child support program. Of these 17 million cases, only 61.5 percent had child support orders in place. Data reported at the end of 2000 indicate that out of $23 billion in current support due, the program collected only $13 billion, or 56 percent. Of the $84 billion still outstanding from previous years, only $6 billion, or 7 percent, was collected.[4]

But before we move into a discussion of the historical treatment of this issue in greater detail, we must first begin building a new toolbox for understanding the trajectory of all entrepreneurial systems using our new, long-run approach. In piecing together this toolbox, the disciplines of political science and economics have had a lot to say. Only recently, however, have they been talking to each other.

WHO ARE POLICY ENTREPRENEURS? ENTREPRENEURIAL MOVEMENTS AT WORK

A theory of policy entrepreneurship must take into account the diversity of actors who are involved in policy change over long periods of time. In fact, while individual stories tend to dominate what is presented to us in popular culture, the political science literature describing who these entrepreneurs are does not necessarily demand autonomous actors. Rather, instead of honing in on definable personality types, major theoretical breakthroughs in political science have tended to describe three entrepreneurial characteristics: *alertness*, *persistence*, and *rhetorical ingenuity*. Notably, each of these characteristics, as we will see, can be displayed by a wide variety of actors. That is, as long as they have these characteristics,

---

[4] See the 2001 *FY2000 Preliminary Data Preview Report*. Washington, DC: Office of Child Support Enforcement, pp. 1–5.

policy entrepreneurs can be politicians, interest groups, bureaucrats, parties, or ordinary citizens.

John Kingdon's work is responsible for our most comprehensive knowledge on the characteristics of policy leaders.[5] In Kingdon's view, there are numerous societal problems and potential solutions "floating around" at a given time. Reflecting his permeable and fluid view of the world, Kingdom contends that each of these problems and solutions can merge at any point in time; the primary issue is when this merger will take place. Policy entrepreneurs act as alert facilitators by appearing on the political scene at opportune times and matching their preferred policy solution to the problem at hand. Inherent in this definition of the policy entrepreneur is the notion of a clearly defined "window of opportunity" for action; the entrepreneur enters the fray by articulating a problem in a specific way, succeeds in establishing his or her program, and then exits from the policy stage.

Other researchers have attempted to formalize the concept of alertness by specifying the exact conditions under which society can expect entrepreneurs to emerge. In these models, there is an identifiable pool of talent that has the potential to exhibit entrepreneurial behaviors. The scope of talent is based on a number of individual factors, including income and education levels. Environmental conditions, however, determine the extent to which such leaders choose to devote their lives to activities in the public rather than the private arena. More specifically, slack budgetary resources in government may encourage entrepreneurs to take their chances on redirecting their energies away from private pursuits and toward their preferred policy goals.[6]

Other political scientists have focused on a second component of entrepreneurial behavior: persistence. Because the opportunities for policy action are uncertain, entrepreneurs must be patient. They must wait for the most opportune time to present their preferred policy alternatives to the public at large. Scholars writing in this tradition point to the need to distinguish policy entrepreneurs from policy opportunists in governmental politics. Entrepreneurs are those individuals respected for their skill set who have been consistently interested in the policy at hand; opportunists, on the other hand, are more likely to associate themselves with the issue

---

[5] John Kingdon. 1984. *Agendas, Alternatives and Public Policies*. Boston: Little, Brown.
[6] Martin Rickets. 1987. *The New Industrial Economics*. New York: St. Martin's Press; Mark Schneider and Paul Teske. 1995. *Public Entrepreneurs: Agents for Change in American Government*. Princeton, NJ: Princeton University Press.

when they see a chance for a substantial impact on the policy agenda. Entrepreneurs – those who remain firmly linked to an issue over time – tend to be much more effective legislators than their opportunistic peers. Researchers have reinforced these findings across various policy areas, including school choice and women's issues.[7]

The third task pinpointed by political scientists as critical to entrepreneurship is the proactive use of rhetorical ingenuity. Rhetorical ingenuity refers specifically to the entrepreneur's ability to frame issues in such a way as to maximize the chance for legislative action. Ingenuity is especially important because of the puzzle articulated in Arrow's Impossibility Theorem, which states that in a world of diverse tastes and preferences, equilibrium in terms of an established policy outcome is difficult to achieve. More specifically, in the early 1950s, the mathematical economist Kenneth Arrow showed that when individuals rank their policy preferences among three or more alternatives, no single voting procedure can always determine which outcome will ultimately be selected.[8] And as the number of individuals and alternative situations to be ranked increases, the likelihood that the individuals' rankings and social rankings will diverge also increases. Instead of stability, then, we should witness only a steady cycling of policy options with no clear outcomes. But empirical observation did not bear these predictions out – decisions were made, and new policies were implemented. The idea that institutions themselves could produce stable outcomes – also known as structure-induced equilibrium – provided the foundation for William Riker's influential work on the use of language in communicating ideas.[9]

If institutions could produce structure-induced equilibrium with respect to policy outcomes, then when would we witness policy change?

---

[7] Carol Weissert. 1991. "Policy Entrepreneurs, Policy Opportunists, and Legislative Effectiveness." *American Politics Quarterly* 19(2): 262–274; Michael Mintrom. 1997. "Policy Entrepreneurs and the Diffusion of Innovation." *American Journal of Political Science* 41(3): 738–770; Nelson W. Polsby. 1994. *Political Innovation in America: The Politics of Policy Initiation*. New Haven, CT: Yale University Press; Sue Thomas. 1991. "The Impact of Women on State Legislative Policies." *The Journal of Politics* 53(4): 958–976; Sue Thomas. 1994. *How Women Legislate*. New York: Oxford University Press; Michael Mintrom. 2000. *Policy Entrepreneurs and School Choice*. Washington, DC: Georgetown University Press.

[8] Kenneth Arrow. 1951. *Social Choice and Individual Values*. New York: Wiley.

[9] Kenneth Shepsle. 1979. "Institutional Arrangements and Equilibrium in Multidimensional Voting Models." *American Journal of Political Science* 23(1): 27–59; William Riker. 1980. "Implications from the Disequilibrium of Majority Rule for the Study of Institutions." *American Political Science Review* 74(2): 1235–1247; William Riker. 1986. *The Art of Political Manipulation*. New Haven, CT: Yale University Press.

Riker's central insight was that the policy entrepreneur has the ability to destabilize any equilibrium by casting his or her preferred policy option in a new way. Riker described these tactics as "heresthetics," or the methodic manipulation of the policy choice set. To Riker, policy actors are motivated to win, or to ensure that their preferred policy ideas are chosen over all of the alternatives. In order to win, they must behave creatively, employing the written word, oral arguments, and visual strategies to improve their chances of success. A classic example of such tactics is provided by the two sides involved in the abortion debate. Those who favor abortion rights call themselves "pro-choice," setting up their opponents as the enemies of freedom and individual liberty. Those who oppose abortion rights, on the other hand, call themselves "pro-life," implying that anyone who disagrees with them is in favor of death to the unborn. In this case, as well as in others, then, entrepreneurs are those individuals who have the verbal skills necessary to destroy past systems of stability and initiate new ones.[10]

Image shaping is an integral part of entrepreneurship, but as Frank R. Baumgartner and Bryan D. Jones point out, venue shopping might be equally important.[11] Entrepreneurs must not only be creative in reshaping policy proposals to their advantage, they must also be skilled in shopping for the most advantageous venue in which to present their new ideas. This is especially true in the United States, where the separation of powers as well as federalism generate multiple access points for those seeking to advance a specific agenda. Again, continuing with the abortion example, opponents of abortion have in recent years pursued restrictive laws in their state legislatures, because the Supreme Court has refused to overturn its 1973 decision in *Roe v. Wade*, which permits abortion under certain conditions. Another notable example of venue shopping is the current effort by advocacy groups in many states, such as New Jersey, in favor of greater funding for urban schools. Because their arguments have not been convincing to state legislators, these groups have now moved to the state courts in order to push their agenda forward.[12] Only if the right mix of

[10] For a thorough account of these strategies at work in the area of drunken driving, see Joseph R. Gusfield. 1981. *The Culture of Public Problems: Drinking-Driving and the Symbolic Order*. Chicago: University of Chicago Press.

[11] Frank R. Baumgartner and Bryan D. Jones. 1993. *Agendas and Instability in American Politics*. Chicago: University of Chicago Press.

[12] See *Abbott v. Burke*, 100 N.J. 269, 495 A.2d 376 (1985) ("Abbott I"); 119 N.J. 287, 575 A.2d 359 (1990) ("Abbott II"); 136 N.J. 444, 643 A.2d 575 (1994) ("Abbott III"); 149 N.J. 145, 693 A.2d 417 (1997) ("Abbott IV"); 153 N.J. 480, 710 A.2d 450 (1998)

policy images and venues is cast can innovators then reap the rewards of a period of "punctuated equilibrium," or stability of policy after a sudden disruption.

The primary characteristics of the entrepreneur, then, are fairly well defined. In order to increase the probability for success, entrepreneurs must be alert to new opportunities, persist in advocating their ideas, and employ rhetorical ingenuity to frame their ideas in novel ways. Notably, nothing in these definitions suggests that entrepreneurs must be autonomous individuals. Rather, the skill sets described by these scholars all point to the ways in which various types of groups can influence the public agenda. We can call these groups of unified individuals *entrepreneurial movements*.

This insight is critical, because it can help build bridges of policy research across the various disciplines of social science. For example, we can explore the ways in which legislative caucuses, using these skills in ways that are very similar to those employed by interest groups, form coalitions across issues. We can also be more attuned to the means by which social movements as wide-ranging transforming initiatives also attend to the characteristics outlined earlier in achieving their goals. In sum, broadening the scope of the entrepreneurship research agenda to include legislators, interest groups, social movements, professional organizations, and other mobilized forces enables us to explore more deeply the endless cycle of policy overhaul that is typical of policymaking today.

A Word about Who Is *Not* an Entrepreneur

Broadening the definition of entrepreneur to include entire *movements* of like-minded individuals is not helpful if the term becomes so elastic that it is rendered meaningless. However, simply stating that entrepreneurs can be more than a single individual hardly pushes us in the direction of definitional chaos.

We know that entrepreneurs must be alert, persistent, and able to use rhetorical ingenuity in crafting their arguments. These three criteria necessitate that we exclude certain categories of people as entrepreneurs. Members of Congress who cosponsor a bill after it begins to ride a wave of publicity surely would not be considered entrepreneurial under this definition. Celebrities who meet the president and mention their pet projects in passing are not entrepreneurial. Corporate shareholders who

("Abbott V"); 163 N.J. 95, 748 A.2d 82 (2000) ("Abbott VI"); 164 N.J. 84, 751 A.2d 1032 (2000) ("Abbott VII"); 170 N.J. 537, 790 A.2d 842 (2002) ("Abbott VIII").

pass on some of their profits to political campaigns definitely are not entrepreneurs. The local school board that lobbies on behalf of a one-time expenditure to improve the appearance of the high school is not acting in an entrepreneurial fashion.

The important point is that we can distinguish, using our definition, between exactly who is and who is not an entrepreneur. *Being entrepreneurial requires real work.* There must be a true mission, a true passion, and a true higher aim. No one can wake up one day and decide to move a policy mountain. Brief interludes with the power structure simply do not qualify. Entrepreneurs must be in the game for the long run.

WHY DO ENTREPRENEURS INNOVATE?

While political science research on the topic of entrepreneurship has focused on the *who* of innovation, economics has concentrated much more on the *why* and the *how* of new ideas. First, let us consider the *why*. Of pivotal interest to economists is the primary impetus behind entrepreneurial behavior. That is, why do firms behave as they do in the market? Why do they strategize? The answer economists have offered is the profit motive. Firms seek to maximize profits within a particular set of constraints.

Clearly, policy entrepreneurs do not seek out profits in the way that private firms do. Instead, we can think of entrepreneurs as seekers of rents.[13] Rent seeking is the process by which individuals aim to restructure public policy in ways that are beneficial to their own interests. Gordon Tullock, in his now much-cited essay "The Welfare Costs of Tariffs, Monopolies, and Theft," and later Anne O. Krueger began work in this direction by exploring the role of government as an economic player in modern society.[14] Building on the insights of the University of Chicago economist George Stigler, Tullock and Krueger argued that government was neither simply a producer of public goods nor a controller of externalities.[15] Rather, government functioned as a distributor of wealth and an allocator of costs.

---

[13] For an excellent review of this rent-seeking literature, see William C. Mitchell and Michael C. Munger. 1991. "Economic Models of Interest Groups: An Introductory Survey." *American Journal of Political Science* 35(2): 512–546.

[14] Anne O. Krueger. 1974. "The Political Economy of the Rent-Seeking Society." *American Economic Review* 64(3): 291–303; Gordon Tullock. 1967. "The Welfare Costs of Tariffs, Monopolies, and Theft." *Western Economic Journal* 5(3): 224–232.

[15] George Stigler. 1971. "The Theory of Economic Regulation." *Bell Journal of Economics and Management Science* 2(1): 3–21.

Since James M. Buchanan, Robert D. Tollison, and Gordon Tullock's seminal work on this topic, *Toward a Theory of the Rent-Seeking Society*, economists have come to understand the nature of this crucial governmental role as an arbiter of rents.[16] Central to this arbitration is the distinction between how the economy as a whole reacts to the creation of waste and how isolated individuals react. Waste in the marketplace occurs when an alternative use of a resource would have produced a higher level of output than its current use. The trigger for waste is imperfect information. Producers may not have the knowledge needed to deploy their resources in more efficient ways. Adding to this complexity is the set of governmental institutions that may delay more efficient deployment of these resources. Yet ironically, while for the economy as a whole these types of institutional barriers might be burdensome, from the perspective of the individual, searching out governmental inefficiencies is a highly rational – and often profitable – act.

In this view, individuals attempt to influence policymakers to grant them special rights or protections so as to shield themselves from heightened levels of competition. Classic examples include the regulation/deregulation of large-scale industries, the allocation of import licenses, and the imposition of tariffs.[17] In each of these cases, there are always potential winners and potential losers. For example, a domestic producer of rice has a strong interest in lobbying the government for protective trade legislation. To the extent that the industry is successful, consumers may suffer a loss in the form of higher rice prices, but the producers gain a "bonus" from the government that shields them from the vicissitudes of free market competition.

Applying these ideas to public policy, we can argue that the primary business of all policy entrepreneurs is rent seeking. All groups aim to promote their ideas as superior to every other group's ideas. Groups strategically position themselves in an attempt to insure that their ideas are ultimately the ones adopted, because if they can attain a legally binding agreement from the government in their favor, then their future stream of policy rewards will be large. They will, in effect, have gained a government-sanctioned monopoly of power over a particular policy realm.

[16] James M. Buchanan, Robert D. Tollison, and Gordon Tullock, eds. 1980. *Toward a Theory of the Rent-Seeking Society*. College Station, TX: Texas A&M Press.
[17] Richard A. Posner. 1974. "Theories of Economic Regulation." *Bell Journal of Economics and Management Science* 5(2): 335–358; George Stigler. 1971. "The Theory of Economic Regulation." *Bell Journal of Economics and Management Science* 2(1): 3–21.

But what, exactly, constitutes this future stream of rewards for policy entrepreneurs? Similar to the case in economics, rents may be primarily financial in nature. Entrepreneurs may gain access to new resources, succeed in transferring wealth from one group to another, reduce their tax burden, and so on. However, rents for policy entrepreneurs may also be more psychological in nature. Entrepreneurs may aim to become pivotal leaders, opinion makers, and notable decision makers, changing the course of history over time. In sum, financial as well as psychological rewards serve as strong motivators of rent-seeking behavior in the policy world.

HOW DO ENTREPRENEURS INNOVATE?

Specifying the motivation behind entrepreneurial behavior is the second fundamental component of a more comprehensive theory concerning innovative action; however, we must also consider the tactics used in this battle to come out on top in the arena of ideas. How does one group gain ascendance over another? What factors determine how long a particular group will be in charge of one specific policy area? Are certain strategies more effective than others in achieving policy prominence?

Once again, economics offers several useful concepts that can aid us in mapping out this part of the entrepreneurial strategy. Two key ideas related to the mechanics of innovation are the capacity to endure risk and the ability to induce a "shakeout" of the competition.

Risk

For years, economists have recognized that entrepreneurs, at least in the market for goods and services, represent a unique category of individuals with higher levels of initiative, foresight, and ingenuity than the rest of the population. Entrepreneurs are able to see market opportunities and to seize upon them. Most distinguishable of all, they take chances in the pursuit of innovation, without a guarantee of a future payoff. But because of their drive for an overarching theory of economic behavior that left little room for individual "heroes," economists have had an uneven history of incorporating entrepreneurial activities into their models of market change.

During the first wave of theorizing in the late eighteenth century, several prominent economists embraced the concept of the risk taker as central to the economic process. Richard Cantillon and Jean Batiste Say first offered insight into this topic by describing entrepreneurs as individuals with a special role to play in the economy – more specifically, as persons capable of directing resources into more efficient uses.[18] In their writings, the entrepreneur began to take his or her rightful place among the other major actors in the economy: the landowner, the capitalist, and the worker. With a purposeful niche all their own, entrepreneurs were the engines of change in all economic systems, producing new combinations of factor inputs and ultimately contributing to the overall economic growth of society at large.

With the advent of the marginal utility revolution in neoclassical economics during the late nineteenth century, however, the focus of scholarly study became equilibrium analysis and the theory of the firm. In this Walrasian world, the price mechanism methodically moved markets toward stability. Change took place largely exogenously, as increases in the factors of production or the introduction of new technologies temporarily created periods of disequilibrium. While disequilibrium generated economic profits for certain segments of the population, such profiteering was always short-lived. Because neoclassical economics assumed that all economic players had complete information, above-normal profits introduced competition into the market, ultimately driving the initial economic profits to zero. In this model, then, there was little room for the entrepreneur; no one was supposed to have an informational advantage over his or her neighbor and thereby to assume a leadership role in propelling innovation.

There were, however, numerous economists who continued to write about the importance of the entrepreneur and his or her centrality in dynamic market transformations. Interestingly, their arguments were by no means uniform. Theorists alternatively described entrepreneurs as decision makers, arbitrageurs, industrial leaders, and coordinators of resources. Gradually, however, they aggregated into several schools of thought related to the entrepreneurial purpose.[19] For this analysis, the most significant theoretical contribution came from the Chicago School,

---

[18] For a comprehensive overview of economists' changing views toward entrepreneurship, see Sven Ripsas. 1998. "Towards an Interdisciplinary Theory of Entrepreneurship." *Small Business Economics* 10(2): 103–115.

[19] For example, there are scholars who view entrepreneurs as decision makers (John Maynard Keynes and Francis Walker), as arbitrageurs (Leon Walras and Israel Kirzner), as industrial leaders (Amasa Walker and Friedrich von Wieser), and as coordinators of resources (Ronald Coase and Werner Sombart). In general, the three schools of thought on entrepreneurial behavior are as follows: (1) the Austrian School, which emphasized discovery; (2) the Schumpeterian tradition, which highlighted the importance of innovation; and (3) the Chicago School, which stressed the notion of risk taking.

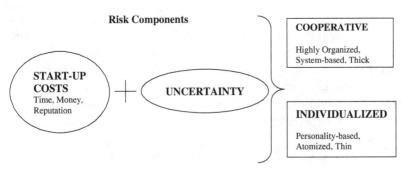

FIGURE I.I. Risk-reduction strategies.

which began the first systematic treatment of risk bearing in entre-preneurial theory.

For economists from the Chicago School, risk involves both (1) the necessity of underwriting start-up costs for a particular venture, and (2) the ability to endure uncertainty. First, in order to begin any project, an entrepreneur must find a way to fund him- or herself "into the market." Because of the novelty of the enterprise, these financial investments can be enormous. In addition to fronting start-up costs, the entrepreneur must also be willing to accept a certain degree of uncertainty. Frank Knight of the Chicago School was one of the earliest articulators of the types of risk facing the modern entrepreneur. According to Knight, uncertainty in the market arises from one primary factor: producers simply are not directly familiar with the needs and preferences of all consumers.[20] They therefore must forecast, to a certain extent, the degree of demand for the good under production. Not everyone, of course, is willing to assume such a risk. The entrepreneur, as a unique type, embraces this uncertainty.

Applying these ideas to policymaking provides us with insightful new ways of understanding the process by which policy leaders move to en-act change (see Figure 1.1). In the first stage of innovation, policy en-trepreneurs must decide how much risk they are willing to bear in pre-senting their ideas. Risk, as defined here, consists of two key components: the necessity of underwriting start-up costs and the capacity to endure uncertainty in order to promote a new idea. In the policy world, start-up

[20] Frank Knight. 1921. *Risk, Uncertainty, and Profit.* Boston: Houghton Mifflin.

costs involve the capital an individual or group must expend in order to enter the political fray. This capital could include money, time, reputational concerns, privacy issues, and so forth. At the same time, if we assume that all innovators want to maximize their impact on a specific policy area, a risk-taking position is also one where the chance for success is uncertain. This uncertainty derives from the simple fact that any policy position may be accepted, ignored, or rejected outright by the general public.

One of the key factors, then, in predicting whether or not a policy entrepreneur will be successful is how he or she goes about reducing the risks involved in starting a new venture. We can array potential strategies from the least powerful to the most powerful in terms of producing change. To increase the likelihood of idea passage and sustainability, entrepreneurs can engage in cooperative organization building. This means that from the very inception of their idea, entrepreneurs become focused on spreading the risk of confronting both start-up costs and uncertainty across the widest, most durable set of interested parties. On the other hand, entrepreneurs may select the much weaker individualized strategy for adapting to risk. An individualized strategy signals that the entrepreneur is relying primarily on him- or herself to move the idea forward, without the benefit of an organizational structure to sustain the innovation over the long run. Entrepreneurs selecting this strategy mistakenly believe that the force and power of their personalities alone will be enough to convince others to front their start-up costs and diminish their uncertainty. Entrepreneurs choosing the individualized risk-reduction strategy thus expose themselves to increased threats from the competition vis-à-vis entrepreneurs who select a more cooperative plan of action.

Shakeout

The willingness to undertake risk is only the first step in exploring the *how* of the entrepreneurial process. The second stage of innovation, beginning once again from economic theory, includes tracking the course of competition that emerges once any new good or service becomes an institutionalized component of production. Joseph Schumpeter defined entrepreneurship as a process of "creative destruction."[21] In his view, the

---

[21] Joseph Schumpeter. 1934. *Theory of Economic Development: An Inquiry into Profits, Capital, Credit, Interest, and the Business Cycle.* Cambridge, MA: Harvard University Press; Joseph Schumpeter. 1954. *History of Economic Analysis.* New York: Oxford University Press.

entrepreneur succeeds in dismantling any type of equilibrium that may have previously existed by creating a new market combination of inputs and outputs. For firms, the main motivation for creative destruction is the search for above-normal profits (positive economic profits). Ultimately, if these firms are successful, incomes are rearranged, the mix of goods and services that society produces and consumes changes, and the path of economic growth is altered, at least temporarily.

Schumpeter was also quick to note that the upward spiral of accumulation does not go on forever. Instead, competition generated by the free flow of firms into and out of the marketplace gradually chips away at the profits accruing to the market's innovators. After a short period of time, the economy moves back into equilibrium, once again ready for the destabilizing impact of another round of entrepreneurial activity.

Similar to the competition for profits in the profit-seeking world, there is also competition for rents in the rent-seeking world. In economics, there is considerable debate over the magnitude of social waste created by rent seeking, including the resources expended by groups in order to obtain rents, the resources expended by the government in order to determine them, and the distortions created by the introduction of such monopolistic rights over production. There is, however, a fair amount of consensus over how the market for rents reaches equilibrium. Rent seekers will enter the market to the point that the total amount invested in obtaining the rents dissipates the total amount of rents to be received.[22]

This leads to a critical question. How do entrepreneurs attempt to gain an advantage over their rivals in the competition over rents? Once again, economists have developed useful ideas related to industrial evolution that can help clarify this process. When an industry is new, many firms enter as producers, product innovation is high, and market shares among firms are extremely volatile. As the industry matures, however, product innovation slows, and fewer firms enter the market. Later, exit dominates entry as less efficient producers lose their economic viability. This process is known as an industry "shakeout." Of course, the goal of each firm is to survive this shakeout process and emerge as an industry leader.

[22] This result is based on a number of assumptions, including that (1) rent seekers are risk-neutral, (2) rent seekers are in symmetrical positions, and (3) there is free entry into the rent-seeking market. See Dennis Mueller. 1989. *Public Choice II*. Cambridge: Cambridge University Press, pp. 229–246.

Economists remain divided over the causes of shakeout. For James Utterback and Fernando Suarez, the key to leading a shakeout is developing and exploiting a "dominant design" for a new product.[23] In the early stages of an industry, the market is permeable to new approaches and novel ways of generating a particular good. In addition, because consumer preferences are uncertain, firms are generally flexible as they attempt to craft a new good. Over time, however, the majority of firms begin to converge on one primary model of product development. This model may emerge because of technological insights, regulatory-imposed standards, or first-mover advantages. In the case of the famous QWERTY typewriter, for example, certain firms began producing machines with this odd, yet quickly adopted keyboard design. Despite its awkwardness, the QWERTY setup rapidly became the dominant design for all typewriters.

According to Utterback and Suarez, shakeout occurs when this convergence dynamic – such as in the QWERTY example – gets under way. With industry agreement on accepted standards of production, opportunities for innovation recede, thereby discouraging new entrants. Firms that have already adopted the dominant design begin to focus on capital investment, and those firms that either failed to adopt this layout or lagged in developing the right manufacturing infrastructure eventually drop out of the market. In sum, shakeout occurs as a result of both the decline in firm entry and the rise in firm exit over the course of time.

Other economists, such as Steven Klepper, have emphasized the centrality of continuous change in the industry life cycle in explaining patterns of survival.[24] Crucial to Klepper's theory are two types of research and development, or R&D, strategies: process and product. Process R&D improves the means by which a good is produced, thereby reducing the average cost of production. Since a reduction in the average cost of production is related to a firm's level of output, larger firms tend to reap the greatest benefits. At the same time, product R&D proceeds apace, independent of a firm's size. Product R&D relates to improvements in a product's features, which opens up new submarkets for firms to exploit.

For Klepper, early entrants into the market usually develop advantages over their later counterparts because they are quick to invest in process R&D. Once these systems are in place, the "rich get richer" and the

---

[23] James Utterbeck and Fernando Suarez. 1993. "Innovation, Competition, and Industry Structure." *Research Policy* 22(1): 1–21.

[24] Steven Klepper. 1996. "Entry, Exit, Growth, and Innovation over the Product Life Cycle." *American Economic Review* 86(3): 562–583.

early firms become larger, ultimately forcing later entrants to invest in extraordinarily expensive capital equipment. As these early firms experience increasing returns and their costs of production are pushed down even further, smaller and less efficient firms become less likely to enter the market. Additionally, firms that cannot compete with these lower costs eventually drop out. The shakeout process thus gives large, R&D-intensive firms an advantage in survival.

A third set of explanations for shakeout involves the refinement of existing technology. According to Boyan Jovanovic and Glenn M. MacDonald, most new industries go through a period of rapid expansion, as firms attempt to develop a new product and take advantage of above-normal profits.[25] In their scheme, all firms produce the optimal level of output, and entry occurs until economic profits are driven to zero. As this process evolves, a refinement in the product occurs, which many firms, but not all, succeed in developing. This is the beginning of the shakeout phase.

At first, the refinement prompts entry into the new market. Firms scramble to enter as quickly as possible in order to take advantage of this new industry niche. However, incumbents already involved in manufacturing the product retain an advantage over these later firms owing to their accumulated experience in production. As all of these firms move into overdrive in order to incorporate the refinement, they increase their optimal level of output, causing prices to fall. Shakeout occurs when a substantial number of firms are unable to react rapidly enough with respect to this product improvement. With prices falling, exit follows, as firms that have failed to innovate leave the industry.

The commonality shared by all of these theories of shakeout is their description of surviving firms' behavior as superior to that of their competitors in the production of a specific good. Winners might propose or quickly incorporate a technological design toward which all firms converge, or they might develop large R&D operations that swamp the technological efforts of their competition. They might even develop or adopt a refinement for a product that other firms have difficulty replicating. In each of these cases, their actions result in a shakeout of less alert firms.

Shakeout in policy entrepreneurship proceeds along a similar trajectory (see Figure 1.2). Each group attempts to control the agenda, in such a way

---

[25] Boyan Jovanovic and Glenn M. MacDonald. 1994. "The Life Cycle of a Competitive Industry." *Journal of Political Economy* 102(2): 322–347.

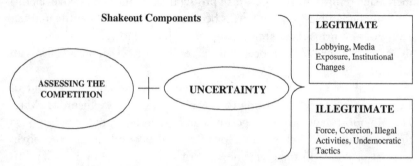

FIGURE 1.2. Shakeout strategies.

that its policy proposals are ultimately adopted. This competition means that all rival groups are interested in removing those who have assumed power in the past in order to gain an advantage for themselves in the present. In the policy world, let us define a shakeout strategy as the set of tactics executed by an emerging competitor in order to dislodge the current controller of the issue domain. As in the case of risk, uncertainty plays a role in the development of a shakeout strategy. Entrepreneurs never know which techniques will be effective enough to remove their competitors from the policy arena.

Similar to the continuum along which we can array risk reduction tactics as either helpful or hurtful to innovation, we can also map out the primary dimension along which shakeout tactics are likely to be either effective or ineffective in moving change forward. This primary dimension is *perceived legitimacy*. If the general public approves of the strategies undertaken by entrepreneurs in order to weaken their opponents, the likelihood of success automatically increases. Examples of legitimate shakeout strategies include lobbying, media exposés, redirecting rules and procedures that currently favor one's opponents, and the like. If, on the other hand, the public perceives an entrepreneurial shakeout strategy as illegitimate, then it is likely that no innovation will be forthcoming. Illegitimate shakeout strategies include, but are not limited to, the use of violence, harassment, illegal manipulation of the rules of the game, intentional false portrayals of the opposition, and so forth.

THE WHO, WHY, AND HOW OF POLICY ENTREPRENEURSHIP: PUTTING THE STRATEGIES TOGETHER

Combining the *who, why*, and *how* of entrepreneurship into one theoretical model helps us to understand the overall process of policy change. There will be periods of success, or of innovation politics; periods of inaction, or of status quo politics; as well as everything in between. But before providing specific examples of these resulting types of politics, let us first sketch the broad outlines of how the three components of this entrepreneurial theory work together (see Figure 1.3).

Let us assume for illustrative purposes that a current holder of policy power has successfully persuaded the government to adopt his or her ideas at some time in the past. Let us call this individual or set of

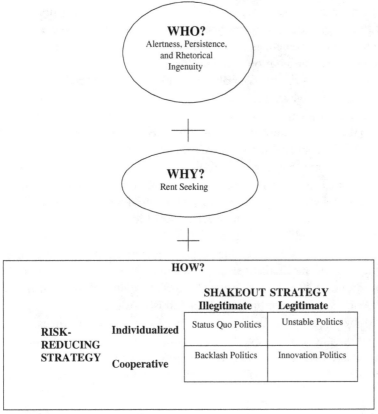

FIGURE 1.3. The who, why, and how of policy entrepreneurship.

individuals the Incumbent Entrepreneur. With the passage of time, other groups begin to mobilize around the same issue and fight for the same privileged consideration from the government. Each competitor pursues a strategy to discredit the current holder of power. Let us call one such competitor the Challenger Entrepreneur.[26] If his or her entrepreneurial strategies are successful, he or she can reallocate resources toward his or her preferred policy outcome, thereby weakening and/or excluding the Incumbent Entrepreneur from the policy bargaining table.

In order to take control, the Challenger Entrepreneur first must exhibit the *who* of policy entrepreneurship – the characteristics identified by many researchers as fundamental to policy success. The Challenger Entrepreneur must be alert to new opportunities, must be persistent in presenting his or her claims, and must employ rhetorical ingenuity in order to frame the issue in an appealing way. Second, the Challenger Entrepreneur must have a clearly defined rent-seeking position as a motivator – the *why* of entrepreneurship. Third, whether or not the Challenger Entrepreneur is successful in policy innovation is ultimately bound up in the combination of risk-reducing and shakeout strategies that he or she pursues – the *how* of policy entrepreneurship. More specifically, if we have a case where the entrepreneur not only utilizes a cooperative risk-reducing strategy but also executes a legitimate shakeout plan, then the probability that "innovation politics" will obtain is high. Using our terminology, this would mean that the Challenger Entrepreneur has engaged in a highly effective entrepreneurial plan of attack against the Incumbent Entrepreneur. This signals danger for the Incumbent Entrepreneur, whose hold on the policy spotlight begins to weaken. In this case, the Incumbent Entrepreneur's rents are driven to zero, as old ideas are dismantled and new ones are placed in their stead. The Incumbent Entrepreneur, in other words, must relinquish his or her primary seat at the policy bargaining table in favor of the Challenger Entrepreneur.

The automobile safety movement represents innovation politics at work. Prior to 1966, the motor vehicle industry was an extremely powerful lobbying group in Washington, D.C. Consumers had virtually no information about the safety of the vehicles they purchased, and as late as 1965, Frederic G. Donner, the head of General Motors (GM), argued that turn signals as well as seat belts should remain optional

---

[26] Note that the use of only two actors in this example is for purposes of simplicity only. As long as there is the potential for any group to accrue rents, the number of potential competitors will vary.

features. Any individual attempting to fight the industry – the Incumbent Entrepreneurs – faced mounting a costly campaign against formidable corporate giants with a proven record of silencing their opponents. Despite these odds, Ralph Nader, a young Harvard-educated lawyer, as well as a series of like-minded activists, decided to undertake the task of becoming the Challenger Entrepreneurs.

First, Nader reduced the risk of entrepreneurial activity by working cooperatively with a variety of like-minded citizen activists. In pursuing his case against the automobile industry, he created the Center for Study of Responsive Law, which, in its early years, brought together 200 young attorneys to ferret out corruption and misinformation within the corporate and political worlds. By 1970, Nader had institutionalized his advocacy activities in three other organizations. The first, the Center for Auto Safety, remained completely dedicated not only to lobbying the automakers for safety improvements, but also to reporting citizen complaints to the appropriate governmental agencies. The second, the Project on Corporate Responsibility, focused almost exclusively on urging major corporations such as GM to consider the rights of everyday consumers in their business practices. And the third, the Public Interest Research Group (PIRG), served as the foundation for a wide range of consumer investigative missions that ultimately moved beyond car safety issues.

Second, Nader and his colleagues pursued highly legitimate shakeout strategies against their competition, namely, the publication of hard-hitting reports and the holding of explosive public hearings. With Nader's 1965 book *Unsafe at Any Speed: The Designed-in Dangers of the American Automobile*, the American public finally became informed about the dangers of driving in substandard vehicles. Citing his detailed account of the hazards posed by automobiles, Nader lobbied for the creation of the National Highway Traffic Safety Administration, which within ten years issued regulations regarding the installation of shoulder harnesses, head restraints, and more durable types of fuel tanks. Based on the work of Nader and his colleagues, consumer activists also helped launch the process of automobile recall, whereby the federal government acquired the authority to force the industry into taking responsibility for potential safety hazards. Nader also utilized public hearings, first in Iowa under Attorney General Lawrence Scalise and then in Washington, D.C., under Senator Abraham Ribicoff in the Senate Subcommittee on Executive Reorganization in March 1966, to promote his ideas. As a result of these strategies, from this period forward, Congress has consistently considered consumer groups' insights and recommendations regarding improving safety features, from mandatory crash testing through the requirement of air bags and automatic seat belts in the 1990s.[27]

A second possibility in terms of entrepreneurial politics is that the Challenger Entrepreneur will pursue an individualized risk-reduction strategy and at the same time follow a legitimate shakeout strategy. On one hand, the Challenger neglects to establish a broad foundation of support that would allow his or her new idea to be sustained over the long run. This oversight, of course, prevents the idea from receiving the full influx of resources offered by more stable, institutionalized groups. On the other hand, because the Challenger has utilized legitimate ways of weakening his or her opponents, there is a strong chance that the new idea will be considered by the public. This twofold course of action often leads to a period of "unstable politics," whereby the Challenger is able to shape policy issues, but usually only marginally and in a fleeting way. Meanwhile, the Incumbent Entrepreneur remains only one step away from regaining full policy power.

As an example of unstable politics, consider the revolutionary changes that are currently taking place in the tobacco industry. For over forty years, tobacco firms, as the Incumbent Entrepreneurs, controlled the regulatory process related to cigarettes. The position the industry took toward government interference in their business practices was simple: scientists could not prove that smoking directly causes any illness, and therefore any further regulation beyond simple package health warnings was unnecessary. As long as they could restrict the number of rules under which they were forced to operate, RJR Nabisco Holdings Corporation, B.A.T. Industries, Brown and Williamson, the Philip Morris Companies, Loews Corporations Lorillard, and the Liggett Corporation could reap the rewards of rent-maximizing behavior. Legislators simply would not touch them.

All was well until a Challenger set of policy entrepreneurs – the state attorneys general – entered the arena during the mid-1990s. Their shakeout strategy against the tobacco competition was seen as highly legitimate. Instead of pursuing scattered lawsuits based on health damages suffered by individual citizens, the attorneys general would instead attempt to recoup Medicaid expenditures in class action lawsuits. This strategy would force

---

[27] For two in-depth analyses of this case, see Ralph Nader. 1965. *Unsafe at Any Speed: The Designed-in Dangers of the American Automobile*. New York: Grossman; and Jerry L. Mashaw and David L. Harfst. 1990. *The Struggle for Auto Safety*. Cambridge, MA: Harvard University Press.

the cigarette companies into defending their sales tactics in a completely new and untested arena.

Yet, while the shakeout strategy was legitimate, the risk-reduction strategy was highly individualized and dependent upon the unique tenacity of Mississippi Attorney General Michael Moore. More specifically, the demands on the most vulnerable firm, Liggett, began only in 1994 after Moore initiated a lawsuit against all tobacco manufacturers to recoup cigarette-related Medicaid expenditures. Flying across the country, Moore convinced other attorneys general from states such as Minnesota, West Virginia, Florida, and Massachusetts to join his suit, leading to the first case breakthrough when the Liggett Corporation decided to settle in 1996. Meanwhile, the other major tobacco companies continued to deny their responsibility with respect to smokers' health care costs. Yet Moore persisted in working behind the scenes to force a settlement. Finally, in 1997, Liggett CEO Bennett LeBow agreed to provide internal industry documents that proved that the tobacco companies had knowingly deceived the public regarding the addictiveness of the materials contained in most cigarettes. This decision ultimately led to the final $365-billion-dollar settlement against the entire industry.

Notably, however, even after eventually being forced to pay billions of dollars in damages, the tobacco companies have been weakened, but not destroyed.[28] The state attorneys general obviously have responsibilities other than pursuing cigarette companies, and Moore never erected an organizational infrastructure to continue handling these smoking-related complaints. The one major resource the attorneys general did create, the internet-based State Tobacco Information Center (STIC), now serves only as a tobacco document archival depository, not as an active lobbying arm of state-based law enforcement. In sum, the public's attention has undoubtedly been heightened with respect to the practices of the Big Tobacco firms, but without a solid foundation of organizational activism, the future of regulatory action is unclear.

A third possibility in terms of policy change is that the Challenger Entrepreneur is very effective in pursuing a cooperative risk-reduction strategy and in putting his or her ideas forward. The infrastructure for change, in this case, is methodically created, maintained, and fortified.

---

[28] For a historical account of the tobacco wars, see Richard Kluger. 1996. *Ashes to Ashes: America's Hundred-Year Cigarette War, the Public Health, and the Unabashed Triumph of Philip Morris*. New York: Alfred A. Knopf; Peter Pringle. 1998. *Cornered: Big Tobacco at the Bar of Justice*. New York: Holt.

At the same time, however, the Challenger pursues a highly illegitimate shakeout strategy. The public disapproves of these tactics so strongly that a period of "backlash politics" ensues, thereby enabling the Incumbent Entrepreneur to turn back the clock, denying all of the Challenger's stated goals.

The rise of the Challenger Black Power movement against the Incumbent Johnson and Nixon administrations in the area of race relations is a primary case in point. During the late 1960s, increasing numbers of black Americans became frustrated at not achieving the social progress promised to them at the height of the civil rights era. Their risk-reduction strategy to effect change was extremely well coordinated across a variety of different groups. For example, the Student Non-violent Coordinating Committee (SNCC), the Black Panther Party for Self-Defense, the Congress of Racial Equality (CORE), and the Black Liberation Army (BLA) each worked to achieve the movement's overarching goals of self-improvement, self-reliance, and self-determination. In building their new organizational structure, they explicitly separated from such integrationist groups as the National Association for the Advancement of Colored People (NAACP), the National Urban League, and the Southern Christian Leadership Conference (SCLC).

The general public, however, often perceived their shakeout strategies as highly illegitimate. Gone were the days of Dr. Martin Luther King, when civil disobedience was the dominant protest activity. In this new era, followers of Malcolm X dismissed King's strategies as too passive. To effect change, blacks had to demand change, violently if necessary. Riots in Harlem, Detroit, and Newark made this rhetoric come to horrific life for the millions of white Americans who watched the news reports of violent confrontations nightly on their television screens.

A backlash quickly ensued. In the minds of most whites, not only were blacks consuming a large chunk of the government's resources in unworkable welfare programs run by incompetent social workers, they also were wreaking havoc across the country with their urban warfare and looting. Something had to change. And Richard M. Nixon, who seized the 1968 presidential election by wooing a sizable percentage of George Wallace's segregationist following, knew exactly what to do. He promised voters that he would call for a sharp reduction in taxes and decreased spending on social programs. Moreover, he courted the white southern vote by promising an end to affirmative action programs and by placing a strong emphasis on law-and-order policies. By the early 1970s, then, the entrepreneurial activities of the Black Power movement had not only been stopped, they had been, at least temporarily, reversed.[29]

Finally, there is always the possibility for "status quo politics," the result of a combination of two failed entrepreneurial strategies. This occurs when an entrepreneur pursues not only a highly individualized strategy to reduce risk, but also an illegitimate course of action in shaking out the competition. Simply put, this means that the Challenger Entrepreneur has failed to create a successful alternative to the status quo, thereby insuring that the Incumbent Entrepreneur's ideas remain intact. Not only does the Incumbent Entrepreneur continue to accrue rents in the process, but he or she is also guaranteed a seat at the policy table for some time to come.

In 1991, when Senator John Heinz from Pennsylvania died unexpectedly in a plane crash, a special election pitted Harris Wofford, a moderate Democrat, against a popular Republican and Bush administration official, Richard Thornburgh. When the face-off began, most political observers considered Wofford to be an underdog who needed a serious issue "spark" to ignite his campaign. In his cross-state travels, Wofford discovered his spark – a latent demand for better health care provision in the United States – and encouraged then–presidential candidate Bill Clinton and other reformers to make health care reform one of their primary issues. With Wofford's dramatic victory, it seemed that the Challenger Entrepreneurs – all those arguing for reform – would have an easy time overcoming the Incumbent Entrepreneurs – the health care professionals who were interested in protecting the status quo. Both the risk-reduction and shakeout strategies pursued by the Challenger reformers, however, would prevent Wofford's vision from becoming a reality.

First, reform advocates had extreme difficulty in moving away from an individualized approach to risk reduction to a more coordinated, cooperative approach. Until the first years of the Clinton administration, government programs such as Medicaid and Medicare, as well as doctors, hospitals, and insurance companies, had coexisted for over twenty-five years in providing health services to the American public. Despite this somewhat peaceful cooperation, the health care system was plagued with major problems. Employers were burdened with heavy medical expenditures; hospitals were folding because they were not being reimbursed by the government at adequate rates; and consumers were angry at the

---

[29] For a systematic treatment of the rise and fall of the Black Power movement, see Doug McAdam. 1985. *Political Process and the Development of Black Insurgency, 1930–1970.* Chicago: University of Chicago Press.

overinflated prices of routine physical examinations. The problem was that these reformers could not find a way to make all of these discontented parties speak with one voice. Each player had a unique set of complaints, and reformers failed to create an umbrella organization to unify them.

Second, the Challenger's shakeout strategy was seen as highly illegitimate by the American public. Advocates for change, led by Hillary Rodham Clinton, became convinced that if they could convene an expert group of domestic policy advisors in private meetings and encourage them to put forth a series of strong recommendations, they could persuade the American public that a new model of health care could effectively supersede the status quo. They ended up meeting in the secure confines of the President's Task Force on Health Care Reform. This shakeout strategy, however, did not anticipate the level of opposition or the intensity with which opponents of reform would rebel against this secrecy.

By the time the president presented the major components of his proposed Health Security Act to the American public in 1993, a counteroffensive had already sprung into action. More specifically, while the proposed Act called for new bureaucracies, the extension of health maintenance groups, and mandatory premium contributions, highly mobilized groups touted a variety of different strategies to deal with the crisis. These included national health insurance, pay-as-you-go schemes, and tax credits for individuals seeking to buy insurance at reduced rates. In the end, because of the limited organizational basis for reform as well as the closed nature of the shakeout strategy, the health care reform movement failed miserably. On September 26, 1994, Senate Majority Leader George Mitchell announced that the prospects for reform were dead in Congress, at least for that legislative session. The new rent-seeking competition given a voice in the Health Security Act simply was not strong enough to alter the status quo.[30]

These examples demonstrate the ways in which we can combine notions of risk and shakeout strategies into one comprehensive theory of the "how" behind the entrepreneurial process. In this view, the progression from an idea to its fruition as a workable public policy is a clearly delineated process with specific, identifiable signposts. If entrepreneurs are victorious in promoting their ideas – that is, if the "politics of innovation" obtains – they can continue to accrue rents by ensuring that their

---

[30] For a thorough policy history of Clinton's health care reform proposal, see Theda Skocpol. 1996. *Boomerang: Clinton's Health Security Effort and the Turn against Government in U.S. Politics.* New York: Norton.

innovative vision remains a part of government policy as long as possible. Such longevity, however, is always threatened by the activities of other rent-seeking groups. Competition encompassed in new risk and shakeout strategies inevitably leads to the partial or complete replacement of past ideas by new ways of conducting business. It is important, however, to note that there is no finality in this process. Once each set of cutting-edge policies is ultimately in place, the cycle starts to repeat itself once again.

THE POLITICS OF INNOVATION: THE CASE OF CHILD SUPPORT ENFORCEMENT

As we have seen, not all entrepreneurial efforts turn out successfully to produce innovation politics. Depending on the critical combination of risk and shakeout strategies, potential reformers can also produce status quo politics, unstable politics, or backlash politics. The key to effecting change is executing a precise entrepreneurial strategy. Only entrepreneurs who carefully utilize cooperative risk reduction techniques and legitimate shakeout mechanisms will produce the politics of innovation. And innovation, as we have seen, always invites more political actors to enter the entrepreneurial game. This book is about this kind of success – or rather, about the various cycles of the politics of innovation that have emerged over time on the issue of child support enforcement.

As the child support problem has lingered for well over one hundred years, it should come as no surprise that, after the initial set of policies established by charity workers and local law enforcement personnel through the 1900s, four different sets of political entrepreneurs have grappled with potential solutions. They include social workers from the turn of the century through the 1960s, conservatives during the 1970s, women's groups and women legislators in the 1980s and early 1990s, and fathers' rights groups in the late 1990s and beyond (see Table 1.1). Each group came to the political bargaining table with its own skills and demands, and, as we will see, each was able to transform the policy agenda in its own, personalized way.

As described earlier, our methodology in examining this issue will be unique, in that we will explore changes in the approach to child support enforcement over the long run. What are the advantages of examining entrepreneurial activity on this issue over time? It is instructive to consider the alternative. More specifically, if we were to examine snapshots of policy development rather than the full evolution of the issue, we would then collect the following pieces of innovation history.

TABLE I.I. *The politics of innovation in child support enforcement*

Period	Entrepreneurs	Rent-Seeking Position
Nineteenth Century	Charity Workers/Law Enforcement	Money to Single Mothers/Extensive Social Monitoring
1900–1960s	Social workers	Extend social services to single mothers
1970s	Conservatives	Pursue fathers of children on welfare
1980s and early 1990s	Women legislators and women's groups	Extend enforcement services to nonwelfare families
Late 1990s–present	Fathers' rights groups	Reduce child support awards

Consider the late nineteenth century. At that time, charity workers "treated" poverty in single-parent households by giving families of lesser means the food, clothing, and shelter that they so desperately needed to survive. They also monitored mothers' behavior to make sure that they were providing "suitable" homes for their children. Mothers who could not live up to these standards were cut off from support. Children born out of wedlock and African-American children received very little protection, and children whose fathers had passed away frequently received only subsistence-level benefits.

From the 1900s to the 1960s, however, social workers began to argue that the poor required more than simply material goods in order to thrive. More specifically, the disadvantaged needed a multiplicity of services to help lift them from the ranks of deprivation. In a short period of time, the social workers stepped up to effect change. In doing so, they tried to apply their traditionally individualistic approach to service provision on a mass level to entire communities that were under economic duress.

Despite this uncertainty, social workers – trained in the areas of counseling, outreach, and community education – began their mission with single-minded enthusiasm. In particular, they proposed offering mothers who received Aid to Families with Dependent Children much more than cash assistance to support their children. If these mothers could no longer be financially tied to their former partners – for whatever reason – social workers could direct them to all of the in-kind benefits for which they qualified, as well as enroll them in job training and educational programs.

Fast forward to the 1970s. The social workers are no longer in control; conservatives have taken the reins of power. Their influence began when

President Gerald R. Ford signed the first substantive piece of legislation – the Social Security Amendments of 1975 – that created a federal child support program.[31] The program was designed to operate as a partnership between the federal government and the states. Under the direction of the U.S. Department of Health, Education, and Welfare (HEW) and later under the Department of Health and Human Services (DHHS), the Administration for Children and Families began to run the Office of Child Support Enforcement (OCSE) in Washington, D.C. From that office, the federal government provided the states with policy direction, legislative supervision, and technical assistance for implementing new laws. The states, in turn, started to control the program's actual day-to-day operations by locating parents, establishing paternity, issuing support orders, and enforcing support. Financially, costs for the program were shared between the federal and state governments, with the federal government funding most of the operating expenses.

In its initial form, the federal child support enforcement program had a single focus: welfare cost recovery. Demographic changes during the 1960s and early 1970s – such as an escalating divorce rate and the growth of single parenthood – had contributed to a vast increase in the number of children living below the poverty line. Concurrently, many conservatives began to worry that the recent liberalization of welfare laws, which had greatly expanded eligibility, was contributing to an undesirable social outcome, namely, the observed rising tendency of single mothers to rely on welfare for financial support in lieu of potentially available private support. Evidence of this behavioral trend mounted as both welfare rolls and expenditures increased during this period. By the late 1970s, then, conservative legislators touted the child support program as an important means by which to reduce the costs of AFDC, the central welfare vehicle for helping poor, usually fatherless families. In this original child support program, the states and the federal government retained all child support collected from fathers in order to reimburse the taxpayers for outlays already made through the welfare system.

Jump to 1984. By this time, the balance of policy power has shifted once again, this time in favor of women legislators and women's organizations. In the past, women who were not relying on AFDC had to turn to the state court system in order to receive child support. Unfortunately for them,

---

[31] The Social Security Amendments passed in 1950, 1965, and 1967 (described in Chapter 2) began the process of granting the states the authority to access information to locate noncustodial parents. These laws represented the foundation upon which the program was launched in 1975.

each state was unique in its method of deciding these cases, and many times multiple courts had jurisdiction over the same case. Moreover, even if the court records showed that another order existed, judges would often exercise their independence by modifying these earlier decisions anyway. Linked to this duplication problem was a similarly frustrating issue – the fragmentation of responsibility in the judicial system, which prevented support cases from being processed in an orderly way. Regardless of the particular problem, the bottom line was the same. Women were not receiving the child support to which they were entitled. Reforms were clearly necessary.

With women legislators and women's organizations hearing these pleas and thus leading the drive, Congress finally passed the Child Support Enforcement Amendments of 1984. This legislation required not only that the states continue providing services to AFDC families, but also that they serve any non-AFDC family that requested government aid in enforcing support.[32] In addition, instead of being channeled to the state coffers, as in the case of AFDC collections, all financial support would go directly to the nonwelfare families. With this new legislation, women across the socioeconomic spectrum would be helped.

Now flash forward to the present. What group of entrepreneurs is currently at the helm of policy leadership? Although it is still too early to know for certain, fathers' rights groups have been gaining increased visibility at all levels of government. While fathers' rights groups are numerous and their goals varied, reducing child support awards remains a paramount concern. First, numerous organizations have complained that low-income fathers simply do not have the financial resources to pay support on a timely and consistent basis. They advocate job training programs and "forgiveness for arrears" to help these men in need. Second, fathers' rights groups maintain that the current set of child support guidelines is inequitable and that it places them in an economically untenable position, frequently preventing them from forming and providing for a second family. In order to solve this problem, they demand a revamping of all state award formulas to reflect the true cost of child rearing. Finally, they argue that fathers should be compensated for the time that they spend with their children above and beyond normal visitation hours. In sum, these groups are currently mounting a campaign across the country to address these issues.

---

[32] States had the option of providing services to non-AFDC families beginning in 1975, but most chose to focus on the welfare caseload.

Now let us return to the question of why the long-term approach is more informative in studying entrepreneurship than the snapshot approach. If we were simply to focus on the snapshots just described, we might come to very different conclusions regarding entrepreneurial behavior than if we were to consider all of these episodes in succession. As snapshots, they are stories about individuals and groups and their particular strategies in attacking the child support problem. But when we analyze them together, we can see what the entrepreneurial process looks like over time and begin building a more generalizable theory of innovation as a whole.

More specifically, we will see how during this period – after the charity workers had begun their interventions – the four entrepreneurial groups each entered into the political arena in order to shape child support policy: social workers, conservatives, women legislators and women's groups, and fathers' rights groups. We will investigate how each group had to assume a certain risk by bearing the costs of entering the fray without any guarantee of success. We will also see how each group utilized a variety of techniques to "shake out" the competition and become the dominant set of new policy entrepreneurs. Using our dynamic approach, we will also see that once one group's ideas had become the reigning wisdom about how to deal with the child support problem, other rent-seeking groups with different ideas about the direction of reform entered the political battlefield. Finally, our approach enables us to track how this competition sometimes forced the previous group of entrepreneurs out of the realm of political influence, especially if the emerging groups were able to institute comprehensive changes in the program and not simply incremental ones.

PLAN OF ANALYSIS

From a historical point of view, the number of children living in poverty in the United States has remained an important concern for policy activists for over one hundred years. Because the issue has taken on so many different forms and ever-greater proportions, the notion that a *single* set of policy entrepreneurs would be able to enter the political arena and "solve" the problem once and for all is simply unrealistic. Instead, as the case of child support will demonstrate, public policy problems frequently undergo "treatment" by multiple policy entrepreneurs, each with their own vision of what priorities should be addressed immediately.

This book differs in its approach from many of the important books on public policy issues that have come before it. The most important difference is that it focuses on the long-term time horizon rather than on a series of short-term crises. In doing so, it reveals how different groups have attempted to frame a certain policy issue over decades, rather than how critical players have battled it out within the context of a few years.[33] The second critical difference is how the book highlights the impact of strong-willed individuals in effecting change. More specifically, it focuses on the purposeful results of active change, rather than on situations where rules and procedures have a large role in determining public outcomes.[34] In the same vein of actor-centered mobilization, the book demonstrates how entrepreneurs can tap evolving values in order to support their cause instead of being stymied by seemingly immutable notions of entrenched American culture.[35]

This book compiles important historical materials, statistics, and interviews in order to shed light on the evolving nature of child support enforcement policy. It is organized as follows. First, Chapter 2 describes the current child support system in order to offer insight into how far policymaking in the past has brought us into the policymaking climate of today. It focuses on the general balance of power between the states and the federal government in collecting child support, the composition of the caseload between welfare and nonwelfare families, and the program's current enforcement duties.

Chapter 3 then brings us back to the beginning of our story, to the nineteenth century, where the seeds of child support policy were first planted. It describes how individual mothers and third-party benefactors had to fight for support on their own through the court system, and how charity workers and local law enforcement became involved in the more financially desperate cases. It also explores how out-of-wedlock children, African-American children, and children whose fathers had died sometimes faced even more dire circumstances in their attempts to secure support.

---

[33] For an excellent study of short-term problem resolution in the Social Security Administration, see Martha Derthick. 1990. *Agency under Stress.* Washington, DC: The Brookings Institution Press.

[34] For examples of excellent procedural analyses, see R. Kent Weaver. 1988. *Automatic Government.* Washington, DC: The Brookings Institution Press; Ronald King. 2000. *Budgeting Entitlements: The Politics of Food Stamps.* Washington, DC: Georgetown University Press; John Witte. 1985. *The Politics and Development of the Federal Income Tax.* Madison, WI: University of Wisconsin Press.

[35] In contrast to this book's approach, Jill Quadagno makes the case that race played an instrumental role in welfare policy throughout much of the twentieth century. See Jill Quadagno. 1994. *The Color of Welfare.* New York: Oxford University Press.

Chapters 4–7 each describe the emergence of a new set of Challenger Entrepreneurs who face off against the Incumbents who rose to power in the previous chapter. Chapter 4 immediately begins tracing this historical passage by analyzing the policy Challengers of the early twentieth century, the social workers – both who they were and what they accomplished in fighting childhood poverty. Chapter 5 then focuses on the emergence of a new type of policy Challenger – conservatives – who confronted the dual problems of family breakdown and skyrocketing welfare expenditures by establishing a child support program operated by the federal government and the states. Chapter 6 follows this issue through another incarnation, as once again a new set of policy Challengers – this time women legislators and women's groups – argued that the key issue in the child support debate was the failure of the federal government to *prevent* women from having to rely on welfare in the first place. It also describes how these new advocates were able to convince President Ronald Reagan to expand and strengthen services for millions of new recipients. Next, Chapter 7 turns to the rise of fathers' rights groups as the primary Challengers and advocates for reducing awards in the late 1990s.

It is important to note that while these chapters revolve around a single set of Challenger Entrepreneurs confronting the set of Incumbents who came before them, this organizational scheme may result in something of an oversimplification of the entrepreneurial trajectory. For example, one question that might emerge from this type of organizational plan is, does the set of Challenger Entrepreneurs suddenly appear out of nowhere to challenge the Incumbents? Of course not. For the sake of clarity, each chapter focuses on a single set of Challenger Entrepreneurs – the ones who overtake the Incumbents – but this does not mean that future sets of Challengers are completely missing from important policy debates. For example, although Chapter 6 highlights the importance of women's groups and women legislators in successfully overtaking the incumbent conservatives, fathers' rights groups – not discussed until Chapter 7 – also participated in this debate. However, their voices are not highlighted until later in the book, when they become louder and more effective in transforming the nature of the child support debate.

There is a second oversimplification that might emerge from the organizational scheme of this book. This oversimplification revolves around the following question: do Challenger Entrepreneurs *completely* replace the Incumbents and cast them into policy obscurity? Again, the answer is, of course not. As described in each of the chapters, the Challengers are successful in overtaking the Incumbents in the marketplace of ideas, but this does not mean that that Incumbents are rendered voiceless. In fact, more often than not they continue to play an important public policy role, but from a background rather than a foreground position. And as the theory of potential entrepreneurial victory laid out earlier suggests, these replaced Incumbents have ample opportunity to stage a policy comeback.

Chapter 8 concludes with several predictions regarding the future of child support policy given the state of competition among current and emerging groups of entrepreneurs. It also offers insights into how entrepreneurial change fits within the overall system of American government, not just in the area of child support enforcement but in other hotly debated issue areas as well.

2

Child Support Enforcement

The Current System

In order to understand the ways in which different cycles of policy entrepreneurs have impacted child support over the past two centuries, it is important to map out the contemporary support program. Recent legislators, governors, and successive presidents have made child support recovery a primary goal of their tenures in office. Their statements have been grand; their actions have been markedly aggressive. Yet, despite this unanimity in mission, they have all squabbled over their territorial rights to execute this policy. How have past decisions regarding the split between the duties of the states and the federal government structured the current approach to the program? How large is the caseload, and what does it look like? And finally, what are the major responsibilities of the program now in place in guaranteeing support for families in need? These are the questions to which this chapter now turns.

THE FEDERAL-STATE BALANCE

Currently, the United States has a child support enforcement system that is the product of a strong federal-state partnership with highly particularized niches of authority. The balance of power within this partnership, however, has not always been stable. Early initiatives, those taken prior to the creation of a comprehensive program, emanated from Washington, D.C., as national legislators focused on strengthening each state's Aid to Families with Dependent Children program – the primary cash assistance vehicle serving low-income families – as a means to support families in need. Later efforts involved building the new child support program itself, and debates about the federal-state balance were largely decided in the states' favor. In the twenty-first century, states find themselves once again in an evolving relationship with the federal government. National policymakers have increasingly placed new requirements on the states to meet specific policy goals, but the states have retained a certain degree of autonomy in meeting those goals.

In the years immediately prior to the creation of the child support enforcement program, national legislators played the dominant policy role as they attempted to encourage states to address the problem through their AFDC programs. First, in 1950, Congress passed Section 402(a)(11), an addition to the Social Security Act, which required that state welfare agencies notify appropriate law enforcement officials upon disbursing AFDC payments if the child in question had been either abandoned or deserted.[1] Amendments added in 1965 (Public Law 89–97) provided state welfare agencies with the authority to obtain addresses from the Department of Health, Education, and Welfare in locating absent parents. The 1967 Amendments (Public Law 90–248) went even further by enabling states to gain access to highly sensitive Internal Revenue Service (IRS) location information. At this time, legislators also added Sections 402(a)(17), (18), (21), and (22) to the Social Security Act of 1935. As part of its AFDC program, each state now had to create a single organizational unit in charge of establishing paternity, as well as enter into cooperative agreements with other state courts on behalf of all families receiving welfare benefits. Notably, non-AFDC families were not included in these early phases of legislative development. Table 2.1 lays out these initial legislative developments and tracks major support legislation to the present.

By the 1970s, the mood of the country had shifted toward a much more concrete approach to the problem at hand. Federal initiatives were clearly not doing the job of resolving the child support problem, and most observers commented on the need for a separate program – distinct from the AFDC program – to deal with the issue by itself. Proposals differed, however, in terms of how far the federal government should go in addressing this issue.

Jumping headfirst into the fray, Senator Henry Bellmon (R-Okla.) introduced S. 1842 on May 17, 1973. This bill proposed the creation of a new parent locator service and a new child support program to be run out of the national attorney general's office. In his vision of child

---

[1] For a general history of this early legislation, see the *First Annual Report to Congress*. 1976. Washington, DC: Office of Child Support Enforcement.

TABLE 2.1. *Major federal child support legislation, 1950–present*

Year	Legislation
1950	42 USC 602(a)(11) • State welfare agencies had to notify law enforcement personnel when child is abandoned or deserted. • Uniform Reciprocal Enforcement of Support Act (URESA) approved.
1965	Public Law (P.L.) 89-97/Social Security Amendments of 1965 • Allowed state welfare agency to access absent parent's address information from the Department of Health, Education, and Welfare (HEW).
1967	P.L. 90-248/Social Security Amendments of 1967 • States had to organize separate administrative units to establish paternity and collect support for AFDC children. • States could access Internal Revenue Service (IRS) records for delinquent parents' addresses.
1975	P.L. 93-647/Social Security Amendments of 1975 • Made HEW responsible for supervising states in establishing independent child support agencies. • Incentive payments established for states to collect support on behalf of AFDC families. • New eligibility requirements added to AFDC program forcing mothers to cooperate with the state in identifying and locating their children's fathers.
1981	P.L. 97-35/Omnibus Reconciliation Act of 1981 • Allowed the IRS to withhold refunds to pay for child support. • Required states to withhold percentage of unemployment benefits for child support. • States had to collect spousal support for AFDC families.
1984	P.L. 98-378/ Child Support Enforcement Amendments of 1984 • Required states to provide equal services for AFDC and non-AFDC families. • Mandated that states establish award guidelines. • Made withholding mandatory for all families if support payments are delinquent by one month. • Made liens against real property in the amount of the overdue support mandatory for all families. • Required withholding of state/federal tax refunds for all families when there was a delinquency. • Established new state incentive payments for AFDC and non-AFDC cases. • Made delinquencies available to credit agencies upon request for all families. • Required persons who have been delinquent in the past to post a bond or other type of security to insure payment for all families.

(continued)

TABLE 2.1 *(continued)*

Year	Legislation
	• Mandated that states adopt expedited (administrative) processes for establishing a child support order rather than the standard court order. • Permitted the state to establish paternity until the child's eighteenth birthday for all families.
1988	P.L. 100-485/Family Support Act of 1988 • Required judges to use award guidelines in determining award amounts. • Created new paternity establishment goals. • Required automatic wage withholding for all new cases. • Ordered new states to have computerized systems in place.
1992	P.L. 102-521/Child Support Recovery Act of 1992 • Imposed a federal criminal penalty for nonpayment of interstate support. P.L. 102-537/Ted Weiss Child Support Enforcement Act of 1992 • Amended Fair Credit Reporting Act to require consumer credit agencies to include child support delinquencies.
1994	P.L. 103-383/Full Faith and Credit for Child Support Orders Act • Required states to enforce child support orders from other states by clarifying issues of jurisdiction. P.L. 103-394/Bankruptcy Reform Act of 1994 • Prevented child support from being discharged in bankruptcy proceedings.
1996	P.L. 104-193/Personal Responsibility and Work Opportunity Reconciliation Act of 1996 (PRWORA) • Strengthened rules for locating and tracking missing parents. • Mandated that all states pass the Uniform Interstate Family Support Act (UIFSA) to replace URESA. • Required all states to pass employer reporting of new hires (W-4) legislation. • Ordered states to implement administrative processes instead of court orders for issuing subpoenas, genetic testing, etc.
1998	P.L. 105-187/Deadbeat Parents Punishment Act of 1998 • Imposed a two-year maximum prison term for avoiding interstate support in the amount of $5,000 or more. P.L. 105-200/Child Support Performance and Incentive Act of 1998 • Created a new incentive structure to encourage states to operate efficient programs.

Source: U.S. Department of Health and Human Services, Administration for Children and Families, Office of Planning, Research and Evaluation; and *The Green Book.* Various years. Committee on Ways and Means, United States House of Representatives. Washington, DC: U.S. Government Printing Office.

support, the federal government would provide subsidies, or "fill in the gap," in order to make up any money that the fathers neglected to pay to their families. The delinquent fathers, in turn, would become indebted to the federal government, subject to all laws and penalties generated by such an outstanding obligation.

The opposition to the federal government making up the difference between monies owed and monies actually received by needy families was intense. Dissatisfied with Bellmon's plan, Senators Sam Nunn (D-Ga.) and Herman Talmadge (D-Ga.) produced a competing vision of child support reform on June 25, 1973, in S. 2081. This bill endorsed the concept of the attorney general as the primary locus of power in the child support program, but rejected the idea that the federal government should help supplement child support payments in the event that a father became delinquent.

There were also other issues to resolve involving jurisdictional infighting between HEW and the Justice Department. HEW's position was clear: child support must be administratively linked to the state-run AFDC programs in order to succeed. And, since HEW ran the AFDC program, it only made sense that it should take charge of the child support program as well. On the other hand, representatives from the Justice Department argued that the child support problem was one of inadequate enforcement, not one of insufficient family services; in this view, only an institution with prosecutorial powers could bring the full weight of the law against the delinquent fathers.

Considering these options, members of Congress were finally able to reach a compromise in H.R. 3153, which created a new program to be organized by the federal government, but to be run on a practical day-to-day basis by the states. Under this bill, ultimately guided through Congress by Senator Russell B. Long (D-La.), the overarching responsibility for the program would be within HEW rather than in the attorney general's office.[2] The attorney general, therefore, would not become the debtee of last resort for delinquent fathers. Instead, the states would play the most important role in devising solutions to the enforcement problem. The conference committee later incorporated H.R. 3153 into a larger bill, and Congress passed it on January 4, 1975. President Ford signed the bill on the same day, officially creating the 1975 Child Support Enforcement Program under Title IV of the Social Security Act.

[2] For more on this decision, see Ronald Mincy and Hillard Pouncy. 1997. "Paternalism, Child Support Enforcement, and Fragile Families." In *The New Paternalism*, ed. Lawrence M. Mead. Washington, DC: The Brookings Institution.

In sum, collecting child support for AFDC families started out as a Washington-led initiative, with Congress passing incremental laws to improve enforcement. By 1975, however, the Ford administration had adopted the "new federalist" belief that familial support – that is, support transferred from fathers to mothers – should remain as state-based a matter as possible. Ford echoed these concerns when he signed the bill into law.

The second element of this bill involves the collection of child support payments from absent parents. I strongly agree with the objectives of this legislation.... I am particularly pleased that this legislation follows a desirable trend in Federal-State relations. It will improve the results of programs previously hampered by unrealistic assumptions of Federal review and control. Those decisions related to local conditions and needs will be made at the State level, while Federal responsibilities are clearly delineated. Indeed, the interests of not only the Federal and State governments but also producers and consumers are recognized and protected.[3]

In his own words, then, Ford foresaw a program that would help the federal government to recoup at least part of its welfare expenditures, but one that would not provide excessive guidance to the states in establishing policy.

In recent years, however, the child support program has had much more of a federal flavor, although states retain some flexibility in designing the specifics of policy implementation. With a growing caseload, national policymakers have been concerned that some states seem to be lagging behind the rest of the nation across a whole host of program indicators. The federal response, a new system of "supervised devolution,"[4] means that, in practical terms, the federal government uses both the carrot of financial incentives and the stick of financial penalties to encourage states to design policies with specific goals in mind.

Carrots are easy to identify. Currently, the federal government pays 66 percent of all program operating expenses, as well as 90 percent of all information technology and genetic testing expenses. When the program first began, states were able to retain between 6 percent and 10 percent of all collections they made on behalf of welfare families;

---

[3] From President Gerald R. Ford. January 4, 1975. "Statement on Signing the Social Service Amendments of 1974." *Public Papers of the President 1975*. Washington, DC: U.S. Government Printing Office.

[4] This phrase comes from Jocelyn Elise Crowley. 2000. "Supervised Devolution: The Case of Child Support Enforcement." *Publius: The Journal of Federalism* 30(1/2): 99–117.

the Child Support Enforcement Amendments of 1984 extended these incentive payments to apply to collections made on behalf of nonwelfare families as well. From 1984 to 1996, these incentives were based only on the states' collection-to-cost ratios. The more a state was able to collect at the lowest cost, the higher the percentage of collections the state was able to retain. Through the Personal Responsibility and Work Opportunity Reconciliation Act (PRWORA) of 1996, the Welfare Reform Technical Amendments Act of 1997, and the Child Support Performance and Incentive Act of 1998, states will now be able to receive incentive payments based on their performance in establishing paternity, establishing orders, collecting current payments, and pursuing arrearages.

States also face financial sticks from the federal government in this new policy regime. Prior to 1996, the states only faced financial penalties if they failed to meet certain paternity establishment standards as required by the Omnibus Reconciliation Act of 1993. With PRWORA, states also have to perform in the following areas: (1) number of orders established, and (2) current monies collected out of total monies due. Penalties are 1 percent of the state's total Temporary Assistance for Needy Families (TANF) block grant in the first year of such a failure to meet these standards, and 2 percent in the second year.[5]

THE COMPOSITION OF THE CASELOAD

As the balance between federal and state authority has shifted over time, so has the composition of the child support caseload. Prior to the 1970s, women receiving welfare faced a unique policy regime with respect to support. Required by their states' AFDC agencies to cooperate in naming their children's father, these mothers had to comply or face welfare sanctions. In the case of non-AFDC families, on the other hand, state court judges rather than state agencies made individually based decisions on the support question, deciding if and when support should be awarded at all. Along with these distinct systems for setting awards, each clientele also faced its own set of enforcement mechanisms that were triggered in the case of a delinquency.

The creation of the child support program in 1975 brought these two caseloads together for the first time in history, and currently the program

---

[5] TANF, a system of block grants to the states for welfare payments to families, replaced the AFDC system in 1996.

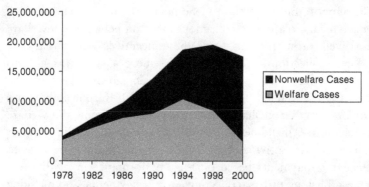

FIGURE 2.1. Child support caseload for welfare and nonwelfare families, 1978–2000. *Source: Annual Reports to Congress.* Various years. Washington, DC: Office of Child Support Enforcement.

handles about 50 percent of all child support cases in the country.[6] There are, however, several important distinctions to note. First, the full range of services offered by the program to nonwelfare families did not come into existence until the Child Support Enforcement Amendments of 1984. Prior to that year, states were relatively free to decide which services they wanted to offer to working-, middle-, and upper-class families. Second, there are differences in terms of program eligibility and compliance. Welfare families are required by law to be part of the child support program. When they apply for welfare benefits, they must agree to enroll in the program, and they assign their support rights to the state. This means that any support that the states are able to collect on their behalf from their former partners goes immediately back to the public coffers to replace welfare monies already expended.[7] Nonwelfare families, on the other hand, are not required to take part in the child support program, although anyone, regardless of income, is eligible for services. Any support that the states collect on behalf of these families is redistributed back to them within a designated period of time.

As Figure 2.1 indicates, the composition of the child support caseload has changed dramatically over time. When the program first began in the

---

[6] The other 50 percent of cases are processed by private attorneys, private child support collection agencies, locally funded child support agencies, or by mutual agreement of the parents. See United States House of Representatives Committee on Ways and Means. 2000. *The 2000 Green Book.* Washington, DC: U.S. Government Printing Office, p. 505.

[7] During one stage of the program (1984–96), states had to "pass through" the first $50 collected from fathers to the family receiving welfare.

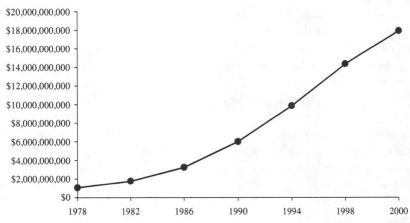

FIGURE 2.2. Total child support collections, 1978–2000. *Sources:* Data taken from *The 2000 Green Book.* 2000. United States House of Representatives, Committee on Ways and Means. Washington, DC: U.S. Government Printing Office, p. 467; *Annual Reports to Congress.* Various years. Washington, DC: Office of Child Support Enforcement.

mid-1970s, welfare cases dominated the caseload – 3.5 million welfare cases to approximately 604,000 nonwelfare families. However, with the full availability of services offered to nonwelfare families in 1984, the types of families applying for services also changed. Nonwelfare families, frustrated by their experiences with the courts, began to enroll by the thousands into the new program. Changes in the country's welfare programs also hastened this trend. PRWORA, which placed time limitations on benefit receipt, has resulted in fewer cases on the rolls, and thus fewer welfare-related child support cases. Indeed, by 2000, nonwelfare families became dominant in the system, which served approximately 14.2 million nonwelfare families and 3.3 million welfare families. And in aiding these families, the program collected over $17.9 billion in outstanding support in 2000, up from approximately $1 billion in 1978 (Figure 2.2).

DUTIES OF THE CURRENT CHILD SUPPORT PROGRAM

With this ever-changing caseload, how has the current child support system coped? What are the duties of the child support program in America today? There are no easy answers to these questions. Most social programs in America proceed along a natural life cycle. They begin with a clearly defined mission, and all employees focus upon achieving carefully

articulated goals. As the program ages, however, new goals are added to
the old goals, so that staff must adapt to changes in the organizational
mission and redirect their energies accordingly. This natural evolution has
applied to the child support system as well. In recent years, the program
has witnessed the "adding on" of multiple new duties, such as offering
job training to program recipients and their families, educating parents
about their proper role in their children's lives, and establishing and enforcing medical support orders. Yet, despite these "add-ons," we can still
conceptualize the program as having four core duties: (1) locating absent
parents, (2) establishing paternity, (3) setting orders and awards, and (4)
enforcing the orders.

1. Locating Absent Parents

The first step in collecting child support is to locate the parent charged
with the responsibility of paying. In the initial stages of screening, the
state child support agency gathers as much information as possible from
the custodial mother about her former partner's whereabouts. If the state
cannot succeed in locating the absent parent from its data records (motor
vehicle registrations, telephone directories, etc.), it can appeal to the Federal Parent Locator Service (FPLS) for assistance. The FPLS is a unique
data management system that holds records pertaining to individuals with
relationships to the Selective Service System, the Department of Defense,
the Veterans Administration, the National Personnel Records Center, the
Internal Revenue Service, the Social Security Administration, and the
State Employment Security Agencies. The FPLS runs weekly data matches
against the records of these agencies in order to locate missing parents.
The child support enforcement program as a whole has succeeded in increasing the number of parents located from 454,000 in 1978 to 6,585,000
in 1998 (see Figure 2.3).

One of the most important new parent locator tools authorized by
PRWORA in 1996 is the use of W-4 forms. In order for child support
enforcement to be effective, the states must have at their disposal reliable
location and income data from the noncustodial father. This is difficult
when the father works seasonally, intermittently, or tends to change jobs
quickly.[8] PRWORA requires that all employers forward a copy of the

---

[8] Ronald Mincy and Hillard Pouncy. 1997. "Paternalism, Child Support Enforcement, and
Fragile Families." In *The New Paternalism*, ed. Lawrence M. Mead. Washington, DC: The
Brookings Institution; Marcia Mobilia Boumil and Joel Friedman. 1996. *Deadbeat Dads:
A National Child Support Scandal*. Westport: Praeger.

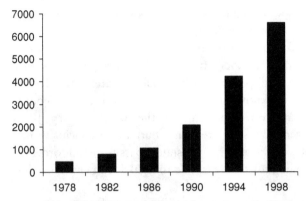

FIGURE 2.3. Absent parents located, 1978–1998 (in thousands). *Source:* Data taken from *The 2000 Green Book*. 2000. United States House of Representatives, Committee on Ways and Means. Washington, DC: U.S. Government Printing Office, p. 467. Data from the year 2000 is no longer reported by the federal Office of Child Support Enforcement.

W-4 form to the state employment security or child support enforcement agency within twenty days after a new worker is hired. State employees then match this information against current child support caseload data in order to locate missing or delinquent parents. They can also match this data to the National Directory of New Hires (NDNH), which is located in the FPLS. NDNH collects new hire data, quarterly wage data, and unemployment insurance information from the fifty states in order to improve support outcomes. Overall, these new initiatives have been successful in locating absent parents. In many states, the introduction of the W-4 system has reduced the amount of time that custodial parents have had to wait for their support from months to days.

2. Establishing Paternity

In order for child support to be effective, families must also establish paternity. The Child Support Enforcement Amendments of 1984 and the Family Support Act of 1988 required states to establish paternity up to a child's eighteenth birthday. As further incentives for state action, the 1988 law introduced standards of paternity establishment across the country, and it offered financial assistance to those states pursuing DNA laboratory testing to match putative fathers with their children. The Omnibus Reconciliation Act of 1993 furthered these trends by instituting financial penalties for those states unable to meet predesignated establishment standards.

States have also sought to streamline the methods by which parents can establish paternity. In the past, paternity establishment has automatically meant an extended and frequently frustrating court process for the mother and father.[9] The Omnibus Reconciliation Act of 1993 required that each state adopt a voluntary civil process for establishing paternity.[10] To give the measure teeth, this acknowledgement also had to create a rebuttal or a conclusive presumption of paternity in the states. The 1993 law also mandated that genetic testing create a rebuttal or a conclusive presumption of paternity, and it required the states to issue default orders of paternity on fathers who refused to respond to legal documents regarding parentage.

Recently, PRWORA required that states introduce voluntary paternity acknowledgment programs that ask fathers to accept their legal responsibilities for their children after the mothers give birth at the hospital. The idea here is to catch the fathers when they are most likely to be involved with their children.[11] While unmarried births represent a greater problem for welfare families than for nonwelfare families, voluntary in-hospital paternity acknowledgment programs have a track record of success for both types of families.[12] As a result of these new programs, paternity establishments have increased from 111,000 in 1978 to 1,556,000 in 2000 (see Figure 2.4).

3. Setting Orders and Awards

Child support orders involve both legally establishing a parent as responsible for the support of his child and setting the award amount.

---

[9] Sandra Danziger and Ann Nichols-Casebolt. 1990. "Child Support in Paternity Cases." *Social Service Review* 64(3): 458–474.

[10] For details of this transition from court-based systems to administrative systems for deciding paternity cases, see Jocelyn Elise Crowley. 2001. "Who Institutionalizes Institutions? The Case of Paternity Establishment in the United States." *Social Science Quarterly* 82(2): 312–328.

[11] Ronald Mincy and Hillard Pouncy. 1997. "Paternalism, Child Support Enforcement, and Fragile Families." In *The New Paternalism*, ed. Lawrence M. Mead. Washington, DC: The Brookings Institution.

[12] Several evaluations of these programs have been produced. These include *Massachusetts Paternity Acknowledgment Program: Implementation Analysis and Program Results*. 1995. Denver: Policy Studies; *Massachusetts Paternity Acknowledgment Program Addendum to the 1995 Executive Summary*. 1997. Cambridge, MA: Massachusetts Department of Revenue, Child Support Enforcement Division; *Massachusetts Paternity Acknowledgment Program: Survey of Selected Maternity Hospitals*. 1997. Cambridge, MA: Paternity Projects, Massachusetts Department of Revenue, Child Support Enforcement Division.

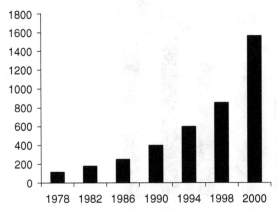

FIGURE 2.4. Paternities established, 1978–2000 (in thousands). *Sources:* See Figure 2.2.

Before 1984, the judicial system was solely responsible for issuing support awards. However, with the growth in the caseload and the delays involved in the judicial processes for assessing these claims, single-parent families quickly fell behind their two-parent counterparts in paying for their children's daily needs. Congress responded with a provision in the 1984 Child Support Enforcement Amendments that required that the states establish an expedited administrative procedure for issuing these awards.

Prior to 1984 as well, local judges decided how much support to award each single-parent family. Amounts to be paid varied widely, resulting in the drafting of another section of the 1984 Child Support Enforcement Amendments related to awards; now, each state had to establish guidelines for setting award levels. Later, the 1988 Family Support Act mandated that each state utilize these guidelines or document the reasons behind its deviation. In general, these laws have created stability across the country, as most states have chosen to set the awards using a relatively limited set of models.[13] State agencies have pursued establishing these orders with increased success over time, as Figure 2.5 indicates. Orders have grown from 315,000 in 1978 to 1.1 million in 2000.

PRWORA also gave states further power to modify awards when appropriate. All program participants must be informed of their right to

---

[13] The main guidelines used include a percentage-of-income standard, the income shares model, the Melson formula, and hybrid formulas. These formulas are discussed in greater detail in Chapter 7.

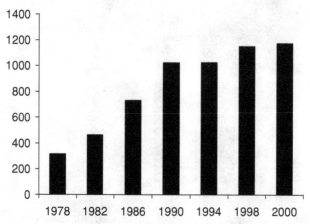

FIGURE 2.5. Child support orders established, 1978–2000 (in thousands). *Sources:* See Figure 2.2.

have their case reviewed at least every three years. Moreover, any case must be reviewed if either parent requests such a review. States can either use their current guidelines to modify award levels, adjust with respect to the inflation rate, or employ an automated method to identify and alter those awards that are flagged by the computer as in need of adjustment.

4. Enforcing the Orders

Locating parents, establishing paternity, and setting awards are all precursors to perhaps the most important function of the child support system: enforcing support. Three enforcement techniques dominate the ways in which child support agencies around the country collect and distribute money from noncustodial to custodial parents: income withholding, tax intercepts, and unemployment intercepts. The Family Support Act of 1988 required all states to utilize income withholding as a means for collecting support beginning in 1990 for all new or modified orders. Income withholding simply means that a father's child support payments are automatically deducted from his paycheck and then distributed back to his family. The tax intercept system, introduced as a result of the Child Support Enforcement Amendments of 1984, uses fathers' social security numbers to seize federal and state tax refunds and then disburse these monies back to the families in need. The unemployment compensation intercept program, a product of the 1981 Omnibus Reconciliation Act, withholds a portion of a father's unemployment benefits and redirects it to his family.[14]

In addition to these techniques, the federal government and the states have teamed up in devising new strategies to enforce support. Property liens, credit reporting, and the passport denial program are in operation across all of the states. In addition to these techniques, one of the most powerful new enforcement tools adopted by the states is license revocation, a procedure mandated by PRWORA. State legislatures have passed laws that authorize the suspension of professional, trade, sporting, business, and driver's licenses for individuals who are delinquent in their support payments. Restrictions such as these have proved especially strong in motivating the self-employed and others who are dependent on such licenses for their livelihoods to pay their support on time.[15]

States have also been active in improving interstate enforcement. Interstate cases represent a special category of orders that are particularly difficult to enforce.[16] In 1990, interstate cases represented approximately one-fourth of the total caseload, translating into slightly over 2.5 million mothers reporting that the noncustodial father lived in a different state.[17] (This excludes the approximately 10.7 percent of all cases where the mother had no knowledge of where the father was currently residing.)[18]

Since child support enforcement is a state-run program, in the past, if nonsupport became an issue for such a custodial mother, her only option was to seek the government's aid in pursuing extradition measures against her former partner. Of course, she rarely employed this strategy. Extradition procedures were simply too costly for the mother, her attorney, and the two states that were involved. Moreover, at that time the states were having enough trouble enforcing *intrastate* support orders to become involved in cases that were almost impossible to prosecute.

In 1950, the states first attempted to improve interstate enforcement through the adoption of the Uniform Reciprocal Enforcement of

---

[14] Of course, if the families are receiving welfare, the money collected is returned to the state.

[15] Marcia Mobilia Boumil and Joel Friedman. 1996. *Deadbeat Dads: A National Child Support Scandal.* Westport: Praeger.

[16] Marcia Mobilia Boumil and Joel Friedman. 1996. *Deadbeat Dads: A National Child Support Scandal.* Westport: Praeger; Andrea H. Beller and John W. Graham. 1993. *Small Change: The Economics of Child Support.* New Haven, CT: Yale University Press.

[17] *Interstate Child Support: Mothers Report Receiving Less Support from Out-of-State Fathers.* 1992. GAO/HRD-92-FS.

[18] *Interstate Child Support: Mothers Report Receiving Less Support from Out-of-State Fathers.* 1992. GAO/HRD-92-FS.

Support Act (URESA). Although strengthened through amendments several times over the following forty years, URESA still proved inadequate to ensure that interstate orders were enforced.[19] For example, many states had incompatible versions of the URESA law on their books, producing two problems: (1) an enormous amount of confusion over which state was actually in charge of the order, and (2) frustration over how long a state could take to respond to another state that was requesting help in enforcing support. In addition, more often than not, the courts in the two states produced multiple and conflicting orders awarding support that were then typically ignored by all of the parties involved.

In an important attempt to solve these problems, the Family Support Act of 1988 mandated the creation of a new Commission on Interstate Enforcement with the sole purpose of recommending improvements to the interstate support system. This effort prompted the National Conference of Commissioners on Uniform State Laws (NCCUSL), an organization dedicated to improving cooperation among the individual state legal systems, to draft revisions of URESA for subsequent adoption by Congress. The Uniform Interstate Family Support Act (UIFSA), passed by the commissioners in 1992, aimed to address these issues by providing for the validity of only one support order at a time, establishing mechanisms by which the states could use long-arm jurisdiction rules (regulations clarifying jurisdictional authority over interstate cases) to implement wage-withholding orders, and fixing time limits under which states must respond to requests for interstate aid in enforcing support. PRWORA mandated the adoption of UIFSA for all states by the end of 1998.

CONCLUSIONS

Throughout the past several decades, we have witnessed jockeying for power between the states and the federal government for control of the child support program. In the early years, Congress passed laws from distant Washington, D.C., that members believed would be sufficient to deal with the problem, but they were soon overwhelmed by the sheer magnitude of single-parent families in need of financial assistance. By the late

---

[19] *Interstate Child Support: Better Information Needed on Absent Parents for Case Pursuit.* 1990. GAO/HRD-90-41; *Interstate Child Support: Case Data Limitations, Enforcement Problems, Views on Improvements Needed.* 1989. GAO/HRD-89-25; *Interstate Child Support: Mothers Report Receiving Less Support from Out-of-State Fathers.* 1992. GAO/HRD-92-FS; *Interstate Child Support: Wage Withholding Not Fulfilling Expectations.* 1992a. GAO/HRD-92-65BR.

1970s and early 1980s, the states seemed to have the competitive edge over national policymakers, as they designed unique ways of determining paternity, setting awards, and collecting support. More recently, the federal government has taken on a supervisory role over the states, granting them freedom in specific areas but making sure that they do not deviate from the direction that members of Congress want the program to take in the years to come.

Despite these ebbs and flows of competitive power, the United States today has a strong system of child support enforcement, almost like a well-oiled machine of legal compulsion. If we do not know where a father is, policymakers can find him in one of many available databases. If we do not know which man is the father of a particular child, administrative agencies can order DNA tests. Formulas spit out order awards, and remote computers assess award levels. Support is deducted from individuals' paychecks before they even know it was there to begin with. And money is sent back to the recipient families, so that housing, food, and utility bills can all be paid on time.

Now that we have a better idea of where we are in terms of the child support system, it is important to understand how we got here. These complex systems of income redistribution within former family units did not materialize out of nowhere. Instead, they are the product of the efforts of a series of policy entrepreneurs who each perceived the child support problem in a different way, and organized to achieve their goals accordingly. In the nineteenth century, the charity workers along with local law enforcement, as we will see in the next chapter, laid the foundation of early American child support policy that subsequent waves of entrepreneurs would later attempt to transform.

3

Charity Workers and Local Law Enforcement

The Beginnings of American Child Support Policy

In taking up my work over eight years ago, I found everything comparatively easy to dispose of except these married vagabonds, who hid behind the wife and flock of little children. I consulted the law, and found there was plenty of law; but the application was not such as to remedy the evil. Such men are often willing to enter a jail, and be well fed and kept warm, and, as a general thing, have nothing to do but read trashy literature, leaving their families to starve or be supported by towns or by benevolent people. I awoke one morning with a determination to see what I could do toward making the law a means to an end. I visited the judge of our city court, and laid my plan before him. I said to him: "I find that in your administration of justice in this court, from time to time, you suspend judgment in the cases of certain men. I want these men to understand that the next time they are presented to this court for non-support of their families, instead of giving them from thirty to sixty days, you will give them the full penalty of the law, and then allow me to give them an opportunity to choose between two things."

"Go ahead," said the judge, "and we will see what we can accomplish."

The first case to come up was a Scotchman. I had seen him in the prisoner's dock time and again. He had a wife and four little children, was a skilled workman, and able to earn three dollars a day. He expected to get his usual thirty days. His wife would get two dollars and half a week in coal, and they would try to work the Charity Organization Society for some help. The man was proved guilty, and it was then the opportunity to try my experiment. I walked over to him, and said: "Dave, you are here again; and I will engage that you will get six months this time." He changed color: he did not like that.

"Now," I said, "wouldn't you like to turn around and be a better man, support yourself respectably and take care of your family?"

"What can a fellow do," he asked, "when everyone hates him?"

"Well," I said, "if I will stand by and be your friend, will you do as I want you to?" He said that he would. I had had some blanks printed that read: "Mr. _____: Please pay to G.W. Swan the money due me for wages for the next six months," or "a year," due David _____," and he signed it. I presented the signed document to the judge of the court, and made a plea for the suspension of judgement for sixty days. I gave a little bond for the man's appearance, and he went to work. When pay-day came, I took his money; and that money did not go into the family, to be got away from the wife by threats or coaxing. I adopted the system of tickets, sending her to the grocery store, allowing a limited amount of groceries to be received, so many dollars' worth a week. A similar arrangement was made with the butcher and with all those from whom David's necessaries were bought. If something were wanted from the dry-goods store, a special order was given for that. We kept a strict book account, and at the end of each month we called the man in and rendered an account to him of what had been spent. That man today is the best man in the employ of C.F. Rogers & Co. His home at that time was anything but cheerful. The condition of affairs had made his wife a scold. There were no carpets on the floors, the furniture was broken, there was only an apology for a stove, and the equipment of the larder was mainly empty whiskey bottles. Go in today, and you will find five rooms nicely furnished, five children – for another one has come into the home – well cared for, well clothed, and four of them in school; and above all, you will find a happy wife. They attend church, and the children go to Sunday school; and the man has a snug little bank account.

G. W. Swan, attendee at the Twenty-second Conference of Charities and Correction, 1895.[1]

Proper child support is an issue that has confronted American society for over a century. Today, we see the most conspicuous ramifications of this problem everywhere, from those impacted children living in desperate poverty to those who go to bed hungry every night to those who lack basic medical care. Perhaps even more widespread are those effects that are less overt but equally invidious – children who perceive, because of their lack of financial support, that their parents do not care about their well-being. These are the children who end up dropping out of school, becoming pregnant, having scuffles with the law, and becoming involved with drugs. In each of these cases, the underlying problem remains the same. What do we, as a society, do when a father, usually the primary breadwinner of the family, cannot or will not provide for the children he brings into this world?

[1] G. W. Swan. 1895. "Remarks." *Twenty Second Conference of Charities and Correction.* Boston: Geo. H. Ellis, pp. 519–520.

Clearly, there are no easy answers to this question, but that has not stopped a variety of groups – policy entrepreneurs – from entering into the political arena and attempting to offer their best guess. In nineteenth-century America, two methods of child support enforcement dominated. The first type involved cases where a third-party benefactor or a mother sued for support. These cases generally involved the well-off, and for the most part the courts decided these cases individually and privately.

The second type of cases involved families of lesser means. Charity workers and local law enforcement comprised one of the first sets of policy leaders to enter the child support debate here. At first, as we will see, their approach was highly paternalistic. As demonstrated in the passage just quoted from Mr. Swan, the charity workers aimed to control many aspects of a family's life in order to help put them back on the right financial road. This involved tracking down wayward fathers, serving as intermediaries between them and their families, and making sure that the "proper" purchases were made for their children's survival. In this paradigm, external financial relief was to be avoided at all costs, as it potentially corrupted the character of the recipients. Only in dire circumstances would private charities be tapped to meet a family's basic needs. This chapter provides a brief introduction to the beginnings of child support policy in the United States.

INDIVIDUALS AS COMPLAINANTS

Third Party Benefactors as Complainants

Both during and immediately after the Revolution, American courts lacked a common law version of a child support duty.[2] This was because most American laws were based on English precedent, and there was no basis in English law for mothers to collect support from their former spouses. In fact, all that the English law provided was a "principle of natural law" that all parents should support their children; no third party – including a mother – could attempt to collect money from her former spouse to help her raise her children.

American courts thus "invented" the common law notion of child support, without reference to any European standard, in the early nineteenth

---

[2] For an excellent discussion of early child support law, see Drew D. Hansen. 1999. "The American Invention of Child Support: Dependency and Punishment in Early American Child Support Law." *Yale Law Journal* 108(5): 1123–1153.

century. The courts first recognized the right of third-party benefactors to sue an alleged father for financial damages. This third party could be a friend, a relative, or simply a merchant who supported the father's children by providing them with a variety of goods and services. In order to win the claim, however, the complainant had to prove that (1) the items purchased were necessities, such as food and clothing, and (2) that the father in question had failed to make available such resources.

One widely cited case that began to articulate the third-party basis for suing was *Van Valkinburgh v. Watson and Watson* (1816).[3] In this New York case, a child attempted to purchase a coat on his father's credit. The merchant sold the child the coat, and then tried to collect the money from the father. The court laid out its legal foundation in favor of all parents' providing for their children by asserting:

A parent is under a natural obligation to furnish necessaries for his infant children; and if the parent neglects that duty, any other person who supplies such necessaries is deemed to have conferred a benefit on the delinquent parent, for which the law raises an implied promise to pay on the part of the parent.[4]

In this case, the justices maintained that the father was actually successfully supporting his son, and that therefore the merchant had no claim in compelling the father to pay for the coat. Thus, while articulating a principle of parental responsibility, the court asserted that only cases where third parties provided necessities to minors could result in enforceable claims.

While the plaintiff could not recover damages in this case, *Van Valkinburgh v. Watson and Watson* did lay the groundwork for the principle of allowing third parties to recover significant child care costs. *Tomkins v. Tomkins* (1858), decided in the New Jersey court system, endorsed this precedent, and in this case found the father liable to a third party.[5] The specifics of the case were as follows. In 1833, Mr. Tomkins left his wife and his child, and he failed thereafter to provide them with any material support. The mother sought aid from an almshouse, and the child went to live with her grandmother. Representatives of the grandmother, the mother, and the child aimed to convince the court that the father had deserted them, and thus sought proper restitution. Lawyers for the father claimed that the father was under no legal requirement to support his

---

[3] *Van Valkinburgh v. Watson and Watson*, 13 Johns 480 (N.Y. 1816).
[4] Ibid.
[5] *Tomkins v. Tomkins*, 11 N.J. Eq. 512 (Ch. 1858).

child, an assertion that the court quickly rejected:

[Lawyers for the father make the claim that] a parent is under no legal obligation to support his child, and that whoever furnishes a child with necessaries, must do it gratuitously; that no recovery can be had for such necessaries, unless they were furnished under an express contract with the parents.... Such is not the law in New Jersey.... A parent is bound to provide his infant children with necessaries; and if he neglects to do so, a third person may supply them, and charge the parent with the amount.[6]

The court went on to further castigate the father in question for his delinquent behavior; at the same time, the justices recognized that they were, in fact, "creating" new law. The court maintained that

[i]f a case can be suggested where the moral obligation of a father to provide for his offspring can be enforced as a legal one, it would be difficult to find one more apposite than this. The complainant left his child, about three or four years of age, with its destitute and heart-broken mother. He abandoned them both to the charities of the world. The mother found shelter in the alms-house. The daughter was forced upon its grandmother, a woman then advanced in life, and of moderate means for her own support. There is no evidence that for the fifteen years the child was under the care of its grandmother, the father ever made any inquiry as to its whereabouts or welfare. Now, in view of all these facts, if there was any doubt as to the legal obligation of the father to provide for his child, and of his legal liability to such as should supply that child with the necessaries of life, the moral obligation is so strong that a court of equity would feel but little inclined to grant relief, on any such ground as that the moral obligation had been converted into a legal one.[7]

In *Tomkins*, the court found the father to be delinquent in his responsibilities toward his family – a breach of what the judges viewed as his natural duty. As reflected in this quotation, part of the finding of fault rested upon the court's visceral reaction to a father's abandonment of his offspring. In the court's opinion, there was an unspoken standard of family life that needed to be protected. Now, with the establishment of this case law, a father's delinquency provided third-party supporters with the ammunition they needed to sue for reimbursement.

Mothers as Complainants

In addition to third parties, mothers themselves who wished to sue for support could also file civil claims. The mothers who made these claims,

[6] Ibid. at 517.
[7] Ibid. at 517–518.

however, faced an additional burden in court. Not only did they have to prove that they were destitute, they also had to show that they were not at fault with respect to the divorce. Significantly, if the wife *were* at fault, then she would not be entitled to collect support.

Connecticut's *Stanton v. Stanton* (1808) was one of the first cases that outlined the legal course of action for mothers acting on behalf of their children.[8] In this case, Eunice Stanton sued the estate of her deceased ex-husband, John Bird, in order to recover expenditures laid out for their children that were subsequently paid for by her second husband, Joshua Stanton. The facts of the case were straightforward. Eunice married John Bird in 1789, had three children, and subsequently divorced him in 1797. She immediately took custody of her two youngest children, William and Maria; her oldest son, John Herman, continued to live with Bird. In 1803, Eunice married Joshua Stanton, after which, in 1805, her eldest son came to live with her (he claimed abuse by Bird). During the time that the three children lived with her and then with her new husband, Eunice Stanton claimed the expenses listed in Table 3.1.

With only the bare bones of a legal precedent establishing a fundamental duty of parents to provide for their children, the justices in the state of Connecticut nonetheless carved out such a duty in their decision by pointing to the financial "dissolution" of the wife upon marriage.

Parents are bound by law to maintain, protect, and educate their legitimate children, during their infancy or nonage. This duty rests on the father; and it is reasonable it should be so, as the personal estate of the wife, and in her possession at the time of the marriage, becomes the property of the husband, and instantly vests in him.... By the divorce, the relation of husband and wife was destroyed; but not the relation between Bird and his children.[9]

As was common law at the time, when a woman became married, all of her assets were transferred to her husband's name. This was the doctrine of coverture, which had evolved as part of English law beginning in the Middle Ages. As the husband was defined as lord of the manor during the Middle Ages, men were defined as "personifying" the entire marital relationship during the eighteenth and early nineteenth centuries in America. The court reasoned that this transferal, while a boon to the husband financially, also bestowed upon him certain responsibilities for his children. The court therefore ordered the estate of John Bird to reimburse his ex-wife for the expenses laid out in Table 3.1.

---

[8] *Stanton v. Stanton*, 3 Day 37 (Conn. 1808).
[9] Ibid. at 55.

TABLE 3.1. *Eunice Stanton's claims against her ex-husband for child support, 1808*

Expense Category	Dollar Amount
Nursing Expenses for William, for 43 weeks, at $1 per week	$43.43
Extra Nursing during William's Sickness	$5.00
Doctor's Bill for William's Sickness	$10.00
Clothing for William	$20.00
Clothing, Boarding, and Nursing for William from March 1798 to September 1803, 6.5 years	$429.00
Schooling for William for 2.5 years at $6	$15.00
Nursing and clothing for William and Maria from June 1, 1797 to May 15, 1798, 49 weeks and 6 days	$74.78
Extra Nursing and Doctor's Bill during Maria's Sickness	$20.00
Boarding and Clothing William from October 1803 to February 1806, 117 weeks and 1 day, at $2.50	$292.87
Schooling for William	$12.00
Boarding for John Herman Bird, from February 1805 to February 1806, 48 weeks and 1 day	$96.30
Books and College Tuition for John Herman Bird	$55.00
Expense Money for John Herman Bird	$20.00

Source: Stanton v. Stanton, 3 Day at 37(1808).

CHARITY ORGANIZATIONS AND LOCAL LAW ENFORCEMENT
AS COMPLAINANTS

While the courts were beginning to establish a common, civil basis for third-party benefactors and mothers in search of child support, certain social trends during the latter half of the nineteenth century prompted the legislative branch to address the nonsupport issue as well. The first set of trends involved the changing nature of the American family, and the second revolved around the breakdown of the poor relief system that had served as the primary safety net for decades across American towns. These trends gave rise to the most powerful agents for action in the child support system prior to the early 1900s – private charity organizations working with local law enforcement.[10]

[10] For a broad overview of some of these changes, see Herma Hill Kay. 2000. "Symposium on Law in the Twentieth Century: From the Second Sex to the Joint Venture: An Overview of Women's Rights and Family Law in the United States during the Twentieth Century." *California Law Review* 88(6): 2017–2093.

   Divorce was rare in the American colonies, as the early settlers brought with them from England the most strictly interpreted traditional and religious ideas concerning the sanctity of marital vows. Once the Americans achieved independence, however, they began to experiment with new ways of developing family law. The states first eliminated the private bills of divorce granted by the legislatures that had been common in the initial years of the republic, replacing them with general divorce statutes applicable to all divorce-seeking parties. Despite this liberalizing trend, the number of couples filing for divorce remained quite low. With the country still heavily reliant on agriculture to fuel the economy, families were wedded to one another in tight-knit communities. These interconnections provided strong social sanctions against any type of misbehavior, such as adultery or desertion, that might serve as a precursor to divorce.

   The rise of industrialization in the latter part of the nineteenth century, however, brought with it a massive disruption in the social order of American life. For the first time, the cities drew workers by the thousands to labor in factories, offices, and all types of manufacturing plants. With the transplantation of families from the rural countryside to the urban centers also came the anonymity of city life and the newfound freedoms associated with such a constantly mobile existence. No longer subject to the community sanctions that had preserved family units in the countryside, workers – in particular, male laborers – were much more willing to flout their responsibilities to their wives and children in the name of individual financial, emotional, or sexual gain.

   Changes in state divorce laws reflected these new economic realities, although these transformations were by no means uniform. By 1905, while South Carolina still disallowed absolute divorce, and New York permitted divorce only in cases of adultery, most other states had enumerated a much longer list of justifiable actionable causes. These included bigamy, extreme cruelty, conviction of a felony, habitual drunkenness, as well as other factors. These more liberal divorce laws provided the opportunity for increasing numbers of couples to seek out a legal end to their union. Although early divorce statistics are somewhat sketchy by modern standards, it has been estimated that there were 2.8 divorces per 100 marriages in 1867. By 1890, the number of splits rose to 5.8 per 100 marriages, and by 1910, to 8.8 per 100 unions.[11]

   As divorce was becoming more prevalent, Americans were changing their views of children. In the early 1800s, most Americans viewed

---

[11] Ibid. at 2041.

children as "miniature adults," capable of the same thought processes, emotional responsibilities, and physical tasks as their older counterparts. Children commonly worked in factories, logging in roughly the same hours as the adults seated next to them. This was especially true in working-class families. Children, and not wives, were normally sent out to be the secondary wage earners in their families. Their labor was seen as a normal part of growing up, or simply as the price to be paid for receiving room and board within a traditional family unit. With children seen as economic assets, fathers normally assumed custody in cases of separation or divorce.

One of the most enduring changes brought about by the Progressive movement was the complete transformation in this dominant perception of children. Reformers, as represented by labor unions, women's suffragists, and other charitable organizations, argued that this prevailing notion of children as small adults was not only completely erroneous, but also devastatingly harmful. Activists, largely from the middle and upper classes, argued that children constituted a special class of people, with unique needs, desires, and opportunities for growth. In this new, more romanticized view, children needed to be protected from the harsh vicissitudes of the world, and especially from the filth, abuse, and other ravages of the labor market. As a result of the spread of these new ideas, restrictions on labor market participation and other child protective laws became more commonplace as the century progressed. Between the years 1900 and 1930, the number of children between the ages of ten and thirteen working in nonfarm occupations dropped from 186,358 to 30,000.[12]

With the spread of these new attitudes in the industrial arena, the states themselves took a greater interest in protecting the well-being of the children living within their borders in other respects as well. By the middle of the nineteenth century, most states had adopted some version of the Elizabethan poor laws, which had been developed in England in 1601. One of the laws' central components was the provision that required parents to support their children if the youngsters – in the absence of such support – would otherwise become paupers. But this provision was very loosely interpreted.

---

[12] Viviana A. Zelizer. 1999. "From Child Labor to Child Work: Changing Cultural Conceptions of Children's Economic Roles, 1870s-1930s." In *Ideas, Ideologies, and Social Movements*, ed. Peter Coclanis and Stuart Bruchey. Columbia: University of South Carolina Press.

In brief, a mother's need set in motion a chain of events that was supposed to provide the family with the basics of an income safety net. The triggering mechanism for assistance was simply a mother who requested aid from her town in order to support her children. After her request was registered and money began flowing in her direction, the courts would require fathers to reimburse the towns for the support of their children. The punishment meted out for this violation in England, however, was almost nonexistent. As Blackstone commented, children were expected to work in order to prevent their pauperization, and "the policy of our laws, which are ever watchful to promote industry, did not mean to compel a father to maintain his idle and lazy children in ease and indolence."[13] Initially, American courts replicated this policy by compelling fathers to reimburse the towns only at extremely low levels, if at all.

With the spread of industrialization and the ramifications created by a loosening social structure, however, the towns experienced increased pressure to help families in need. This pressure, interestingly enough, fell upon the charity workers – the precursors of today's professional social workers – who were then laboring in mostly private organizations. As fathers began to desert their families in higher numbers than ever before, charitable organizations were overwhelmed with single mothers requesting financial support. Aid was not disbursed liberally or freely, however. The type of relief that these private groups favored was very specific and pivoted on one specific moral theme: it could not serve to weaken the character of the person receiving the aid.

This vision of a great and upstanding society was propagated by leaders of the Charity Organization Society (COS) movement. The first such organization began 1878 in Buffalo, New York, and the movement spread throughout the country from there. While each local group was different, generally its members shared at least one common belief. In their view, striving to be an affluent member of society should be the goal of every man and woman across the nation. If someone were poor, according to Mary E. Richmond, one of the movement's leaders, it was probably the result of a moral failing on his or her part. Public relief, therefore, had to be condemned at every turn, since it only fed into this depraved moral state. The proper role of charity, then, was simple. Private citizens should set an example for the lowly, inspiring them to find the direction and the

---

[13] William Blackstone. 1841. *Commentaries on the Laws of England.* New York: W. E. Dean, p. 437.

help that they needed through personal efforts and family relationships to rise above their current situation in life. What this meant in practice was that local Charity Organization leaders would take it upon themselves to visit families "in need" in order to determine the true cause of their deprivation. Only truly deserving families would receive financial assistance; the others – the lazy, the slovenly, and the cheats – would have to pull themselves up by their own bootstraps.

The COS movement and all of its affiliated private agencies held fast to this belief system in all areas of welfare work, including the case of deserted children. In her analysis of the issue, Richmond argued that the problems of children being raised by "married vagabonds" were difficult to solve, but not impossible. The teams of "friendly visitors" played an important role in addressing these families' needs, and were much more important than the provision of public relief.

The visitor's tools are moral suasion, the cutting off of supplies from every available source, the frequently renewed offer of work, and last of all, the law. A paid agent may apply these also, so may a clergyman or public official; but the advantage peculiar to the visitor is that, confining her work, as she does, to a very few families, she has better opportunities of becoming well acquainted.[14]

The key to any friendly visitor's success in motivating a father to become more responsible for his children, according to Richmond, was found not in the generosity of assistance but rather in its denial.[15]

In many cases the more heroic treatment of cutting off supplies must be resorted to. So long as charitable people insist that they must forestall the possibility of "letting the innocent suffer" by aiding every neglected family generously, just so long the lazy man has society by the throat. When we find that we are dealing with such a man, it becomes necessary to prove that we have more strength of character to resist temptation to help than he has strength of character to resist temptation to work.[16]

---

[14] Mary Richmond. 1895. "Married Vagabonds." *Twenty-Second Conference of Charities and Correction.* Boston: Geo. H. Ellis, p. 516.

[15] Richmond was actually progressive in many ways for her time. As the historian Michael Katz has pointed out, during the mid nineteenth century, children were commonly separated from their parents owing to the plight of poverty. For example, from the 1850s to the 1890s, the New York Children's Aid Society was responsible for shipping thousands of city children from their homes to live with strangers in the West. Other children were simply institutionalized. See Michael B. Katz. 2001. *The Price of Citizenship.* New York: Holt, pp. 66–71; Michael B. Katz. 1995. *Improving Poor People.* Princeton, N.J.: Princeton University Press, pp. 38–41.

[16] Mary Richmond. 1895. "Married Vagabonds." *Twenty-Second Conference of Charities and Correction.* Boston: Geo. H. Ellis, p. 516.

In order to insure support for families over the long run, then, COS movement leaders advocated a hard-line approach. To the greatest extent possible, aid had to be kept to a minimum. Only when all else had failed would the town provide assistance and use the full extent of the law to pursue the wayward father.

When it came to actually attending to the problems of single mothers, however, charity workers, while mostly attentive, were simply overwhelmed by the task before them. Most of these organizations simply could not meet the demand at hand, and therefore took two forms of remedial action to address the crisis. First, charity workers appealed to the state legislatures to enact stricter criminal penalties for fathers who deserted their families. They advocated jail time, fines, or some combination of the two punishments. These lobbying efforts were critical because, at the turn of the century, only four states considered desertion or abandonment to be a felony, thereby reducing the possibility of punishment for wayward fathers to close to zero. Moreover, even those states that did have laws against desertion on the books typically had low fines (approximately $100) and brief mandatory jail sentences (three months). However, by 1911, organized charity workers had pushed seven states into passing tough new felony laws, and had increased penalties in eighteen other states to fines up to $1,000 and jail sentences of up to one year.[17]

Second, relief workers in private agencies began to serve as important liaisons among mothers, fathers, and the state. The new criminal laws passed by the states enabled the support collected from fathers to be directly transferred to the mothers in question or – even better, from the agencies' point of view – *through* the agencies from the fathers to the mothers. Private agencies took advantage of this legal remedy by acting as intermediaries between these parties: representatives from these groups began bringing charges against specific fathers in the court system in order to compel them to pay. In one 1894 study conducted by the superintendent of the Children's Home Society of Minnesota, Reverend E. P. Savage concluded that there were over 25,000 children who had been deserted by their parents in the United States. In order to "lift from society one of its heavy burdens," Savage encouraged all relief workers to flex the legal and fiscal muscle of the exemplary city of Cincinnati when pursuing delinquent fathers. As Savage pointed out, historical records documented

---

[17] Martha May. 1988. "The Problem of Duty: Family Desertion in the Progressive Era." *Social Service Review* 62(1): 40–59.

that in 1895, the Humane Society of Cincinnati investigated 937 cases of deserting fathers and won arrests for 654 of them, resulting in a total collection of $13,947.94.[18]

In her analysis of the Massachusetts Society for the Prevention of Cruelty to Children (MSPCC) records at the turn of the century, Linda Gordon also found that the relief workers took an active role in bringing support orders against deserting fathers.[19] Private agencies obtained orders from the courts and then insured that the fathers received the orders. Similar to other agencies, the MSPCC became a virtual collection bureau by entering into court-based agreements that required the fathers to pay support directly to the agencies. The MSPCC then engaged in active supervision of all recipient single mothers in order to guarantee that all the monies funneled back to them were spent "correctly" on their children.

An additional complication for the towns that were seeking financial compensation for helping single mothers in need was the problem of interstate flight.[20] As fathers became more mobile and job opportunities opened all over the country, fleeing one's state of origin became a common method for escaping the obligation of supporting one's children. The National Conference of Commissioners on Uniform State Laws (NCCUSL), the organization that encourages uniform legal standards across the country, attempted to deal with this problem on numerous occasions. In 1911, the commission proposed the Uniform Desertion and Non-Support Act (UDNA), which was later adopted by eighteen states. The UDNA made it an offense for a father to willfully desert his children and fail to pay support. Unfortunately, the initial incarnation of this interstate enforcement law was inadequate, because it was difficult to prove whether a father had "willfully" left his family or simply left his hometown temporarily in search of employment. The Uniform Support of Dependents Law (USDL), adopted by several states in 1944, improved upon the UDNA by requiring that fathers support their children in other states that had similar support laws. Yet, despite these improvements, interstate enforcement continued to be an enormous problem.

---

[18] Reverend E. P. Savage. 1897. "Desertion by Parents." *Twenty Fourth Conference of Charities and Correction.* Boston: Geo. H. Ellis, pp. 317–328.
[19] Linda Gordon. 1985. "Single Mothers and Child Neglect, 1880–1920." *American Quarterly* 37(2): 173–192.
[20] See Tina M. Fielding. 1994. "The Uniform Interstate Family Support Act: The New URESA." *Dayton Law Review* 20(Fall): 425.

EXCEPTIONS TO THE RULE: OUT-OF-WEDLOCK, AFRICAN-AMERICAN, AND FATHERLESS CHILDREN

Beyond these laws that applied to the families just described, it is important to point out that there were three categories of children to whom standard child support policy did not pertain: out-of-wedlock children, African-American children, and children with deceased fathers. Society held parents of these children to different standards, and thus meted out either rewards or punishments according to highly particularized rules and norms. By far, out-of-wedlock and African-American children fared the worst, while children of widows received relatively better treatment under the law.

Consider the case of children born out of wedlock. Not only were the towns active in pursuing fathers who deserted their children through separation or divorce, they also became involved in proceedings involving out-of-wedlock children. The combination of a complex court structure and different mechanisms for choosing judges created a unique system in each state in which paternity cases were heard. However, the states *did* share an historical framework for understanding the issue: English common law. Prior to 1576 in England, children born out of wedlock usually became wards of the state; there were no provisions that forced parents into supporting their offspring. However, with new laws passed in 1576, parents began to face incarceration if they did not materially provide for their children. Moreover, because producing an out-of-wedlock child was seen as a violation of both man-made law and God's law, these "bastardy proceedings," as they were called, were considered criminal trials. According to Marygold S. Melli,

In 1576 as the Poor Law statute noted "bastards begotten and born out of lawful matrimony" constituted "an offense against God's law and man's law." Nonmarital sexual intercourse was both a sin and a crime – both a moral and a government offense – in the legal and moral context of the times. Therefore, the alleged father was in fact being accused of a crime. The law reflected this. It was quasi-criminal, providing for the arrest of the father, proof beyond a reasonable doubt and other features of criminal cases.[21]

American law incorporated these Elizabethan ideas into its standard procedures for handling paternity establishment cases.

---

[21] Marygold S. Melli. 1992. "A Brief History of the Legal Structure for Paternity Establishment in the United States." From *Paternity Establishment: A Public Policy Conference, Volume 1* (SR#56A). Madison, WI: Institute for Research on Poverty.

Since illegitimacy was clearly frowned upon, states approached the child support problem with different degrees of punitiveness. Throughout the nineteenth and early twentieth centuries, many states viewed the illegitimate child through the doctrine of *filius nullius,* or "no one's son." While this usually meant that an illegitimate child could not inherit from his or her father, the doctrine also had ramifications for child support enforcement. *Filius nullius* meant that states such as Texas and Idaho could refuse to acknowledge an illegitimate child's right to be supported by his or her father. In Virginia, a father had to support his illegitimate child only if he formally recognized him or her. For those states that *did* require support, the amount was usually minimal and the time frame usually brief. Some states, such as New York, required support until the child reached the age of twenty-one, while other states, such as Massachusetts, mandated support only for a period of up to six years.[22]

During this time period, there were attempts to create a semblance of uniformity in policy across all states in the union. In 1922, the NCCUSL passed the Uniform Illegitimacy Act and asked the states to comply. Like its English forerunners, the resolution provided for a quasi-criminal proceeding whereby the state would issue a warrant for the father's arrest, the courts would hold a preliminary hearing as to probable cause, and the father would have to post bail for his release.

There were, however, many inadequacies in these criminal proceedings. Fathers were reluctant to identify themselves as accountable sources of support, because they could face criminal prosecution. Mothers were reluctant to cooperate, because they did not want to see the fathers of their children jailed. And prosecutors placed these cases at the bottom of their priority lists, because the probable payoff in eventual support was close to zero. Child support awards continued to be spotty among this group.[23]

Standard child support laws also did not apply to African-American families. Under the system of slavery, official marriages between African Americans were largely prohibited by law. Slavery made the white male

---

[22] Harry D. Krause. 1971. *Illegitimacy: Law and Social Policy.* Indianapolis: Bobbs-Merill, pp. 22–25.

[23] There were some reforms later in the mid twentieth century. For example, in 1960 the conference passed the Uniform Act on Paternity, which would, if the states chose to adopt it, replace the Uniform Illegitimacy Act. This act transformed paternity proceedings by encouraging states to replace criminal proceedings with civil ones. However, by the early 1960s, as the problem continued to spiral upward, most states still treated illegitimacy criminally.

slaveholder the head of household for all blacks – adults and children – that he "owned." Even during the post–Civil War era, child support was not an issue, since whites often seized upon black children as indentured laborers under the notorious Black Codes. These practices persisted well into the 1880s, when legal reformers finally managed to overturn these chattel-like arrangements. Prejudice, however, continued unabated, so that few social reformers or law enforcement personnel would assume the responsibility of bringing a case against a deserting African-American father. These children were simply not seen as worth the bother and expense of a legal pursuit.

Finally, standard child support laws also did not apply to widowed mothers, although their fate stood in marked contrast to the situations involving out-of-wedlock and African-American children. Widowed mothers were placed in a special category of assistance, more deserving of guaranteed financial assistance than a divorced mother or the mother of an out-of-wedlock child. During the early part of the twentieth century, the majority of states created "mothers' pensions." If a woman lost her husband through death, and she faced dire economic circumstances, she could apply for state-based aid. This assistance prevented her from having to give up her children to local authorities for lack of support.

Although by 1921 forty states had such programs in place, there were two severe problems that prevented the programs from making a substantial impact on the largest number of potentially eligible women. First, the benefit levels were, by any standard, extremely low. States permitted localities (usually counties) to run these programs, and most never came close to funding the program at an adequate level.[24] In 1930, when the mother's aid committee of the White House Conference on Child Health and Protection recommended average grants of at least $60 per month, only eight cities throughout the United States were meeting this goal. In 1931, the median grant was $21.78 per month.[25] Most mothers therefore had to find supplemental income even if they were able to secure a pension. Second, women had to qualify for the benefit by passing a character test; if caseworkers found that the mothers were unable to provide a suitable home for their children, these women were immediately expelled from the rolls.[26]

---

[24] Many counties simply elected not to have any type of program at all.

[25] See Theda Skocpol. 1992. *Protecting Soldiers and Mothers.* Cambridge, MA: Harvard University Press, p. 472.

[26] Ibid.

Despite such inadequacies in the law, widows continued to be seen as a special class of unfortunates and thus were spared the disgrace of begging for charity. Reflecting widows' privileged circumstances, these state pension programs were subsequently rolled into the Aid to Dependent Children (ADC) program under the Social Security Act of 1935, when the federal government finally agreed to provide subsidies to the states for these grants.

CONCLUSIONS

For the majority of children born to white, divorced parents, the history of child support enforcement up through the early 1900s was dominated by two primary players: individual complainants and private charitable organizations working with local law enforcement personnel. Each of these avenues of recourse presented enormous problems to mothers in need. Individual efforts to attain support through the courts were haphazard and largely tools of the upper classes. When charity workers and local law enforcement became involved, mothers often did not fare any better. Private agencies collaborated with law enforcement personnel by bringing support claims to their attention, securing orders of support from local judges, and working as virtual collection agencies by redistributing the money collected from the fathers back to the mothers. Awards were low, and societal "behavior monitoring" was high. Children born out of wedlock and African-American children were largely ignored, and children whose fathers had passed away received only subsistence-level benefits, if they received any at all.

A new child support system seemed desirable, a system that would guarantee consistency in payments and not discriminate among potential recipients. Yet, with these primary incumbent policy entrepreneurs in power – private relief workers and local law enforcement officials – it would take an enormous effort from new policy entrepreneurs advocating a different approach to effect change. Newly professionalized social workers, as we will see in the next chapter, took up this challenge with vigor.

4

Social Workers as Challenger Entrepreneurs

At the turn of the century, a newly evolving profession – the social workers – began advocating on behalf of a completely revolutionary approach to child support enforcement. In doing so, they entirely overturned the conventional wisdom of the private charity workers and law enforcement personnel who had come before them. According to the social workers, families did not necessarily need to be reunited; in fact, in cases of physical, emotional, or substance abuse, family unification would be a harmful outcome. Of course, by making this argument, they placed themselves at the center of the policy solution. According to their new perspective, instead of focusing on rehabilitating fathers, social workers would champion the cause of single mothers. Women needed as much help as possible in raising their children, including education, day care, and job training. And since these were such enormous tasks, private charities could not do the job alone. The federal government needed to step in with a massive infusion of aid to get these women back on their feet. The only question was when these social workers could make their move and pitch their agenda effectively to the American public, and they found their opportunity during the Eisenhower, Kennedy, and Johnson administrations.

This chapter proceeds as follows. The first section presents the major rent-seeking position of the social work profession – that is, the profession's emphasis on providing goods and services to single mothers as "child support" rather than on trying to locate absentee fathers. The second section then discusses the risk-reduction strategies used by the social workers to gain an edge on their entrepreneurial competitors. It focuses on the ways in which their cooperative strategies – such as building a uniform professional organization, creating educational standards, and

TABLE 4.1. *Poverty statistics for female-headed households, 1959–64*

Year	White Number (000)	White Percentage	Black Number (000)	Black Percentage
1959	7,115	43.8	3,275	73.5
1960	7,207	42.3	3,456	76.7
1961	7,048	41.9	3,750	75.1
1962	7,015	41.8	4,216	77.3
1963	6,982	39.9	4,115	75.8
1964	7,046	38.3	3,925	71.3

Source: Characteristics of the Population below the Poverty Level, various years. March Supplement to the Current Population Survey (CPS), United States Bureau of the Census.

developing a unique disciplinary identity – provided them with the necessary strength to push their agenda forward. The third section then turns to their shakeout strategy, a presidential administration infiltration plan that was perceived as highly legitimate by the American public. The fourth section summarizes their victories, and the fifth section offers several conclusions regarding the ramifications of the social workers' influence on the reform of child support policy in the United States.

DEFINING A RENT-SEEKING POSITION

One of the most disturbing crises facing the country, a problem "discovered" during the mid twentieth century, was the high percentage of Americans living in poverty, particularly those households headed by women. Postwar television, movies, and newspapers all portrayed a booming America with an expanding industrial sector and many new service professions. But while the economy was indeed growing, a large segment of the population was being left behind. In fact, in 1959, 43.8 percent of all white, female-headed households were living below the poverty line. For blacks, the comparable figure was an alarming 73.5 percent.[1] Table 4.1 summarizes these trends. For many reasons, at the time not fully understood, children living only with their mothers were suffering from severe economic deprivation. Children were in need, and as American citizens became increasingly aware of the problem, they turned to the government to help explore possible solutions.

---

[1] From *Characteristics of the Population below the Poverty Level*. Various Years. March supplement to the Current Population Survey (CPS), United States Bureau of the Census.

In contrast to earlier periods in American history, when local churches, towns, and extended families provided the social safety net for those in need, the primary advocates for the poor during the early to mid twentieth century were the newly professionalized social workers.[2] At first, they were generally divided into two camps. During the post–World War I period, a sizeable segment of social workers began treating a larger middle-class clientele. Drawn primarily from the psychiatric tradition, these newly trained social workers offered an innovative type of "talk therapy" to a certain part of the American population. Indeed, during the 1920s and 1930s, psychotherapy came into fashion, and those with available resources to explore the origins of their problems started visiting members of the profession to help solve them. Freudian analysis served to bring thousands of new clients into contact with the social work profession for the first time, and terms like the Oedipus complex, dream analysis, and the subconscious all became part of the national jargon.[3]

At the same time, other, more activist-oriented social workers were drawn to work in the public welfare system. They viewed their primary role as one of helping the more disadvantaged population achieve economic and personal independence. They based their arguments on such works as Bradley Buell's influential *Community Planning for Human Services*, which argued that welfare recipients often suffered from a wide array of problems that demanded the attention of several agencies at once.[4] In this model, what was needed was a skilled group of individuals committed to the coordination of services for troubled families across the country.

Notably, social workers working in the public arena who aimed to develop a plan of action for families in need focused predominantly on women rather than men. With the phrase "child support" as yet nonexistent in policy circles, social workers pinned their aspirations on improving the economic prospects of mothers in need. Their diagnoses involved job training services, education, and day care centers for single women designed to help wean them from the dole. This position was inspired both by a core belief system as to what might work and by self-interest regarding their profession's future. In other words, their motivations were

---

[2] Much of the following discussion is based upon James Leiby's 1978 comprehensive work, *A History of Social Work in the United States*. New York: Columbia University Press.

[3] Mark Courtney. 1992. "Psychiatric Social Workers and the Early Days of Private Practice." *Social Service Review* 66(2): 199–214.

[4] Bradley Buell. 1952. *Community Planning for Human Services*. New York: Columbia University Press.

twofold. On one hand, research on poverty had suggested the need for increased services to help families to attain self-sufficiency. On the other hand, if leaders of the profession were to choose any other course of action, they would be reducing their own importance in solving this crucial social problem.

This was the case because prior to the early twentieth century, as we have seen in the previous chapter, it was primarily private agencies and local law enforcement, and not the social workers, who controlled the child support agenda. Social workers, indeed, were up against a formidable set of opponents in wresting control of this issue and becoming its primary entrepreneurs. Not only did private agencies and law enforcement have a strong working relationship with one another, they also had a completely different target than the new publicly oriented social workers. The earlier groups focused their attention on rehabilitation and punishment of the fathers accused of abandoning their children, rather than on helping the mothers to live independently.

Beginning in the early nineteenth century, the United States was known as a country where private charities, churches, and other philanthropic organizations were the sole service-oriented entities to take care of those in need. The Charity Organization Movement had institutionalized a series of policies and procedures to deal with the problems of the poor. This involved using "friendly visitors" and intensive casework to help correct the perceived moral failings of those in need. Movement organizers frowned upon public relief while extolling the virtues of private volunteers to assist in moving families out from the ranks of poverty. While the Great Depression and the resulting New Deal programs had somewhat softened the nation's attitude toward increased governmental involvement in the economy, reliance on private charities with their focus on holding fathers accountable continued to be the dominant social service safety net paradigm.

In addition to opposition from private charities, social workers advocating a larger public role for themselves also encountered difficulties from state law enforcement personnel. Since the nonpayment of child support was considered a criminal act, it was up to the local police to apprehend these offenders. Police did not consider the mothers to be the problem – it was the fathers who needed jail time and local rehabilitation. District attorneys agreed with this approach, and repeatedly filed charges against fathers who had abandoned their most basic of duties – the financial support of their families. Social workers who advocated a new public role for their profession thus faced two sets of incumbent policy entrepreneurs that would be difficult to thwart. They therefore had to carefully craft highly effective and cooperative risk-reduction strategies in order to move their case forward.

RISK-REDUCTION STRATEGIES

The Great Depression highlighted divisions within the occupation of social work that had been brewing for several decades. On one hand, thousands of social workers continued to support the efforts of private charity societies to handle the economic devastation of the early 1930s. They insisted that casework was still the most appropriate model for handling poverty in single-parent families, and they rejected the notion that social workers should engage in cooperative relationships with federal officials in order to achieve certain societal goals. Moreover, they frowned on what they viewed as the dilution of their membership by untrained, unskilled relief workers who had no commitment to the occupation's status as a whole. By remaining insulated from these external pressures, they hoped to preserve the integrity of the profession.

Social workers who advocated on behalf of a more public approach to their profession, of course, viewed their role vis-à-vis society completely differently. The massive dislocation of workers during the 1930s had infused in them a new mission and sense of urgency. With the number of needy families increasing exponentially all around them, these publicly oriented social workers welcomed the financial support they received from the federal government in such legislation as the Federal Emergency Relief Act and the Social Security Act. They recognized that with the weaknesses inherent in the modern economy, they could no longer work in isolation from the public purse. Instead, they needed to work *in conjunction* with federal programs in order to best achieve their goal of a more affluent and productive society.[5]

Social workers emerging from the public welfare tradition could easily articulate their arguments for a new approach to child support. They wanted to move away from the more punitive, private, father-oriented approach to advocate a more service-driven, public, mother-oriented approach that would allow them maximum influence. Before they entered the fray, however, they first had to work on reducing the risks of becoming

---

[5] They also wanted to distinguish their work from the "check-writing" functions of bureaucrats in the Social Security program. See Edward D. Berkowitz. 1991. *America's Welfare State: From Roosevelt to Reagan.* Baltimore: Johns Hopkins University Press.

involved in this particular political battle. In reducing their risks, they had two options. They could crown a single representative of their interests, and inexorably link their fortunes to the rise and fall of a unique personality; or they could pursue a more cooperative approach, uniting their rank-and-file members from the bottom up. Publicly oriented social workers wisely coalesced around the latter approach as they developed a single organizational voice, promoted strong professional standards, and advocated on behalf of their own disciplinary practices.

Organization Building

The American Association of Social Workers (AASW), begun in 1921, was one of the first organizations developed with the primary aim of improving the visibility and increasing the power of the social work profession.[6] Its membership was broad, and it was theoretically open to any practicing social worker who wanted a voice in the development of the profession. For the most part, AASW members hailed from large cities such as New York, Philadelphia, and Chicago, and the overwhelming majority worked for large municipal agencies. Their educational backgrounds also tilted decidedly in one direction, with over 40 percent of all AASW members holding a high school diploma or less, and only 9 percent boasting a graduate degree.[7] During these initial years, the AASW struggled with reconciling the sometimes opposing tasks of encouraging increased membership while at the same time trying to raise educational standards. As the major association wavered in these decisions among many others, several other groups sprang up to cater to the needs of social workers who desired a stronger and more specialized organizational home.

This dissension was very real. For example, there were three major groups organized in the medical community. These groups had begun coalescing at the turn of the century and were extremely reluctant to relinquish any of their authority to some overarching umbrella organization such as the AASW. The first, the American Association of Medical

---

[6] Much of the discussion on the risk-reduction and shakeout strategies of the social workers is based upon Leslie Leighninger. 1987. *Social Work: Search for Identity*. New York: Greenwood Press; Walter Trattner. 1989. *From Poor Law to Welfare State*. New York: The Free Press; June Axinn and Herman Levin. 1997. *Social Welfare: A History of the American Response to Need*. New York: Longman; Gary R. Lowe and P. Nelson Reid, eds. 1999. *The Professionalization of Poverty*. New York: Aldine De Gruyter.

[7] Leslie Leighninger. 1987. *Social Work: Search for Identity*. New York: Greenwood Press, p. 13.

Social Workers (AAMSW), was begun in 1918 under Professor Richard A. Cabot and the social worker Ida M. Cannon in response to a perceived need to help the ill and infirm. Medical social workers argued that their calling was to pool the resources of the friends, the family, and the community of those receiving hospital care. Only when these emotional and financial resources were centralized, they argued, would the patient have the maximum chance for recovery. In 1926, a splinter group broke off from the AAMSW to form the American Association of Psychiatric Social Workers (AAPSW). While its members originally worked solely in psychiatric hospitals, the group later broadened its scope to include any social worker who desired psychiatric training. The last medical organization was mobilized in the school systems. The National Association of Visiting Teachers, later renamed the National Association of School Social Workers (NASSW), was begun in 1919 with the broad-based mission of insuring that all children in public schools were as well adjusted as possible to the demands of modern life. Many found full-time jobs in individual schools or worked as consultants to a number of school districts in a given area.

While the AAMSW, AAPSW, and NASSW all took as their organizational base the setting where they practiced, other specialty groups that formed during this period coalesced around a particular occupational technique. Rather than utilizing the case method, which stressed attentiveness to individual needs, the American Association of Social and Group Workers, formed in 1936, advocated a more communal approach to problem solving. Reorganized in 1946 as the American Association of Group Workers (AAGW), the organization sought out practitioners in a variety of fields, such as recreation and youth services, in order to attack contemporary societal ills. The Association for the Study of Community Organization (ASCO), which was begun in 1946, possessed a similar outlook, namely, that the development of strong peer relationships served a special purpose in buttressing individuals against mental duress. Lastly, the Social Work Research Group (SWRG), organized in 1949, aimed to bring together social work researchers in universities and other academic settings in order to facilitate the exchange of scholarly ideas.

The movement to reunify social work as a profession began during the 1950s, when the disparate groups just described began to coalesce into broad, far-reaching organizations. A variety of factors contributed to this drive, perhaps the most important being the concern over an overzealous McCarthyism that targeted social workers as secret communists. Social workers, finding themselves subject to extraordinarily hostile political diatribes, quickly recognized the virtues of banding together in common defense. Moreover, the social conservatism of the 1950s brought with it many attacks on the social welfare system in general, such as the Jenner Amendment, which permitted states to release the names of all public welfare recipients. Viewing these legislative initiatives as threats to their profession's dignity, increasing numbers of social workers became convinced of the need to pull their forces together and defend their work against what they viewed as unrestrained fanaticism.

The original AASW took the lead in this direction by proposing various resolutions aimed at bringing the disparate factions of the profession together into one unified whole. First, in 1946, the AASW passed measures that called for the organization to bring together all splinter groups. Then, in 1948, it encouraged all types of social workers to speak out on proposed antiwelfare legislation being formulated at all levels of government. By 1949, the AASW had formed the Committee on Interassociation Structure, which brought together members not only of AASW, but also of the AAMSW, AAPSW, NASSW, and SWRG. ASCO was excluded for a variety of reasons, including its uneven commitment to professional development. The recommendations of the committee were relatively straightforward. The primary goal was to bring all social workers under one broad umbrella organization. Subdivisions would be preserved only to the extent that specialty concerns would still need to be addressed by practitioners in certain fields.

Although these initial measures were not immediately adopted, they did lay the groundwork for further discussions on the nature of the profession's evolutionary development in the years to come. In 1950, the AASW renamed the Committee on Interassociation Structure the Temporary Inter-Association Council of Social Work Membership Organizations (TIAC). After hammering out differences with respect to training and common goals, the profession finally came together to form the National Association of Social Workers (NASW) in 1955. NASW contained the original five social worker groups, and provided ASCO with a committee status to organize its membership. Table 4.2 summarizes the origins and consolidation of these early organizations.

Within the first five years of its existence, NASW had successfully laid the foundation of a strong organizational structure. The group not only developed a standardized code of ethics, it also began the process of studying certification and licensing procedures across the fifty states. The association also turned its efforts toward the possibilities for increased political action, including consulting with governmental allies and cultivating

TABLE 4.2. *Social work organizations in the early to mid twentieth century*

Organization	Abbreviation	Date of Origin	Mission
American Association of Medical Social Workers	AAMSW	1918	Mobilize resources for people receiving hospital care
American Association of Schools of Social Work	AASSW	1919	Accredit social work programs with an emphasis on graduate training
National Association of School Social Workers (previously National Association of Visiting Teachers)	NASSW	1919	Help school children adjust to their surroundings
American Association of Social Workers	AASW	1921	Improve the visibility of the profession
American Association of Psychiatric Social Workers	AAPSW	1926	Promote training of social workers tending to the mentally ill
American Association of Group Workers (previously American Association of Social and Group Workers)	AAGA	1936	Support youth and recreation services
National Association of Schools of Social Administration	NASSA	1942	Accredit social work programs with an emphasis on undergraduate training
Association for the Study of Community Organization	ASCO	1946	Advance the development of peer relationships in society
Social Work Research Group	SWRG	1949	Bring social workers into academic settings
Temporary Inter-Association Council of Social Work Membership Organizations (previously the Committee on Interassociation Structure)	TIAC	1949	Propose ideas to unify the profession into one organization
National Association of Social Workers	NASW	1955	Unite social workers under one associational umbrella

Note: When an organization was formed and then later reconstituted under a different name, the original founding date is listed here.

members for the provision of expert testimony. Despite these centrifugal forces pulling social workers together, however, the profession still needed a more solid identity from which to advocate change. Social workers solved this part of the puzzle by reexamining the profession's commitment to educational requirements.

Educational Standards

While various specialized social work organizations were putting aside their differences and merging to form the NASW, a secondary type of movement was also gaining strength. This was the drive to improve the power and status of the profession through formalized educational standards.

As early as 1897, Mary Richmond had exhorted social workers attending the National Conference of Charities and Correction to establish formal education for those entering the profession. She wanted all of her experience as well as that of others in her field to be systematically presented to persons interested in exploring a social work career. Her early wish came true in the following year when the New York Charity Organization Society pioneered a six-week-long summer program in social work. Students attended lectures by prominent leaders in the field and visited poorhouses, asylums, and other institutions. In 1904, educators at this summer school transformed their program into the year-long New York School of Philanthropy, led by Edward Devine. Graham Taylor, a social gospel minister and leader of the Chicago Commons Settlement House, founded the similar Chicago School of Civics and Philanthropy somewhat earlier, in 1903. Jeffrey Richardson Brackett, who had long worked in the Baltimore charity system, led the effort in Boston, where Harvard University, Simmons Female College, and the Boston Associated Charities joined together to form the Boston School for Social Workers in 1904.

While these schools began with positive intentions to educate the many newcomers who were entering the field, they lacked a coherent vision as to what the academic foundation of their training should be. Early on, these new schools invited as many guest lecturers into their classrooms as possible. Academics, practitioners, and activists provided their own insights into the profession, sometimes with contradictory results. Some courses emphasized theoretical work, with rigorous teaching in economics and sociology. Other classes provided students with more of the nuts and bolts of everyday job experience, including family counseling, child welfare work, and even home repair. Eventually, the wide discrepancy in the quality of the programs, as well as debates over what should be taught, prompted the formation of new organizations within the field designed to resolve these issues.[8]

---

[8] For an excellent discussion of these early social work schools, see Linda Shoemaker. 1998. "Early Conflicts in Social Work Education." *Social Service Review* 72(2): 182–191.

TABLE 4.3. *Number of social workers in the United States, 1910–1970*

Year	Number of Social Workers
1910	19,000
1920	46,000
1930	71,000
1940	119,000
1950	136,000
1960	193,000
1970	311,000

Source: *Historical Statistics of the United States: Colonial Times to 1970*. 1976. Washington, DC: U.S. Bureau of the Census. Figures include social and group workers, as well as religious aides.

The American Association of Schools of Social Work (AASSW) began as the dominant organization in charge of accrediting programs in the discipline. Started in 1919, the group grew to include twenty-eight schools by 1930. By 1932, the association had succeeded in requiring at least one year of graduate education for all new applicant schools.[9] By 1937, the requirement was raised to two years for all schools seeking accreditation. The primary champions of this approach included Edith Abbott and Sophonisba Brekinridge, who wanted to push social work into the realm of respectable occupations such as law and medicine. In their view, prestige came with formal educational programs, and until social workers could boast of one of their own, they would retain the second-class status of paraprofessionals.

At the same time, however, there remained a substantial segment of the social worker population who found fault with this type of educational standardization. These individuals argued that the impending demands on the social work profession necessitated a broader accreditation process. Moreover, the majority of those working in the field had only an undergraduate education or less. As Table 4.3 indicates, at the turn of the century there were only 19,000 social workers. By 1950, there were 136,000 individuals in the profession, most of whom were providing much-needed services without a formal degree.

---

[9] Leslie Leighninger. 1987. *Social Work: Search for Identity*. New York: Greenwood Press, p. 15.

At the end of the 1930s, members of various land grant colleges and state universities began to mount a successful challenge to the AASSW. Their primary demand was that a new accreditation association be formed, one that would recognize the importance of undergraduate training in social work as well as graduate training. At the same time, they desired recognition for the small but growing number of workers who eschewed private agency employment in favor of public employment. They formed the National Association of Schools of Social Administration (NASSA) in 1942, directly in opposition to the AASSW.

Practitioners and educators on both sides of the question recognized the dangers associated with two warring sets of accrediting boards. Rather than propel the field into a greater position of power vis-à-vis other occupational fields, two competing systems would relegate social work to the bottom of the professional ladder. In a move to reconcile the competing views on education, the two sides agreed to conduct a study with the aim of mapping out the most critical issues in curriculum development. They chose Ernest V. Hollis, a respected leader from the United States Office of Education, and Alice Taylor, a prominent social work practitioner, to conduct the study. Hollis and Taylor spent months poring over documents, attending regional conferences, and interviewing leaders in the field in order to fulfill what they saw as a professional obligation of paramount importance.

In the end, on the most pivotal issue, the Hollis-Taylor report sided with the AASSW. Graduate training in the field had to be the core of social work education, and it could not be superseded by even the strongest undergraduate curricula. At the same time, however, Hollis and Taylor recommended that schools of social work broaden their educational mandate away from parochial, private agency concerns to public welfare issues in general. This was a victory for the NASSA, which wanted the profession to wear a more public face in its duties and mission. The Hollis-Taylor report, in sum, served as a broad declaration for the profession to move beyond its educational sparring and unite behind one set of educational rules.

Both the AASSW and the NASSA, although not completely satisfied with all of the recommendations of the report, nonetheless agreed to abide by them. In 1952, they relinquished their autonomous associational units and merged to form the Council on Social Work Education (CSWE). Its primary mission was to standardize social work educational practices, promote uniformity, and accredit schools of social work. The intended end result of this effort was to present a solid educational front to the outside world, an image that would undoubtedly strengthen the group's position in its attempts to influence child support policy.

Professional Identity

Social workers also aimed to strengthen their organizational base by creating unique standards of practice. Other fields that were important in developing public policy had their own distinctive methods of conducting research and implementing their practices and ideas. Economics and political science, for example, conducted surveys, studied cases, and derived testable hypotheses about how the world works. In order to be taken seriously, social work needed to move forward on this methodological front as well.

As we have seen, social work represented a broad group of employees who specialized in a vast variety of fields, including psychiatry, group work, and hospital care. As might be expected, each group developed its own set of practices related to its specialty and guarded those principles ferociously. Yet, just as most social workers recognized the power in numbers that might accrue to the occupation if they organized into one professional organization, they also became cognizant of the importance of creating a unifying methodological text that would define their profession as whole. Like practitioners in law and medicine, social workers craved the professional legitimacy such an official compilation of practices would afford them. They wanted to write their own book on critical problem solving.

One of the first efforts to harmonize these conflicting approaches to service delivery began at an annual social work conference held in Milford, New York. Although the conference was heavily attended by city social workers from Boston, New York, and Philadelphia, members sought to implement a broad-based approach to service delivery wherever in the country such services were needed. Meeting from 1923 to 1925, the conference compiled its list of practices in a volume later published by the American Association of Social Workers in 1928. While this publication represented an early victory for those searching for a professional synthesis of practice, the volume had severe weaknesses. Instead of providing a blueprint for diagnosis, it simply categorized the practices already in use by the plethora of specialties within the field. Social work as a field remained divided, and by the early 1930s, two separate foundations for scientific practice were emerging, each hoping to claim victory as the "last word" and the primary canon of the field.

On one hand were those social workers heavily influenced by the fields of psychology, psychiatry, and, in particular, the writings of Sigmund Freud. According to this approach, social workers should aim to uncover the deep, hidden roots of individual clients' problems before designing plans of corrective action. On the other hand were social workers who based their ideas on sociology. These workers looked toward the environment facing a particular client and the ways in which individual needs and societal pressures could be fused together in a more positive direction in order to address personal problems. In each case, however, social workers faced barriers with respect to the large-scale reproduction of these techniques. Academics researching psychiatry and sociology in their "pure" forms were loathe to coordinate with the "practical" social workers. Like those in every other academic field, they wanted to establish their own set of theoretical principles uncontaminated by proponents of social action. Moreover, while these two approaches offered social workers a method for approaching their own questions, they still did not constitute a "social work paradigm" that could stand on its own. The methodological crisis in the profession needed a savior, and luckily it found one in the extraordinary efforts of the Russell Sage Foundation (RSF) in its work on behalf of social change.

Under the direction of Donald Young, the RSF became actively involved in pushing the social work discipline to create its own dictionary of knowledge. Founded in 1907, RSF began as a grant-disbursing organization with the primary mission of enhancing the living conditions of persons residing within the United States. By the time Young took the helm in the late 1940s, RSF was floundering owing to its lack of centralized purpose, and it began looking for new and exciting ways to allocate its resources. Young, a strong advocate of infusing a solid foundation of social science into social work, helped to sponsor two innovative programs directed toward the organization's new goals.

The first involved the development of a unique social work / social science doctoral program at the University of Michigan. The School of Social Work at Michigan was much younger than its counterparts in New York and Chicago. This youth and fluidity provided just the environment that many academics argued was necessary to experiment with innovative ways of structuring intellectual enterprises. Young helped to organize a Committee on Social Welfare Research, which designed over the next several years a new Ph.D. program, with social science methodologies as its critical backbone. This novel program ensured that students seeking a Ph.D. in the field of social work would have a strong grasp of political science, economics, and sociology as well. Students leaving the program would be trained to be teachers, researchers, and administrators, and they would represent the foundation's "most sustained and successful attempt to influence the shape of social work education."[10]

RSF also sponsored curriculum revision studies at Western Reserve and other universities, which often worked by placing social scientists trained in a variety of fields into social work schools. While these latter experiments had mixed results – in these communities, members from each discipline tended to look at the others with suspicion and uneasiness – they provided the basis for the extension of social work research in the years to come. At Western Reserve, for example, social workers were initially skeptical of the introduction of social science methods into their curricula. They therefore tended to reject the incorporation into their disciplines of new faculty members without experience in the field. Social workers did, however, understand that the future of their profession rested with the consolidation of their own distinct methodologies, and they actively began to incorporate other social science tools into their classroom instruction.[11]

By the end of the first half of the twentieth century, the development of social work's own professional identity had clearly come a long way. Although the profession remained divided into a variety of factions, most practitioners believed in the need for an autonomous set of practices that would distinguish social work from other fields. Drawing from other social sciences as well as creating the field's own knowledge base, social workers started writing their own methodological textbooks. This progress was reflected during the 1950s in the development of Ph.D. programs, which expanded from five in 1950 to twelve by 1958. By the early 1960s, schools were successfully training graduates in a healthy combination of scholarship and action.

SHAKEOUT STRATEGIES

While the profession as a whole was becoming a stronger force in policy debates, millions of families – in particular, single mothers and their children – continued to languish in poverty. Congress responded to the cry to "do something" about the poverty problem with the Amendments to the Social Security Act of 1956. The publication of Michael Harrington's *The*

---

[10] Ibid., p. 166.
[11] Ibid., p. 167.

Other America, which described the interlocking web of forces that tied millions of American children to lives of poverty, helped the measure to receive funding by 1962.[12] But the path to achieving this end was far from simple. Social workers advocating a more service-oriented and mother-oriented approach had to develop intensive shakeout tactics to remove the Incumbent Entrepreneurs – the private charity workers and local law enforcement personnel – from power. At this decision-making crossroads, the social workers could have pursued an illegitimate means – such as coercion, deceit, or violence – to shake out their competition. Instead, they elected to pursue their goals through a highly integrated and legitimate presidential administration infiltration strategy.

They found their opportunity to change the course of policy at the nexus of two successive presidential administrations: those of Dwight D. Eisenhower and John F. Kennedy. Eisenhower enabled the social workers to knock at the door of innovation, and Kennedy was the one who opened it. The foundations for change were thus laid in the 1950s.

Passage of the 1956 Social Security Amendments marked an important day for social workers as they attempted to offer a variety of services to women in need of financial support. The end product represented the long and hard lobbying efforts of Elizabeth Wickendon, advocating on behalf of the American Public Welfare Association (APWA). Wickendon, who had argued for the incorporation of social services into the old ADC program as early as 1949, had acquired access to the top tiers of government when her friend, Charles Schottland, was named commissioner of Social Security in 1954. Schottland, receptive to the pleas of Wickendon and other like-minded welfare leaders, helped to insert language into the Amendments that ensured that rehabilitative services would be provided to mothers on welfare. Unfortunately, the new law did not require that states enact these provisions, and most localities continued to proceed with business as usual, disbursing only cash through the ADC system. Nonetheless, social work leaders realized that the opportunity to fund these initiatives might be close at hand, and they planned their efforts to ingratiate themselves with successive presidential administrations accordingly.

During the years between 1955 and 1962, the publicly oriented social work community actively worked to shake out its competition – private service agencies and local law enforcement – by forming close relationships with White House officials. As soon as it was founded, the NASW

---

[12] Michael Harrington. 1963. *The Other America: Poverty in the United States.* Baltimore: Penguin.

created the Commission on Social Policy Research, which focused on targeted political action to promote social workers as the new leaders in public welfare. Immediately, the commission worked on forming relationships with high-level officials in the Eisenhower administration and prepared congressional testimony on impending legislation. The NASW also formed a Department of Health, Education, and Welfare Liaison Committee to improve relations with the Social Security Administration as well as other human service agencies.

At the same time, the CSWE formalized its lobbying efforts under the tutelage of its first executive director, Ernest Witte. Witte, a firm believer in the infusion of trained social workers into public welfare agencies, organized massive letter-writing campaigns to encourage Congress to pass reform legislation that would utilize such services. Witte also actively recruited governmental leaders to serve as board members. Jane Hoey, former head of the Bureau of Public Assistance, joined the board, as did Wilbur Cohen, who had taken the lead in developing the first Social Security program during the Depression era.

In addition to engaging in direct and personal lobbying, leading social workers also fought for positions on important government committees designed to study contemporary welfare problems. For example, the Advisory Council on Public Assistance was created by the Social Security Amendments of 1958. Members included Loula Dunn, director of the APWA, and Wilbur Cohen. While advising Eisenhower as to possible reforms, Cohen took a temporary position at the University of Michigan School of Social Work. Although Cohen was not a trained social worker, he acquired an understanding of the key issues being advocated by the profession during his time at Michigan. Later, based on experience gained during his brief academic tenure, he would lead the fight to include service-oriented provisions in future welfare proposals.

After assuming office in 1961, Kennedy appointed Cohen to serve as chair of his Task Force on Health and Social Security. Cohen and his committee, which included Wickendon, endorsed the recommendations of Eisenhower's advisory council. These recommendations included federal funding for general assistance and full funding of the 1956 Social Security Amendments. However, Kennedy's task force went one step further by arguing for the unification of the Children's Bureau, which provided social services to low-income children, and the Bureau of Public Assistance, which offered more general services to low-income families. Proponents of this organizational scheme argued that unification under one division at HEW would provide synergistic effects for the clienteles impacted by the various programs.

Meanwhile, Wickendon herself worked to promote the incorporation of social workers into a new and revised version of the ADC program. Although not a social worker herself, Wickendon had long been an advocate for governmental aid to low-income families. With help from the director of the New York School of Social Work at Columbia University, Fred DelliQuadri, Wickendon began a comprehensive series of studies to explore the possibilities for service delivery reform in the country's welfare system. With the support of NASW's executive directors, the Child Welfare League, and the Family Social Service Association of America, Wickendon mailed out a ten-question survey to leaders in the social work field asking them for their input on organizational reform. In their final report of 1961, the study's primary investigators articulated three main findings. First, the researchers advocated the merger of all federal public assistance and child welfare programs into one division under HEW. Second, the report argued that the federal government should ensure that all states receive grants to develop their own sets of area-specific services. Finally, the report encouraged the federal government to provide funds for the purpose of training social workers for employment in the public sector. Strategically, Wickendon sent a copy of the page proofs to Abraham Ribicoff, whom President Kennedy had just nominated as the new secretary of HEW. Fortunately as well for the social workers, Ribicoff immediately chose Wilbur Cohen as his assistant secretary for legislation.

The last committee created to influence social welfare policy was arguably the most important. Immediately upon assuming office, Ribicoff asked Cohen to establish an Ad Hoc Committee on Public Welfare in order to investigate all potential ways of improving the welfare system. Members of the NASW, CSWE, and APWA lobbied for positions on the committee, and Cohen granted their requests. The committee's final report echoed the findings of the reports that had come before it, including increased funding for services, the creation of a general assistance category of aid, and new funding for social work education.

By 1962, these reports had deeply influenced Kennedy. Kennedy had entered office with a mind open to new ideas, especially when it came to dealing with such seemingly intractable problems as poverty. Invigorated by youth and a sense of eternal optimism for the country, Kennedy became the first president to deliver a message to Congress entirely on the subject of welfare. In this speech, he articulated what he believed were the necessary components for building a new American policy related to the problems of single-parent families: rehabilitation, the promotion of new skills, and the tailoring of general programs to meet specific needs.[13]

With the president on their side, social workers were able to silence their chief competitors for power, private charities and local law enforcement personnel. They flooded the 1962 congressional testimony calendar with their representatives, including Dr. Ellen Winston, a past president of the APWA, Norman V. Lourie, the current president of the NASW, Robert E. Bondy, the director of the National Social Welfare Assembly (an organization begun during World War II to plan social welfare provision), and Elizabeth Wickendon herself, in her new role as the director of the Project on Public Services for Families and Children at the New York School of Social Work. They were joined in providing testimony before Congress by their administration allies, Wilbur J. Cohen and Secretary Ribicoff. Interestingly, the primary representatives of the private charities – and the only ones invited to offer public testimony before the House Ways and Means Committee – were the Reverend Monsignor Raymond J. Gallagher of the National Conference of Catholic Charities and Bradshaw Mintener from the National Council of the Churches of Christ in the U.S.A.

For years, Catholic Charities had opposed the efforts of the NASW and the APWA to overtake its duties. As early as the mid-1950s, the organization had criticized the government's haste in passing new service "add-ons" to public assistance without formal academic study.[14] As Monsignor John O'Grady, secretary of the National Conference of Catholic Charities and editor of the *Catholic Charities Review*, testified before Congress in 1956, these studies had to be undertaken by neutral academics, because "studies made by those who are charged with the administration of assistance . . . have a tendency to glamorize assistance." To O'Grady, "We must constantly keep in mind that public assistance is admittedly the least desirable of all methods of taking care of human needs."[15]

In addition to these criticisms concerning the lack of research on programmatic expansion, leaders of Catholic Charities argued that private and local agencies simply did a better job of helping families in need. In his comments on the emerging legislation in 1961, O'Grady asserted

[13] President John F. Kennedy. "Special Message to the Congress on Public Welfare Programs." February 1, 1962. ⟨www.presidency.ucsb.edu⟩
[14] Monsignor John O'Grady. 1956. "Planning without the Facts." *The Catholic Charities Review* 40(3): 1–2.
[15] Ibid., quoted in Betty Parker Taylor. "A Case Illustration: Improving Family Relationships through Casework Treatment." *The Catholic Charities Review* 40(3): 8.

that new federal initiatives in the areas of helping dependent families "do not take into account local programs of self-help and community organization. . . . These local community programs are in harmony with the best traditions of our time and with our best Christian traditions."[16] By 1962, Monsignor Raymond J. Gallagher had replaced Monsignor O'Grady as secretary of the National Conference of Catholic Charities and editor of the *Catholic Charities Review*, and his attacks on the public social workers were even sharper.

[The 1962 Amendments] propose[s] public welfare solutions to a variety of problems from other fields. For a field already beset by many articulate critics for failing to accomplish its stated purpose relative to needy persons, it hardly seems prudent for public welfare to seek as its responsibility matters that have their genesis in entirely different fields.[17]

Later, Monsignor Gallagher went on to castigate these public welfare groups for seeking this new role of social service provision "rather than [using] their ingenuity and resourcefulness to find other ways to meet the problem with no greater expense and much less risk to the persons involved."[18] To Gallagher, passage of the 1962 Amendments would "handicap [Catholic Charities] seriously."[19]

In their 1962 testimony on the actual legislation before Congress, both Monsignor Gallagher and Mr. Mintener voiced concerns over how the shakeout strategies of the publicly oriented social workers had effectively silenced service providers from their own camps. Monsignor Gallagher, for example, expressed a worry that the new program would result in

the drying up of interest and activity on the part of people to use their own ingenuity and initiative to help meet their own problems or the problems of a neighbor or others in their general vicinity. For this reason we are anxious to have voluntary effort espoused in whatever way is possible to do so, so that this ingredient of citizenship may never be lost or become inactive in a large number of our people. . . .[20]

---

[16] Monsignor John O'Grady. 1961. "Research as Basis for New Social Programs." *The Catholic Charities Review* 45(4): 1.

[17] Monsignor Raymond J. Gallagher. 1962. "Public Welfare – 1962 Model." *The Catholic Charities Review* 46(3): 2.

[18] Monsignor Raymond J. Gallagher. 1962. "Who Has the Answer?" *The Catholic Charities Review* 46(6): 3.

[19] Ibid.

[20] Monsignor Raymond J. Gallagher. 1962. Testimony on "Public Welfare Amendments of 1962." Hearing before the Ways and Means Committee, United States House of Representatives. Washington, DC: U.S. Government Printing Office, p. 590.

Mr. Mintener reiterated this point and argued that private agencies and other nonprofits groups should not be cut out of this new funding scheme. Maintaining that "private agencies have a great tradition of pioneering service in this country and will continue to contribute an indispensable share of the total health and welfare services of the nation," Mintener lobbied to include legislative language that would prevent bias against private groups in service delivery.[21] By the time the hearings were held, however, the voices advocating a more public approach were clearly the loudest ones on the political stage.

As for the district attorneys and local police, the chief law enforcement personnel responsible for capturing nonsupporting fathers, they were not invited to testify at the 1962 hearings. In fact, the only reference to their role in the child support crisis came from a Republican congressman from the state of Iowa, Neal Smith, who wanted law enforcement to continue to play a strong role. But as his statements reflect, his interest in enlisting the support of law enforcement had a secondary motivation as well:

The first thing I would mention with regard to this is that enforcement is very important. Most states have laws that we call child desertion laws, or they are criminal laws of some kind, that make it a felony to desert the family. I found back when I was working as a state's attorney assigned to the welfare board that some men that were in another state really were in close contact with the family; yet the wife would go down and make her application for ADC claiming the husband had deserted and she would get it and know that there was no danger of the husband being thrown in jail because the state would not extradite him.

I would point out in many states, and I found this through the national welfare conferences we had at that time, the Governors will pay for the extradition of a fellow that wrote a bad $10 check, but they usually won't extradite a child deserter even though the family is drawing a couple thousand dollars a year from the county, state, and federal governments.

In 1951, we extradited three deserters that were in other states and almost immediately a couple dozen women came down and said they no longer needed ADC and that their husbands suddenly had returned. We know in many of these cases the husbands just went to the other state and got a job and the wife applied for ADC because they knew they would get away with it. In our case, extradition seemed to work all right until one the Governor looked at his extradition costs and saw that that account had been reduced. He stopped extraditing child deserters – and this is not unique to Iowa – the invitation was again extended to those who wanted to cheat.

---

[21] Bradshaw Mintener. 1962. Testimony on "Public Welfare Amendments of 1962." Hearing before the Ways and Means Committee, United States House of Representatives. Washington, DC: U.S. Government Printing Office, p. 573.

This is going on in many states, so the first thing I think should be done in this area is to work with the states to encourage extradition of child deserters that go across to other states. Extradition and child desertion proceedings are purely within the police powers of the state. It has to be a cooperative venture of some kind and I do not think you can just pass a Federal law and that is the end of it. It has to be something cooperative with the states. But something should be done to encourage better enforcement of child desertion laws.[22]

Interestingly, Smith was concerned with capturing fathers in order to prevent welfare fraud, not simply in order to hold fathers accountable to their offspring. This sentiment clearly indicated that the public social workers had shifted the debate successfully away from the fathers, whom they believed they could not control, and toward the mothers, whom they believed they could help with employment and rehabilitative services.

OVERTAKING THE INCUMBENTS

In the end, the social workers achieved exactly what they wanted. Requiring social workers to move beyond the mere provision of material goods, the 1962 Social Security Amendments mandated that all public assistance clients receive medical care, vocational rehabilitation, and referrals to other social service agencies as their needs demanded. In order to receive reimbursement for their programs, the states had to provide an economic "plan of action" for each child enrolled in the new Aid to Families with Dependent Children (AFDC) program, which replaced ADC, as well as offer resources to individuals not yet receiving federal aid but on the cusp of becoming recipients. The 1962 law changed the formulas by which states received aid so that up to 75 percent of service–related expenditures would be reimbursed by the federal government. This added up to costs of approximately $40 million per year.[23]

States also had to establish a broad definition of child welfare services, make them available in every county, and enforce predetermined standards of performance. In addition to authorizing protective payments (for neglected children) and foster care payments to institutions, the Amendments also provided for training programs that would enable parents to prepare for entry into the labor market. Child welfare services also were

[22] Neal Smith. 1962. Testimony on "Public Welfare Amendments of 1962." Hearing before the Ways and Means Committee, United States House of Representatives. Washington, DC: U.S. Government Printing Office, p. 422.

[23] Data from the John F. Kennedy Library website: ⟨http://www.cs.umb.edu/jfklibrary/jfk_leg_record4.html#Social Security, 1962.⟩. Accessed on July 10, 2002.

increased: from $25 million a year to $30 million in 1963, $35 million in 1964, $40 million in 1965 and 1966, $45 million in 1967 and 1968, and $50 million in 1969 and thereafter. The legislation earmarked $5 million of this amount for day care services in 1963 and $10 million in subsequent years.[24] Finally, the legislation contained measures to help train social workers to provide these new services.

In addition to the services promised to welfare recipients, the 1962 Amendments were of most significance because of their institutionalization of publicly oriented social workers into American social policy. As early as 1933, Harry Hopkins, director of numerous relief programs during the Great Depression, including the Federal Emergency Relief Administration, had been a leading opponent of social workers' assuming any larger public presence. In describing the Federal Emergency Relief Act to the National Conference of Social Workers, Hopkins stated that all relief efforts should be targeted toward families experiencing the worst effects of the Great Depression. The intent of federal aid was not, therefore, "to develop a great social work organization throughout the United States."[25] Relief was to be targeted and then terminated wherever possible.

But by 1962, the publicly oriented social workers had altered the course of their profession. They had made themselves invaluable by incorporating their own members into the enactment and eventual implementation of the nation's new welfare system. Whether it was in developing individualized plans of family action or meeting the requirements of the Social Security commissioner that in order to be effective, family services required "caseloads of no more than sixty per (social) worker, one supervisor for each five workers, and home visiting as frequently as necessary," publicly oriented social workers were now inextricably linked to the future of America's child support policy.[26]

CONCLUSIONS

With the 1962 Amendments to the Social Security Act, social workers had achieved a startling victory. They were the new holders of power with respect to child support enforcement policy. The battle, of course, had not been easy. Entrenched policy incumbents, led by local private charitable

[24] Ibid.
[25] Harry Hopkins. 1933. "The Developing Program of National Relief." *Proceedings: National Conference of Social Workers*, pp. 65–67, 71.
[26] U.S. Department of Health, Education, and Welfare Press Release, Social Security Administration. January 6, 1963.

organizations and law enforcement personnel, had been engaged in a partnership that had persisted for decades. However, by pursuing the cooperative, broad-based risk reduction strategies of unification, professionalization, and the creation of a unique body of practice all their own, social workers improved their chances to control the policy agenda. They were ultimately successful when they followed a highly legitimate shakeout strategy – establishing close ties with members of the Eisenhower and Kennedy administrations – in order to fulfill their mission.

In addition, by the mid-sixties, the social workers appeared to be gaining even more power. Several important books pointed to the more entrenched problems experienced by certain segments of the disadvantaged population – in particular, black, female-headed households. Not only did a substantial percentage of this minority live in destitution, they also had to contend with the subtle and not-so-subtle societal barriers associated with racism. Research such as *Black Rage*, by William H. Grier and Price M. Cobbs, and *Dark Ghetto*, by Kenneth Clark, painted a desperate picture of the black psyche, destroyed by years of white discrimination and hatred.[27] Only a thorough revisioning of the values permeating both black and white communities could help to undo this damage.

Partly in response to these painful realities, a new cohort of social workers began to actively argue for another innovative client-employee model for their profession. According to this model, social workers should also strive to encourage community participation in the restructuring of economically disadvantaged neighborhoods rather than concentrate solely on casework. Indeed, members of the Social Welfare Workers Movement, the Association of Black Social Workers, and even the more conservative National Association of Social Workers maintained that individual problems could never be solved if the communities in which the disadvantaged lived were suffering from severe socioeconomic blight. In this paradigm shift, social action should supplement casework as the new model of reform. According to James G. Emerson, executive secretary of the Community Service Society of New York, the country's oldest and largest family service agency,

The situation is not just a matter of persons with problems, but rather of whole areas afflicted with social ills. If the individual is to be helped, someone has to deal with the complex of social ills that bears on the individual, not just on the individual himself. We are convinced that an approach that focuses primarily on

[27] William H. Grier and Price M. Cobbs. 1968. *Black Rage*. New York: Basic Books; Kenneth Clark. 1965. *Dark Ghetto: Dilemmas of Social Power*. New York: Harper and Row.

individuals may help some people, but will not really alleviate the basic problem of a sick community. Instead of starting out by saying that the individual is the client, we're going to say the community is the client.[28]

During the mid-sixties, then, social workers took it upon themselves not only to help individuals adapt to their environments, but also to change these environments themselves into more meaningful places in which to live.

In order to promote their new model of therapy, the social workers needed allies, and they found a ready and willing one in President Lyndon Baines Johnson. Immediately upon taking office, President Johnson encouraged Congress to pass the Economic Opportunity Act, which offered a whole new array of services to families in need. The theory was that as the economic circumstances of individuals improved, they would be less likely to have children who would need government aid as their primary means of support; fewer children, therefore, would have to live in poverty. The Job Corps, for example, provided educational and work opportunities for hundreds of high school dropouts. The Neighborhood Youth Corps, as another example, gave part-time jobs to students while they stayed in school. And, at the extreme end of this democratic experiment, the Community Action Program encouraged "maximum feasible participation" of area residents in neighborhoods undergoing economic rehabilitation. This meant that social work professionals actively engaged the public in improving their own lives by joining with them in challenging the status quo of limited opportunity. Instead of being outsiders, then, social workers were now partners in effecting change. It was truly the heyday of the social work profession's influence on American social policy, and on child support policy in particular. But the heyday could not last forever, and conservatives, unhappy with the social worker revolution of the 1960s, were waiting in the wings to effect a new cycle of policy change.

---

[28] As quoted in Walter Trattner. 1989. *From Poor Law to Welfare State*. New York: The Free Press, p. 312.

5

Conservatives as Challenger Entrepreneurs

No one considered Gerald R. Ford and his Republican colleagues to be likely policy trailblazers. When Richard M. Nixon resigned the presidency effective August 9, 1974, the immediate future of social policy in the United States seemed to be largely predictable – and largely unremarkable, for that matter. Ford, who had served in Congress from Michigan for over twenty-five years and then for one year in the vice-presidency, promised the country stability. And for the most part, stability – some would say immobility – is what he provided.

Some of this paralysis Ford brought upon himself. His September 1974 pardon of Richard Nixon did not help to energize a nation searching for the redress of past injustices. And then there was the devastating impact of the economy. By 1974, inflation was soaring to a rate of 12 percent per year, and unemployment was well over 7 percent. Traditional methods of stimulating the economy, such as tax cuts and increased spending, did not seem to have the impact they had once had in past cycles of boom and bust. Moreover, the deepening energy crisis did nothing to endear Ford to the American public. Citizens all over the country were waiting in long lines for overpriced gas that was in short supply due to the Arab oil embargo of 1973. Adding to the stalemate, Ford himself was continually at odds with the country's overwhelmingly Democratic Congress, and vetoed a record number of bills during his brief tenure in office.

It was surprising, therefore, that Ford would prove to be such a visionary when it came to child support enforcement. In a 1975 speech urging the rapid implementation of child support legislation, Senator Sam

Nunn (D-Ga.) pointed to the President's groundbreaking initiatives in this area.

Many members of Congress and most of the citizens of this country are probably unaware of the President's long commitment to solving the problem of absent parents who fail to support their children and families. In fact, the first proposed legislation I could find concerning the absent parent who failed to provide for the support of his children and family was introduced on May 9, 1949 in H.R. 4580 by a freshman Congressman from Grand Rapids, Michigan. He wasn't too well known then, but his name is now familiar to everyone. He was none other than Gerald R. Ford. On that same day, a similar bill, H.R. 4565, was introduced by Congressman Andrew Jacobs of Indiana. These two bills soon became known as the "runaway pappy" bills. H.R. 4580 provided for the enforcement of support orders in certain state and federal courts, and to make it a crime to move or travel in interstate and foreign commerce to avoid compliance with such orders. Congressman Ford continued to introduce a similar bill in about eight different Congresses. The last such bill was H.R. 2309, which he introduced on January 8, 1973.[1]

When Ford introduced this final bill before becoming vice president, he echoed Nunn's appraisal of his approach – that it would pave the way for an entirely new approach to child support enforcement. Passage of his bill, Ford argued, would "give legal sanction to the moral and social obligations every husband has to take care of his family."[2]

The unlikely innovation that emerged from President Ford's office with the help of his fellow conservatives is the focus of this chapter. How did Ford, in one short-lived presidential administration, harness the energies of his fellow Republicans – both legislators and local activists – in order to transform the child support policy arena from one that focused on providing services to single mothers to one that actively pursued nonpaying fathers in the name of accountability?

The first task, addressed in the first section of the chapter, involved defining a clear-cut rent-seeking position around which all like-minded conservatives could rally. This first section also describes the history of this rent-seeking position and, more specifically, the sociodemographic trends that led to this increased concern over single-parent families. Next, the second section delves into the conservatives' approach to risk reduction,

---

[1] Senator Sam Nunn. 1975. Speech prepared on "Amendments to Child Support Bill." Gerald R. Ford Presidential Library, Spencer C. Johnson Files, Box 3, p. 2. Contrary to Nunn's account, Ford actually introduced his first child support bill earlier, on January 17, 1949, as H.R. 1538.

[2] Quoted in ibid., p. 2.

which involved increasing their representation at all levels of government and creating new grassroots organizations with the sole goal of lobbying top policymakers. The third section then turns to the conservative strategy of "shaking out" the social worker competition by repeatedly championing "automatic" programs such as a new collection-oriented child support agency, or, more simply, programs that did not require social services. The fourth section reviews their victories in the child support arena, and the fifth section concludes.

DEFINING A RENT-SEEKING POSITION

For conservatives, the failure of the social workers to adequately address the problem of single-parent families' turning to welfare for financial support was completely inexcusable. Throughout the 1960s, the profession had received an incredible infusion of funds to buttress their efforts, beginning with the 1962 Social Security Amendments. They had had the full backing of HEW in designing highly tailored response plans for families in need. They had had the ability to offer services to individuals with a variety of employment backgrounds. They had had the enthusiastic support of back-to-back Democratic presidential administrations. And yet the child support crisis, as we shall soon see, had only worsened.

In defining their rent-seeking position, conservatives were motivated by two primary forces. First of all, they were alarmed at the growth in welfare expenditures created by the 1962 Social Security Amendments. The federal government was spending more money on welfare than ever before, yet the results were clearly insufficient. Second, and strongly related to this concern, conservatives became increasingly incensed over the propensity of fathers to recklessly have children and then abandon them to the state for financial support. Any new effort to stem the child support crisis had to instill in these men a distinct and powerful sense of responsibility for the children that they brought into this world.

Because conservatives were primarily interested in addressing what they viewed as the interlinked problems of skyrocketing welfare costs and individual parental accountability, they proposed a new child support program that focused on AFDC families, rather than on all families in need of financial help from their fathers. Their plan would involve a radical departure from past initiatives to ease the financial burdens of single-parent families. Instead of providing rehabilitative and employment services to the *mothers* in question, conservatives proposed a new federal-state partnership to punitively pursue the *fathers* of these children. In other words, the government would not track down these fathers with the "friendly" intent of offering them jobs or training as they had the mothers. No, this time the government would use its full authority as a legitimate wielder of law enforcement power to locate and coerce nonpaying fathers into supporting their offspring.

The program that they envisioned was simple. Each state would create its own office of child support enforcement that would work in conjunction with the Federal Office of Child Support Enforcement to find fathers of families on welfare. They would be aided in their efforts by the mothers, whose receipt of benefits would be conditional upon their disclosure of their former partners' whereabouts. Once the fathers were located, the states would garnish their wages to help reimburse their coffers for the money already laid out on behalf of their families. The states would also have the authority to pursue fathers for all arrearages that had accumulated before the fathers were found.

This solution to the child support problem – the conservatives' rent-seeking position, with the help and guidance of President Ford – seems so commonsensical now that we often forget how groundbreaking it actually was. For decades, social policy in the United States had focused on the women involved in single-parent families. By 1962, this approach, led by the social workers, had reached such a crescendo that the federal government actually funded millions of dollars in new services to help these mothers become more employable. By the early 1970s, with the perceived failure of this approach, conservatives were proposing a new plan. Go after the fathers instead, they argued, with a renewed sense of mission. And while many observers criticized this approach as too punitive, too harsh, or too unworkable, the conservatives themselves quickly marshaled the anecdotal and statistical evidence they needed to enact their new proposals.

The Historical Roots of This Rent-Seeking Position

Even while the social workers were vigorously working on behalf of families during the 1960s, the problem of nonpayment of child support was only worsening. Conservatives were the first to call attention to family breakdown and the enormous jump in the number of welfare recipients, which they argued were the primary contributors to this social policy crisis. Senator Henry Bellmon (R-Okla.) called it "one of the most important social problems that we have in this country."[3] Senator Bob Dole (R-Kans.) described his frustration with the system when he worked as a county attorney:

I was county attorney in a very small county in Kansas for eight years and the easiest thing to do, when the father left a family and moved to some other state was to send the mother down to the welfare office. . . . I understand a 1971 HEW study shows that nationwide in cases where the father was absent from the home, only about 13 percent of the families received any support payments from the absent fathers and less than 10 percent got as much as $50 a month. So, I feel we should recognize that the present law is not working.[4]

Senator Carl T. Curtis (R-Nebr.) complained about the problem in this way:

Some of the people that are supporting their own children and paying their taxes, have not had many educational advantages, they have not inherited any money, and they have not anything else, but they have worked hard and they have sacrificed and they are self-supporting. And the only difference between them and some of these errant fathers is the desire to support their own children. And where the desire is absent, I think society has to impose some compulsion, and I think it is that simple.[5]

These were not just personal claims and opinions designed to bring attention to the problem. The statistics bore out such claims.

Nonmarital Births. First, the overall birthrate (which could potentially increase the number of children needing child support) was declining. The birthrate tripled from 1940 to 1957, but decreased rapidly from the early 1960s through the mid-1970s. More precisely, during the decades between 1961 and 1981, the birthrate dropped from 23.3 to 15.8 per 1,000 in the population.

However, at the same time that the birthrate was dropping, a greater percentage of these births were nonmarital. In 1961, only 5.6 percent of

---

[3] Henry Bellmon. 1973. Testimony on "Child Support and the Work Bonus." Hearing before the Committee on Finance, United States Senate. Washington, DC: U.S. Government Printing Office, p. 69.

[4] Bob Dole. 1973. Testimony on "Child Support and the Work Bonus." Hearing before the Committee on Finance, United States Senate. Washington, DC: U.S. Government Printing Office, p. 116.

[5] Carl T. Curtis. 1973. Testimony on "Child Support and the Work Bonus." Hearing before the Committee on Finance, United States Senate. Washington, DC: U.S. Government Printing Office, p. 128.

all births were to unmarried women. By 1975, this number had climbed to 14.3 percent, reaching 18.9 percent by 1981. With more and more women having babies out of wedlock, the social safety net was bound to be stressed. Mothers without husbands were much more likely to look to the state to provide them with the income that they needed in order to survive.

Of course, many factors contributed to the rising number of nonmarital births. Perhaps most important was the growing number of unmarried women of childbearing age for whom marriage was not a priority.[6] Moreover, while these women were delaying marriage, they were not necessarily putting off sexual activity. A declining abortion rate and more liberal public attitudes toward single motherhood contributed to this evolving phenomenon.[7] Table 5.1 summarizes these trends in greater detail.

Divorce Rates. During the sixties and seventies, divorce in the United States also became more commonplace. The number of divorces increased from approximately 393,000 in 1960 to 1.19 million in 1980, resulting in a jump from 2.2 to a peak rate of 5.2 divorces per thousand in the population.[8]

As with the rising nonmarital birthrate, the causal factors behind the divorce trend are complex. The transition from a fault-based system of deciding marital dissolution cases – based on provable charges, such as adultery and cruelty – to a no-fault system made divorces easier to obtain.[9] Women's economic independence as well as the declining number of "marriageable males" (men with good employment prospects) also played a part.[10] Others point to the ease of obtaining government benefits for income support, thereby making marriage irrelevant to a couple's

[6] *Births to Unmarried Mothers: United States, 1980–1992.* 1995. Series 21, no. 53. Vital and Health Statistics, Centers for Disease Control and Prevention. Washington, DC: U.S. Government Printing Office.

[7] Ailsa Burns and Cath Scott. 1994. *Mother-Headed Families and Why They Have Increased.* Hillsdale, NJ: Erlbaum.

[8] These data taken from *Children of Divorce – Vital and Health Statistics.* 1989. Series 21, no. 46. Washington, DC: U.S. Government Printing Office.

[9] Herbert Jacob. 1988. *Silent Revolution: The Transformation of Divorce Law in the United States.* Chicago: University of Chicago Press.

[10] Gary Becker. 1991. *A Treatise on the Family.* Cambridge, MA: Harvard University Press; William Julius Wilson. 1987. *The Truly Disadvantaged.* Chicago: University of Chicago Press.

TABLE 5.1. *Total births and nonmarital births in the United States, 1961–85*

Year	Total Number of Births	Birth Rate per 1,000 in Population	Number of Births to Unmarried Women	% of all Births to Unmarried Women	Number of Nonmarital Births per 1,000 Live Births
1961	4,268,326	23.3	240,200	5.6	56
1963	4,098,020	21.7	259,400	6.3	63
1965	3,760,358	19.4	291,200	7.7	77
1967	3,520,959	17.8	318,100	9	90
1969	3,600,206	17.9	360,800	10	100
1971	3,555,970	17.2	401,400	11.3	113
1973	3,136,965	14.8	407,300	13	130
1975	3,144,198	14.6	447,900	14.3	143
1977	3,326,632	15.1	515,700	15.5	155
1979	3,494,398	15.6	597,800	17.1	171
1981	3,629,238	15.8	686,605	18.9	189
1983	3,638,933	15.6	737,893	20.3	203
1985	3,760,561	15.8	828,174	22	220

Source: National Vital Statistics Report, October 18, 2000.

economic fortunes.[11] Still others blame changing cultural norms and the rise of cohabitation as a viable marriage substitute.[12]

Regardless of its causes, the rising divorce rate produced a remarkable surge in the number of children experiencing familial break-up. In 1970 alone, approximately 870,000 children were impacted by divorcing parents. By 1980, this number peaked at slightly over 1.17 million, and it remained at historically high levels throughout the early 1980s.[13] For Americans in general, these statistics represented a completely new social phenomenon with far-reaching ramifications. The traditional two-parent family was rapidly becoming a relic of the past, as increasing numbers of young children experienced the tumult of divorce. In combination, the rising nonmarital birthrate and the climbing divorce rate created a social landscape where a significant proportion of American children were living with only one parent at some point in their lives. In 1968, approximately 8.3 million children under the age of eighteen had lived with only one parent at some point during their youth. This number represented 11.8 percent of all children living in the United States. By 1980, this number had jumped to 11.5 million, representing 18.5 percent of all children living in this country. Tables 5.2 and 5.3 and Figure 5.1 summarize these trends.

Rising Numbers of Welfare Recipients. As an additional concern, many conservatives began to worry that the recent liberalization of welfare laws was contributing to another extremely undesirable social outcome. This involved the rising tendency of single mothers to rely on welfare for financial support in lieu of potentially available private support. Providing evidence of this behavioral trend, the welfare rolls exploded during the 1960s and 1970s. From 1962 to 1980, the number of families receiving AFDC jumped from 924,000 to 3.3 million. As a result, welfare expenditures also underwent a massive expansion, from $3.7 billion to $14 billion in constant dollars during the same years (see Table 5.4 and Figures 5.2 and 5.3).

[11] Charles Murray. 1993. "Welfare and the Family: The U.S. Experience." *The Journal of Labor Economics* 11(1): S224–S262; Irwin Garfinkel and Sara S. McLanahan. 1986. *Single Mothers and Their Children*. Washington, DC: The Urban Institute Press.

[12] Larry Bumpass, James Sweet, and Andrew Cherlin. 1991. "The Role of Cohabitation in Declining Marriage Rates." *Journal of Marriage and the Family* 53(4): 913–927; David Popenoe. 1996. *Life without Father*. New York: The Free Press.

[13] *Children of Divorce – Vital and Health Statistics.* 1989. Series 21, no. 46. Washington, DC: U.S. Government Printing Office.

TABLE 5.2. *Children involved in divorce in the United States, 1960–84*

Year	Number of Divorces	Number of Children Involved	Rate per 1,000 Children under 18	Rate per 1,000 in Population
1960	393,000	463,000	7.2	2.2
1962	413,000	532,000	7.9	2.2
1964	450,000	613,000	8.7	2.3
1966	499,000	669,000	9.5	2.5
1968	584,000	784,000	11.1	2.9
1970	708,000	870,000	12.5	3.5
1972	845,000	1,021,000	14.7	4
1974	977,000	1,099,000	16.2	4.6
1976	1,083,000	1,117,000	16.9	5
1978	1,130,000	1,147,000	17.7	5.1
1980	1,189,000	1,174,000	17.3	5.2
1982	1,170,000	1,108,000	17.6	5.1
1984	1,169,000	1,081,000	17.2	5

Source: *Children of Divorce – Vital and Health Statistics.* 1989. Series 21, no. 46. Washington, DC: U.S. Government Printing Office.

TABLE 5.3. *Minors living with one parent in the United States, 1968–85*

Year	Total Number of Children under 18 (in millions)	Total Number of Children under 18 Living with One Parent (in millions)	% of Minors Living with One Parent
1968	70,326	8,332	11.8
1970	70,317	8,509	12.1
1971	69,162	8,200	11.9
1972	70,255	9,478	13.5
1973	68,811	9,664	14.0
1974	67,950	10,093	14.9
1975	67,047	10,489	15.6
1976	66,087	10,245	15.5
1977	65,129	11,121	17.1
1978	64,062	11,311	17.7
1979	63,206	11,710	18.5
1980	62,389	11,528	18.5
1981	63,427	12,466	19.7
1982	62,918	12,619	20.1
1983	62,407	13,701	22.0
1984	62,281	14,006	22.5
1985	62,139	14,024	22.6

Source: "Marital Status and Living Arrangements: March 1998 (Update)." Current Population Reports, series P20-514, U.S. Bureau of the Census. Accessed on ⟨http://www.census.gov⟩ on April 4, 2001.

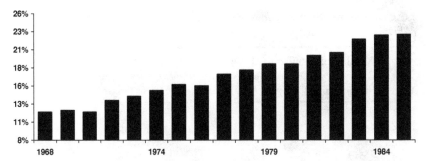

FIGURE 5.1. Percentage of minors living with one parent in the United States, 1968–84. *Source*: "Marital Status and Living Arrangements: March 1988 (Update)" and earlier reports. Current Population Reports, series P20-514, U.S. Bureau of the Census.

For most conservatives, the root causes of these trends were easy to find. The rising number of unmarried welfare recipients was simply an unintended consequence of the generosity and permissiveness of the AFDC program itself. More specifically, changes in the legal environment propelled by such groups as the National Association of Social Workers and the National Welfare Rights Organization (NWRO) had helped to expand eligibility requirements during the late 1960s and early 1970s. In the Supreme Court decision *Shapiro v. Thompson* (1969), for example, the judges struck down as unconstitutional residency requirements preventing newly relocated families (who had moved from one state to another) from accessing benefits, while in *King v. Smith* (1968) and *Lewis v. Martin* (1970), the Court voided man-in-the-house rules, which had prohibited mothers from receiving benefits if they were cohabiting with a man. In addition, *Goldberg v. Kelly* (1970) guaranteed recipients the right to appeal welfare agency decisions that involved a change in their benefit levels.[14]

Beyond expanding the number of eligibles, these decisions, many conservatives had come to believe, had reduced the relevancy of a stable family unit in raising a child. In other words, men and women no longer had to fear an unexpected pregnancy, for the AFDC program would step

[14] See Michael Sosin. 1986. "Legal Rights and Welfare Change, 1960–1980." In *Fighting Poverty*, ed. Sheldon Danziger and Daniel Weinberg. Cambridge: Harvard University Press, pp. 260–286, for a useful review of these court cases: *Shapiro v. Thompson*, 394 U.S. 618, 22 L. Ed. 2d 600, 89 S. Ct. 1322, 1969; *King v. Smith*, 392 U.S. 309, 20 L. Ed. 2d 1118, 88 S. Ct. 2128, 1968; *Lewis v. Martin*, 397 U.S. 552, 25 L. Ed. 2d 561, 90 S. Ct. 1282, 1970; *Goldberg v. Kelly*, 397 U.S. 254, 25 L. Ed. 2d 287, 90 S. Ct. 1011, 1970.

TABLE 5.4. *Growth in the Aid to Families with Dependent Children (AFDC) program, 1962–85*

Year	Number of Families Receiving AFDC (in thousands)	Total Expenditures in Current Dollars (millions)	Total Expenditures in 1996 Constant Dollars (millions)
1962	924	780	3,712
1963	950	830	3,902
1964	984	920	4,274
1965	1,037	1,020	4,683
1966	1,074	1,090	4,889
1967	1,141	1,290	5,608
1968	1,307	1,610	6,790
1969	1,538	2,013	8,138
1970	1,909	2,765	10,650
1971	2,532	3,289	12,100
1972	2,918	3,874	13,765
1973	3,124	4,198	14,357
1974	3,170	4,482	14,148
1975	3,357	5,216	14,948
1976	3,575	5,827	15,662
1977	3,593	6,254	15,648
1978	3,539	6,402	15,051
1979	3,496	6,550	14,138
1980	3,642	7,255	14,042
1981	3,871	7,825	13,791
1982	3,569	7,851	12,916
1983	3,651	8,302	13,116
1984	3,725	8,734	13,222
1985	3,692	9,063	13,231

Source: U.S. Department of Health and Human Services, Administration for Children and Families, Office of Planning, Research and Evaluation; and *The Green Book*. Various years. Committee on Ways and Means, United States House of Representatives. Washington, DC: U.S. Government Printing Office.

in with financial support. Most damaging, however, was the program's perceived sponsorship of a father's right to leave his children. The message was straightforward. AFDC rules did not require fathers to support their children if the mother claimed ignorance concerning who or where he was. Fathers could simply walk away from their children with impunity.

The combination of these various social trends brought the problem of child support enforcement into sharp focus. Left unattended, rising

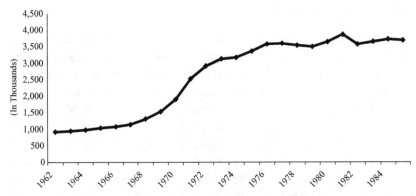

FIGURE 5.2. Growth in the number of families on AFDC. *Source: The Green Book*. Various years. Committee on Ways and Means, United States House of Representatives. Washington, DC: U.S. Government Printing Office.

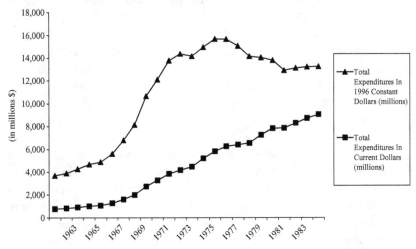

FIGURE 5.3. Total expenditures on the AFDC program. *Source*: See Figure 5.2.

nonmarital birth rates and divorce rates had created a crisis in which an ever-growing percentage of American youth were likely to live with only one parent. Even more devastating for lawmakers in charge of guarding the public purse, welfare expenditures to support these families were sky-rocketing. If these trends were ignored, the federal government as well as the states would be under increasing budgetary duress. The time for change, according to the conservatives, was now.

RISK-REDUCTION STRATEGIES

The aggregation and accumulation of all of these social ills clearly cried out for attention, and conservatives had in their arsenal a methodically contrived plan of attack. By holding fathers accountable for their actions, conservatives hoped to become the new policy entrepreneurs in this issue area. To be successful, however, they had to choose a path of organization. They could rally around a single individual, hoping that this leader would help them to achieve their goals; or they could organize more cooperatively, spreading the risk of political involvement across as many activists as possible. They wisely chose the cooperative risk-reduction strategy and organized in two arenas: the political realm and across America's communities.

During the Kennedy and Johnson administrations, conservatives had faced an uphill battle in pushing their agenda forward. The social upheaval of the 1960s had created a climate in which liberal ideas had become the standard ones in most political decision making. Groups previously marginalized in the American political system, such as minorities and women, were now demanding equality. These and other disenfranchised groups were beginning to open up the government to new ideas, and legislators were becoming more responsive to their claims. Moreover, the emergence of these new groups encouraged lawmakers to think about long-standing issues in novel ways, thereby further expanding the policy process to include progressive ideas.

By the early 1970s, however, the mood of the country had shifted, and resentment toward the political status quo manifested itself in a variety of ways.[15] Divisions in the Democratic Party over the Vietnam War, as well as frustration over the lack of results produced by the Great Society programs, helped to create a new movement in American society toward conservatism. But other factors also contributed to the mass exodus of voters away from the Democrats and toward the Republican Party.[16]

First, business loudly complained about the regulatory reforms that had been passed over the previous ten years. In an increasingly internationally

---

[15] Kevin Phillips. 1969. *The Emerging Republican Majority*. New Rochelle, NY: Arlington House.

[16] For an excellent discussion of this Republican transformation, see Benjamin Ginsberg and Martin Shefter. 1984. "A Critical Realignment? The New Politics, the Reconstituted Right, and the Election of 1984." In *The Elections of 1984*, ed. Michael Nelson. Washington, DC: Congressional Quarterly Press; Austin Ranney, ed. 1985. *The American Elections of 1984*. Washington, DC: American Enterprise Institute.

competitive business environment, American firms were struggling to remain afloat. The layers of environmental and consumer protection legislation that Congress had passed during the 1960s united businesses both large and small in opposition to the Democratic Party. Second, southern Democrats began a mass defection from the party because of what they perceived as its overly liberal positions on civil rights. As the economy slowed, working-class whites' hostility toward policies such as affirmative action and racial preferences intensified into vocal and sometimes violent outrage. Finally, many Protestants and Catholics became alarmed at what they viewed as the extremely permissive positions of the Democratic Party on issues such as school prayer, gay rights, and abortion. As time passed, they began actively searching for what they considered a politically moral alternative.

After the Watergate scandal, the election of Jimmy Carter to the presidency provided only a brief break in the rising tide of conservative sentiment that was then engulfing the country. This conservative tide culminated during Ronald Reagan's campaign for the presidency. In the late 1970s, Ronald Reagan moved to refashion and strengthen Nixon's "Silent Majority," by offering new policies around which his coalition could rally. Nixon had entered office on a platform of opposition – striking back at the Democrats on domestic and foreign policy issues at every turn. Reagan wanted more. Instead of surviving simply by opposing Democratic policies, Reagan hoped to create his own agenda that would solidify conservative dominance over the country.

He accomplished this by promising voters that he would support five major new initiatives if he were elected to the presidency. First, he allied himself with suburban voters by calling for a sharp reduction in taxes and decreased spending on social programs. Second, he courted the white southern vote by promising an end to affirmative action programs. Third, he attracted the attention of corporate leaders by arguing for a reduction in regulations – both environmental and consumer – that were adding millions of dollars to the cost of doing business in the country each year. Fourth, he promised those on the religious right that he would support the policies they favored, such as a ban on abortion and the introduction of prayer into public schools. Finally, he infused new energy into the defense industry by advocating a massive expansion in weapons programs to combat what he viewed as the serious Soviet threat to the United States' national security.

In his efforts to solidify the conservative right, Reagan was enormously successful. He swept the 1980 elections, winning with his vice president,

TABLE 5.5. *Republican gains in national government, 1975–85*

Year	Number of Republicans in House	Number of Republicans in Senate
1975	144	37
1977	143	38
1979	157	41
1981	192	53
1983	165	54
1985	182	53

Source: The Statistical Abstract of the United States. Various years. Bureau of Statistics, Department of the Treasury. Washington, DC: U.S. Government Printing Office.

George H. W. Bush, 50.8 percent of the popular vote to the Carter-Mondale team's 41 percent. On his coattails came a fleet of conservative lawmakers; by 1981, there were 192 Republicans in the House of Representatives and 53 Republican Senators (see Table 5.5). In 1984, Reagan increased his standing with the public by winning 58.8 percent of the popular vote to Mondale-Ferraro's 40.6 percent. By 1985, there were still 182 Republicans in the House and 53 in the Senate.

Not only were conservatives growing in number in Washington, D.C., they were also increasing their effectiveness in terms of working as a unified block. To rival the Democratic Study Group, a liberal-oriented policy group formed in 1959 that encouraged openness in government, conservatives formed the Republican Study Committee in 1973. To provide a counterweight to the Wednesday Club, a group of liberal Senate Republicans formed in 1963, conservatives created the Senate Steering Committee in 1973. Their strategy was simple: they would directly match each more left-leaning legislative group with a right-leaning one of their own.[17]

On the national scene, conservative candidates were also coordinating their efforts financially. Begun in 1975, the National Conservative Political Action Committee (NCPAC), under the direction of Terry Dolan, initiated the "independent expenditure campaign." Simply put, this was a strategy whereby political action committees, or PACs, could spend as much as they wanted either for or against a particular candidate as long as they did not directly contact the candidate running for office. NCPAC first

---

[17] For a history of these organizations, see Edwin J. Feulner. 1983. *Conservatives Stalk the House.* Ottawa, IL: Green Hill.

TABLE 5.6. *Republican gains in state government,*
1976–85

Year	Governors Number of Republicans	State Legislatures Percentage Republican
1976	12	32%
1977	12	32%
1978	22	36%
1979	22	36%
1980	23	39%
1981	23	39%
1982	16	37%
1983	16	37%
1984	16	41%
1985	16	41%

Source: The Statistical Abstract of the United States.
Various Years. Bureau of Statistics, Department of
the Treasury. Washington, DC: U.S. Government
Printing Office.

successfully used independent expenditures against Senator Dick Clark
(D-Iowa) in 1978, who lost to Republican Roger Jepsen. By 1980, NCPAC
had an arsenal of $1 million to use in the most prominent senatorial
races. Employing a carefully planned series of attack ads, NCPAC began
to compile what would eventually become an extremely effective track
record. Four of the six Democratic senators they opposed in 1980 – John
Culver (Iowa), George McGovern (S. Dak.), Frank Church (Idaho), and
Birch Bayh (Ind.) – were ultimately defeated.[18]

These conservative inroads at the national level were mirrored by what
was occurring at the state level (see Table 5.6). In 1976, Republicans controlled only twelve governorships and occupied only 32 percent of all seats
in the state legislatures. By 1981, they had almost doubled their number
of governorships to twenty-three and increased their average legislative
representation to 39 percent. Helping them to sustain these gains was the
American Legislative Exchange Council (ALEC), formed in 1973 by the
conservative activist Paul Weyrich. Designed to keep conservative legislators abreast of pro-business, pro-family, and pro-growth policies, ALEC

---

[18] Candice Nelson. 1990. "Loose Cannons: Independent Expenditures." In *Money, Elections
and Democracy – Reforming Congressional Campaign Finance*, ed. James Thurber and Roger
A. Davidson. Boulder, CO: Westview Press, p. 57. Alan Cranston (D-Calif.) and Thomas
Eagleton (D-Mo.) retained their seats despite NCPAC's efforts.

offered state lawmakers model legislation that would help to strengthen their partisan agenda.

These conservative political gains were reinforced by the creation of a wide variety of right-leaning grassroots organizations that also championed a new approach to social policy. On one level, the landslide defeat of Barry Goldwater for president in 1964 represented a monumental victory in American politics for liberals against the conservative agenda. But the loss also proved to be a rallying point for those whose ideas had been summarily dismissed by the American public at the voting booth. *They* knew they were right regarding the future of the country; they simply had to do a better job of convincing the rest of the country as to the merits of their vision.

And what was their long-range plan? According to political analyst Kevin Phillips, the organizations begun in the 1960s and 1970s that would later be referred to as the New Right were

a group of anti-establishment, middle-class political rebels more interested in issues like abortion, gun control, busing, ERA, quotas, bureaucracy, and the grassroots tax revolt than in capital gains taxation or natural gas deregulation.[19]

One of their most formidable enemies was "Big Government." To these groups, too many lazy and immoral Americans were living off the toil of hardworking Americans. Welfare was a primary example. Fathers needed to do the right thing and support their children, instead of forcing taxpayers to ante up.

A variety of right-leaning organizations sprang up to counter this Big Government trend. The American Conservative Union, formed in 1965, served as the lobbying arm of the conservative movement in its early years. Other early conservative organizations included the Young Americans for Freedom (a youth-oriented membership group), formed in 1960; the Philadelphia Society (a collective of intellectuals), established in 1964; and the Heritage Foundation (a think tank at the national level), created in 1973. These groups ultimately provided the foundation for the Conservative Caucus, begun in 1975. Led by political strategist Howard Phillips, the caucus boasted of 300,000 contributors and an annual budget of $3 million by 1980. Phillips later helped convince Jerry Falwell to lead the Moral Majority, a coalition of politically and socially conservative voters. By mid-1980, the Moral Majority and other Christian organizations

---

[19] Kevin Phillips quoted in Lee Edwards. 1999. *The Conservative Revolution.* New York: The Free Press, p. 184.

had registered over 2.5 million new voters.[20] Clearly, the conservative opportunity to transform the policy agenda, if it were ever to appear, was now at hand.

SHAKEOUT STRATEGIES

Throughout the 1960s and early 1970s, then, conservatives made clear inroads in pursuing cooperative risk-reduction strategies. They increased their levels of representation at all levels of government and built up a wide range of right-leaning organizations to support their claims. However, as we have seen, staking out risk-reduction strategies is only half of the battle. Conservatives also had to "shake out" their competition, using only legitimate means, in order to give their ideas a chance of being heard. This meant discrediting the current holders of power – the social workers – who controlled all aspects of child support policy. Given the social workers' dominance over this policy issue, this shakeout process clearly would not be easy.

Nonetheless, conservatives took up this challenge using one central shakeout strategy: to the extent that they would support any social policy at all, they would primarily support "automatic" social programs. "Automatic" social programs are those initiatives that rely only minimally, if at all, on the skills and resources of social workers.[21] In others words, these programs typically eschew any personalized social service delivery provisions whatsoever. Instead, automatic programs utilize more impersonal, automated ways of offering financial resources to low-income individuals, such as simple cash transfers. By gradually building up their support for such automatic programs, conservatives could achieve two goals. First, they could still claim that they were in favor of certain types of social spending; they were just advocating spending in a different form. Second, they could carefully remove the social workers from power, thereby laying the groundwork for a new type of child support policy with members of their own party at the helm.

By the mid-1960s, conservatives were already working to shake out their competition by actively lobbying for automatic social programs,

---

[20] See ibid., Chapter 10.
[21] In many ways, our definition of "automatic" social programs is analogous to that of R. Kent Weaver in his 1988 book *Automatic Government* (Washington, DC: The Brookings Institution Press). The major difference is that Weaver describes indexation as a means to shift responsibility for programmatic changes, while we are focusing on more radical types of restructuring.

two of which will be considered here. Each of these initiatives provided an integral part of the foundation for the new child support program that they would propose in the following decade. The first, the Social Security Amendments of 1967, was successfully signed into law by President Johnson and dramatically reduced the scope of social workers' power vis-à-vis their welfare clients. The second, Richard Nixon's Family Assistance Plan (FAP), was never enacted into law, but it did significantly change the terms of debate with respect to the types of automatic welfare proposals that were later thought to be politically possible.

The Social Security Amendments of 1967

The 1962 Social Security Amendments provided social workers with enormous power. They had both the funding and the authority to offer single mothers a vast array of services, including job preparation skills, actual employment training, and "soft" life skills to help them cope with the challenges that lay before them on a day-to-day basis. However, the continued growth in the welfare rolls throughout the sixties prompted legislators to take a renewed and skeptical look at AFDC, the primary public assistance plan in operation at the time.[22] Their investigation brought about the Social Security Amendments of 1967, a law that offered some new benefits to recipients, but which mainly aimed to cut back on what was widely perceived as out-of-control government spending. And the mechanism that produced these reductions was the clever severing of social workers from the awarding of assistance payments.

From the start, the 1967 Amendments were a mixed bag of carrots and sticks designed to reduce the welfare rolls. For instance, the Amendments provided welfare recipients with additional incentives to work. Instead of facing a 100 percent tax on their earnings, recipients could keep the first $30, and subsequently one-third of everything they earned, without experiencing a reduction in their benefits. Beyond these incentives, however, the legislation focused almost exclusively on "freezing" the number of new beneficiaries and on imposing new work requirements on those already enrolled in the program. While exempting children in need of aid when the father had passed away or was unemployed, the new law encouraged the states to deny assistance to children born in nonmarital circumstances.

---

[22] For a substantial treatment of this turn away from services to work requirements, see Gilbert Y. Steiner. 1971. *The State of Welfare*. Washington, DC: The Brookings Institution Press.

In a similar, more punitive vein, the Amendments' new jobs program, the Work Incentive Program, or WIN, was instituted to establish a formal link between employment and the receipt of benefits. Welfare recipients now had to "work off" their grants in a variety of employment settings in order to continue to receive government assistance.

While opposition to the enrollment freeze ultimately prompted Congress to repeal pieces of this legislation in 1969, the other parts of the 1967 Amendments were implemented quite rapidly. Most important were the organizational and administrative changes that took place in the wake of this legislative reform. First, the Welfare Administration and the Bureau of Family Services, established in 1962, were abolished. In their stead, the Social and Rehabilitation Service (SRS) took over in the area of public assistance service delivery. The new organizational mission of all SRS employees was to focus primarily on immediate employment training rather than on addressing any of the recipients' other pressing needs.

Second, and perhaps most significantly, the Amendments involved a series of administrative rulings promulgated under the conservative presidential administration of Richard Nixon that formally separated the provision of services from the disbursement of financial assistance. Initially, social workers supported this split, by focussing on the autonomy that such a division would offer welfare clients. For example, the National Association of Social Workers argued that the separation afforded clients new dignity and the right to ask for services only if they really wanted them. The division also established financial assistance as a matter of right, not conditional on the client's interaction with the powers of the state through the service delivery system.

Conservatives, however, supported the split for a much different reason. The separation of services from financial assistance meant that social workers would have less of a hold on welfare recipients as a group. First, social workers would no longer be present during the intake process, informing prospective clients of their rights to a broad range of government assistance programs. Conservatives could then pack these positions with financial accountants and other technical personnel who would be trained to limit rather than expand the eligibility requirements. Second, if recipients were no longer obligated to receive ongoing services, many of them, conservatives argued, would simply elect to receive a check by itself. This would further weaken the power of the social workers, as they would be forced into relinquishing their ongoing day-to-day contact and advocacy relationship with their welfare clientele.

Indeed, federal regulations mandated that all of the states separate the process of disbursing monetary payments from the provision of services by January 1, 1974. California, under conservative governor Ronald Reagan, was one of the more aggressive states in pursuing this split. During his first four years in office, beginning in 1966, Reagan established a strong reputation for rolling back what he viewed as deeply flawed welfare policies. In pursuing this end, his political philosophy was clear. The government should get out of the business of providing financial assistance for able-bodied adults. For far too long, left-leaning social workers had "protected" citizens who wanted to defraud the state. During his tenure, Reagan aimed to remove from office as many of these "protectors" as he could.

After cycling through several welfare directors who were "out of sync" with his philosophy, Reagan finally appointed Robert Carleson to be the new director of the state Department of Social Welfare. The year was 1971, and Reagan was beginning his second term in office. In his role as the new director, Carleson immediately set about the task of reducing the scope and influence of the social workers by crafting the department's new budget behind closed doors. According to Harold E. Simmons, deputy director for employment and rehabilitation at the department,

At the end of January 1971, the completed department budget was submitted to the Governor with closely guarded copies remaining unavailable to staff. The Governor then submitted his budget to the Legislature, so, finally, we obtained a copy from a legislative staff member. We were amazed to find that 153 top level social service management staff had been eliminated, virtually all of such staff. Moreover, the entire Employment and Rehabilitation Branch had been completely obliterated. We searched the pages of the budget in disbelief and then examined Department of Employment and other departmental budgets to determine whether the positions had been transferred, but they could not be found. It was clear that Reagan had ordered a purge of social work administrators and consultants.

As we examined the situation further, it became apparent that a contingency fund had been set up in the budget to employ undesignated types of staff. Further investigation revealed that a civil service examination had been given months earlier for the social administrator series, a group of positions largely excluding social work administrators and including fiscal, technical and management types. The employment lists were ready and waiting to provide manpower to replace the purged social work administrators and the contingency fund would pay their salaries. What clever, secretive planning this was.[23]

---

[23] See Harold E. Simmons. 1975. *California Welfare Reform: Recycling the 1601 Elizabethan Poor Law*. Sacramento, CA: General Welfare Publications, p. 79.

The transformation of the welfare department in California was typical of what was occurring across the country. Either under the direction of a conservative governor, or under pressure from regulations emanating from Washington, social workers were being stripped of their duties. In their place, states were offering jobs to accountants and other financial personnel. In this new vision, welfare would be completely "streamlined." The technocrats would serve as the cutting-edge gatekeepers for eligibility, and the social workers would be relegated to a secondary status – if they could hold onto any type of status at all – of service provision.

The Family Assistance Plan

While the 1967 Social Security Amendments were being implemented at the state level across the country, there was also momentum gathering at the national level to effect another type of dramatic welfare change.[24] Various strains of opposition to Democratic principles helped provide the foundation for Richard Nixon's "Silent Majority," the substantial percentage of the American population that buttressed his reemergence into political life in the late sixties. This Silent Majority helped elect him to the presidency in 1968 and then again in 1972, each time entrusting him to confront the problem of childhood poverty in a novel way.

A significant part of the impetus behind Nixon's willingness to take on the traditional welfare program was political fear. In the 1968 election, Nixon not only had to worry about opposition from his left in the form of Hubert Humphrey, he also had to worry about the groundswell of support that was gaining on his right in the person of George Wallace. Wallace, elected governor of Alabama in 1962, had made his career in politics as a pro–states rights, pro-segregationist candidate. After "standing in the schoolhouse door" to block two African-American students from entering the University of Alabama, Wallace rose to national stature as a leader in the anti-integrationist movement. He made a surprisingly strong showing in the Democratic primaries during the 1964 presidential campaign, but it was the 1968 election that really drew attention to Wallace. He carried five southern states by blasting integration and the liberal welfare state that had made affirmative action policies possible. Reelected governor in 1970, Wallace seemed ready to intrude into

---

[24] For a through account of this proposal, see M. Kenneth Bowler. 1974. *The Nixon Guaranteed Income Proposal.* Cambridge, MA: Ballinger Publishing.

Nixon's hard-won political world as soon as the opportunity became available.

To curry favor with these Wallace voters, Nixon needed a plan.[25] At first, three main issues dominated Nixon's welfare agenda: the adequacy or inadequacy of benefits, the interstate variation in support, and the availability of work incentives. At the same time, Nixon had three plans of action before him. First, there was the report of the Advisory Council on Public Welfare to the Secretary of Health, Education, and Welfare, completed in 1966. Endorsed by the social work profession, this proposal aimed to federalize the AFDC program by guaranteeing a minimum benefit level across the fifty states. A second proposal, favored by a more radical fringe of the social work profession, sought to guarantee children's allowances to all parents, regardless of income. This would remove the stigma of welfare from all recipients, and the government could tax the benefits of those in the middle and upper classes. Nixon, however, favored the third alternative – the Family Assistance Plan, or FAP – which summarily removed social workers from the lives of the disadvantaged altogether.

The Family Assistance Plan, which guaranteed a minimum income to all, provided financial assistance that was reduced by earnings to a break-even point when the family became self-supporting. More specifically, FAP would guarantee a family of four $1,600 per year (at the time, the median income in the country for a family of four was $11,167).[26] FAP would be administered through the Social Security Administration and would serve to replace the AFDC program. In addition, the plan would require state aid for unemployed parents, as well as increase the federal role in providing assistance for the blind, disabled, and aged. With this measure, Nixon caught the public's imagination by establishing an array of incentives and penalties to encourage people to work.

But there was an added bonus. By implementing FAP, Nixon would destroy the power of – or, in his words, "get rid of" – the left-leaning social workers completely.[27] Nixon and the conservatives used three primary modes of attack to discredit the social workers in preparation for

[25] For an excellent discussion of the ways in which race interacted with the development of welfare policy during the Nixon Administration, see Jill Quadagno. 1994. *The Color of Welfare.* New York: Oxford University Press.

[26] See "Table F-8. Size of Family–Families (All Races) by Median and Mean Income: 1947 to 1999." U.S. Census Bureau. Accessed on <http://www.census.gov/hhes/income/histinc/fo8.html> on September 10, 2001.

[27] Vincent Burke. 1974. *Nixon's Good Deed.* New York: Columbia University Press, p. 67.

their push on behalf of FAP.[28] First, conservatives argued that the social work profession lacked the methodological rigor to be in charge of major, sweeping welfare reforms. According to political scientist Daniel Patrick Moynihan, Nixon's domestic policy advisor in his pre-Senate days, social work as a discipline had yet to be firmly established with its own tools for analyzing problems. To Moynihan, the "profession had overestimated how much it knew or could hope to know."[29] Moreover, the profession "lacked ... a working model of social behavior which would enable the practice of social welfare to produce definable social consequences."[30] Given these deficiencies, social workers could not be trusted in devising this country's domestic programs in the years to come.

A second major critique came from those observers who argued that the social workers were not so much concerned with helping others as with helping themselves to aggrandize their own position within the field of public policy. This viewpoint gained momentum as work in other academic fields, notably political science, pointed to the corrupting effects of interest groups who essentially "hijacked" public policy to serve their own specific needs rather than those of the country as a whole.[31] Again, Moynihan became the central critic of the profession when he pointed to its members' transparent self-interest in designing new plans to help the poor.

With astonishing consistency, middle-class professionals – whatever their racial or ethnic backgrounds – when asked to devise ways of improving the condition of lower class groups would come up with schemes of which the first effect would be to improve the condition of middle-class professionals, and the second effect might or might not be that of improving the condition of the poor.[32]

In essence, conservatives were charging the social workers with defrauding the American public into believing that their primary concern was helping the disadvantaged. In fact, as Moynihan suggested, Americans

---

[28] For a thorough discussion of each of these factors, see David A. Rochefort. 1986. *American Social Welfare Policy: Dynamics of Formulation and Change.* Boulder, CO: Westview.

[29] Daniel Patrick Moynihan. 1973. *The Politics of a Guaranteed Income.* New York: Vintage, p. 46.

[30] Ibid., p. 45.

[31] See, for example, Theodore Lowi. 1969. *The End of Liberalism: Ideology, Policy, and the Crisis of Public Authority.* New York: Norton.

[32] Daniel Patrick Moynihan. 1973. *The Politics of a Guaranteed Income.* New York: Vintage, p. 54.

needed to know what their true motivating interests were, especially if they conflicted with their stated professional mission.

The third and final area where conservatives found fault with the social workers was in their "controlling" methods of conducting business. In this view, what the disadvantaged needed was not social workers attending to their every need, but rather a push toward employment using the power of financial penalties. On December 11, 1970, Nixon, in preparation for an upcoming presidential address, directed his speechwriter Ray Price to stress how "getting rid" of the social workers would be not only good for conservatives seeking additional control over welfare reform, but also positive for the welfare recipients themselves. Nixon argued that Price should craft a speech with the following characteristics:

Paint a picture of what a terrible mark [welfare] leaves on the child's life. Point out that [Nixon's welfare reform or FAP] takes away the degradation of social workers snooping around, of making some children seem to be a class apart.... Point out that the greatest [problem] of the present welfare program is the effect that it has on children, and that the greatest benefit of [his proposed reform] is the fact that it will allow the children of all families in America to stand proud with dignity without being singled out as those who are getting food stamps, welfare, or what have you.... [I]n the depression years I remember when my brother had tuberculosis for five years and we had to keep him in a hospital, my mother didn't buy a new dress for five years. We were really quite desperately poor, but as Eisenhower said it much more eloquently at Abilene in his opening campaign statement in 1952, the glory of it was that we didn't know it. The problem today is that the children growing up in welfare families receiving food stamps and government largess [sic] with social workers poking around are poor and *they do know it*.... [33]

Repeated drafting of the legislation in the White House indicated that staff members had to learn "to properly reflect the President's aversion to social workers."[34] The president later echoed this philosophy in his memoirs.

I thought that people should have the responsibility of spending carefully and taking care of themselves. I abhorred the snoopy, patronizing surveillance of the social workers which made children and adults feel stigmatized and separate. The basic premise of the Family Assistance Plan was simple: what the poor need to help them rise out of poverty is money.[35]

[33] Quoted in Tom Wicker. 1991. *One of Us*. New York: Random House, pp. 530–531.
[34] Vincent Burke. 1974. *Nixon's Good Deed*. New York: Columbia University Press, p. 89.
[35] Edward D. Berkowitz. 1994. *America's Welfare State*. Baltimore: Johns Hopkins University Press, p. 128.

In sum, FAP would be the ultimate "automatic program." Families would either qualify for benefits and receive a check from the federal government, or not. The service component to assistance would be minimized, and the "snoopy" social workers would be rendered powerless.

Unlike the Social Security Amendments of 1967, however, which passed quite easily and immobilized a large percentage of the social workers in the process, FAP ran into difficulties in its translation from a bill to a law. While the House Ways and Means Committee and then ultimately the House as a whole easily passed the bill in 1970, FAP encountered much more opposition in the Senate. Liberals in the Senate argued that the guaranteed income level was much too low, while conservatives were concerned that the work incentives, when combined with the notch effects created by other programs, would actually result in increased dependency. When the bill died in the Senate, the House promptly proposed an alternative, H.R. 1, in 1971. This bill raised the guaranteed income level to $2,400 for a family of four and strengthened work requirements, and it again passed the House. By the time the bill reached the Senate, however, two alternatives were already being circulated. Senator Abraham Ribicoff (D-Conn.) backed a bill that would raise the guaranteed income level to $3,000, while the conservative Senator Russell B. Long (D-La.) advocated the adoption of stricter mandatory work requirements for all family heads (with the exception of those with children under six and those attending school on a full-time basis).

By October 1972, the Senate had rejected all three plans before it. Liberals regarded the new approach to assistance as too stingy toward the poor, and conservatives argued that it did not provide welfare recipients with enough incentives to work. However, there was still cause for celebration within conservative circles. Although the plan never passed, FAP's popularity both within and outside the Nixon Administration suggested to conservatives that stripping power away from the social workers was, in fact, a real possibility. In fact, the major debates over FAP's future were about the magnitude of the benefits levels, not about the relative absence of social workers from the program's administration. With social workers already in a weakened position, it now seemed possible for conservatives to strike again with a completely novel way of approaching the child poverty problem: the child support enforcement program.

OVERTAKING THE INCUMBENTS

To the emerging conservative presence across the United States, the inadequacies of past policies in the child support arena were more than self-evident. Conservatives argued that the entire approach that social workers had advocated was wrong. Parents did not refuse to pay child support because they lacked economic opportunity, as the social workers had maintained. Rather, parents did not pay child support because societal norms of appropriate behavior that prohibited family breakdown were simply becoming too lax. It was time to get tough. The government had to get out of the business of taking care of children and force fathers to support their offspring.

On the national stage, however, conservatives were still in the minority in Congress. Social workers and their strong Democratic supporters had lost a significant amount of power in the preceding fights over welfare reform, but they were far from being marginalized in the political arena. Yet, fortuitously for conservatives, there was a brief opportunity for action during the mid-1970s. A little-known Congressman from Michigan, Gerald R. Ford, had been shopping around a new idea to improve child support performance for decades, and with Nixon's resignation in 1974, Ford had unexpectedly assumed a position of national prominence.

As early as 1949, Ford had begun his campaign against what he termed "runaway pappys," or men who willfully abandoned their children, leaving them without financial support. The problem, as Ford perceived it, was that men were not being held responsible for the children that they brought into this world. While the states permitted civil remedies for mothers looking for support from fathers living within the state, problems with interstate enforcement were simply overwhelming. According to W. J. Brockelbank, professor of law at the University of Idaho and contributor to the *American Bar Association Journal* in 1951,

The first obstacle is the inertia of the local prosecuting attorney. If no one has been murdered or no property has been stolen or the one requesting prosecution is not one of his special friends, he will hesitate before spending time and money on a matter so little rewarding in publicity. If charges are preferred against the absconding breadwinner, he must be extradited and brought for trial to the state where the crime was committed. And before he will be given up by the governor of the asylum state, it must be shown that, having committed a crime in the first state, he "fled from justice." Even if [the governor] feels the allegations are true, the governor may still not wish to give the defendant up for he may know him as a self-respecting man of orderly habits and may hesitate to send him out of the state to meet charges that may be either fabricated or incapable of proof. In such a situation there is no way known to the law to force the hand of the governor.[36]

[36] W. J. Brockelbank. 1951. "The Problem of Family Support: A New Uniform Act Offers a Solution." *American Bar Association Journal* 37(February): 94.

Brockelbank ended up concluding with the Council of State Governments that the criminal process for catching up with these fathers needed to be revamped because of "the expensive extradition costs, the limited nature of the criminal statute, and the fact that the arrest of the husband or father destroys the source of wage earnings."[37]

In January 1949, Ford introduced the first of many measures intended to improve interstate enforcement, calling for fines of up to $2,500 and imprisonment for up to three years for men who abandon their children.[38] By May 9 of the same year, Ford had incorporated the suggestions of his colleagues to include language in a newly revised bill that "Congress hereby declares that every individual has a natural, moral, and social obligation to support the members of his immediate family, which transcend the status of debt."[39] Immediately upon the introduction of these bills, Ford attracted the support of local newspapers. The *Grand Rapids Press*, for example, editorialized that something needed to be done about the "galloping daddy" problem and that Ford's bills represented a step in the right direction. Ford's proposed legislation would force these "galloping daddies" to understand that their flight from justice was futile; then maybe more of them "might stay home and support their families."[40] Yet, while local newspapers supported Ford, Congress was not yet prepared to endorse such a dramatically different approach to addressing the child support problem. Social workers were rising in power in the United States, and from their perspective, what was needed were not punitive measures directed toward fathers, but social services designed to help mothers.

By the mid-1970s, however, a new mood of conservative influence had descended upon Washington. From the time hearings began on the child support issue (what would eventually become Part B of the Social Security Act) until Congress passed Public Law 93–647 (the Social Security Amendments of 1975) during the adjournment rush of 1974–75, Congress was simultaneously holding hearings on what would become Part A of the same Social Security Amendments. Part A represented the social workers' last grasp at influence. More specifically, Part A offered welfare recipients a host of new services, including appropriations that would accomplish

---

[37] Ibid.
[38] H.R. 1538, Eighty-first Congress, First Session. Gerald R. Ford Presidential Library. Box F2.
[39] Ibid.
[40] "Galloping Daddies." Editorial from the *Grand Rapids Press*, April 8, 1950. Gerald R. Ford Presidential Library. Box F2.

the following: (1) help recipients achieve economic self-support in order to prevent, reduce, or eliminate dependency; (2) prevent or remedy neglect, abuse, and exploitation of children and adults; (3) prevent or reduce inappropriate institutional care by providing for community-based care and alternatives; and (4) secure referral or admission for institutional care when other forms of care are not appropriate.[41] In return for agreeing to these measures, conservatives demanded funding for the child support program.

The congressional decision to initiate this program most likely was more political than economic.... Thus, at a single point in time, Congress passed amendments to the Social Security Act which provided for the broadest social service programs since the War on Poverty – amendments for which liberals within and outside of two administrations had wrangled – and at the same time set up a second part of the same bureaucratic structure, designed in such a way as to substantially reduce absent fathers of AFDC children.... [Without proof of the program's cost-effectiveness,] it is easier to believe that the bill's potential opponents in Congress, and others who favored the social services provisions [Part A], regarded Part B [the Child Support Amendments] as a price to be paid for conservative congressional support for Part A. After all, "logrolling" is not unheard of in these matters.[42]

In sum, conservatives would support Part A of the Amendments, but only if the social workers were automated out of a substantial part of their jobs under Part B of the same package of legislation.

This "unspoken" agreement is readily apparent when we examine testimony on Part B conducted during 1973. Congress heard testimony on behalf of the new child support program in the Senate Finance Committee, under the direction of the conservative Senator Russell B. Long (D-La.). Granted unlimited time to present testimony, Secretary of Health, Education, and Welfare Caspar Weinberger and Robert B. Carleson, Governor Reagan's former director of the state Department of Social Welfare and later special assistant to the secretary for welfare matters, articulately made the case for a new child support program. In his oral testimony, Weinberger praised the efforts of states like California under Reagan, who were successful in instituting a "new order" in providing for children whose lives were threatened by financial instability. Under this

---

[41] These provisions are reported in Judith Cassetty's book *Child Support and Public Policy.* 1978. Lexington, MA: Lexington Books.
[42] Ibid., pp. 10–15.

new conservative regime, governmental efforts would focus on pursuing fathers rather than providing services for mothers.

A major problem with the current welfare program arises when parents desert their children and are able to contribute to their support but do not. The result is an unnecessary burden on the nation's welfare system. When public welfare supports the family of a parent who has left his children, the public has a stake in assuring that he meets as much of his support obligation as he can.... This concept is beginning to take hold in the states. California has taken the lead in developing, as part of its welfare reform program, a comprehensive effort of increasing requirements that absent parents meet their responsibilities.[43]

Adding to Weinberger's statements, Carleson, recalling his days in California, pointed out that the "public strongly supported an affirmative support enforcement program." To Carleson, the sooner the nation as a whole instituted such a similar program, the better.[44]

In contrast to the time devoted to the conservative point of view concerning the direction of public policy toward children living in poverty, Congress paid scant attention to the social workers. No social worker was called to present oral testimony before Congress; they were all relegated to submitting written testimony. Glenn Allison, director of the Legislative Department of the National Association of Social Workers, submitted a short letter in opposition to the new child support program, arguing that the Association would rather "call ... attention to the need for strong programs to deal with the frightening erosion of healthy family life in the United States."[45] NASW specifically maintained that the program would have a "deleterious effect on families which are already torn and broken. Experience has shown that adversary type actions between family members not only tend to permanently scar the relationship between those directly involved but also have a deep and long-lasting impact on others in the family."[46] As such, the program as a whole

[43] Caspar Weinberger. 1973. Testimony on "Child Support and the Work Bonus." Hearing before the Committee on Finance, United States Senate. Washington, DC: U.S. Government Printing Office, p. 80.

[44] Robert Carleson. 1973. Testimony on "Child Support and the Work Bonus." Hearing before the Committee on Finance, United States Senate. Washington, DC: U.S. Government Printing Office, p. 114.

[45] Glenn Allison. 1973. Letter submitted as testimony on "Child Support and the Work Bonus." Hearing before the Committee on Finance, United States Senate. Washington, DC: U.S. Government Printing Office, p. 255.

[46] "NASW Claims Child Support Rules Threaten Civil Liberty and Privacy." July 1975. *The NASW NEWS* 20(7): 2.

represented "an undesirable Federal intrusion into the realm of domestic relations."

Similarly, Elizabeth Wickendon, representing the old guard of social work prominence through the National Assembly for Social Policy and Development, voiced her opposition to the proposed conservative initiative by asserting that the focus of welfare should be on "an adequate range of jobs, education, housing, income and opportunities for all." She further warned that "social responsibility is the product of a society in which benefits and opportunity are equitably open to all and cannot be instilled by the punishment and hence greater bitterness of an underprivileged subclass."[47] Yet, despite their protestations, Allison's and Wickendon's voices were clearly being supplanted by those with a completely new philosophy for dealing with poverty. Assistance to mothers would now take second place to the punitive pursuit of fathers.

After all of the testimony was presented and reconciled, President Ford signed the first substantive piece of legislation – the Social Security Amendments of 1975 – creating a federally sponsored child support agency, primarily for families on AFDC. In its initial form, the Federal Child Support Enforcement Program was to be funded primarily by the federal government and operated by the states. The Department of Health, Education, and Welfare would be in charge of offering technical assistance to the states, evaluating state programs, and certifying cases for referral to the Internal Revenue Service when support could be intercepted through the tax system. The law also added the requirement that all new AFDC applicants agree to assign their support rights to the state. Finally, the law provided for a monetary incentive scheme for the states based on the amount of AFDC support collections they were able to make.

Because the heart of the program rested with the states, conservative legislators at that level of government soon took charge. They had to establish separate organizational units that would be responsible for establishing paternity and enforcing collections. In addition, they were responsible for entering into cooperative arrangements with the courts, law enforcement officials, and other states in order to enforce support. Additionally, the states had to create their own parent locator services that would be compatible with the Federal Parent Locator Service in Washington, D.C. Beyond meeting these federal mandates, states also

---

[47] Elizabeth Wickendon. 1973. Letter submitted as testimony on "Child Support and the Work Bonus." Hearing before the Committee on Finance, United States Senate. Washington, DC: U.S. Government Printing Office, p. 258.

began to pass their own voluntary laws to enforce support. These included initiatives enabling officials to cross state lines to establish paternity, methods to withhold wages if fathers became delinquent in their payments, and rules regarding the imposition of property liens on fathers' assets.

In sum, during the late 1960s, the problem of child support did not vanish under the tutelage of the social workers. In fact, it worsened, as thousands of families either broke up or were never legally established by a marital contract in the first place. What did change was the emergence of a new class of policy entrepreneurs – conservative legislators and activists – who viewed the problem from a completely different perspective than their social worker predecessors. The child support crisis, in their view, was not caused by a lack of economic opportunity for parents, but rather by familial breakdown and the increasing willingness of young mothers to turn to the government for financial aid. Rather than continue to dole out new government benefits by expanding the AFDC program, these entrepreneurs devised a way to shift the burden of support from the state back to the father. The new child support program, and the subsequent voluntary state initiatives, aimed to make this a reality as soon as possible.

CONCLUSIONS

By the mid-1970s, child support enforcement in the United States had undergone a massive transformation. Gone were the days when social workers controlled the agenda. Gone were the days when the primary focus of this public policy was distributing benefits to mothers and providing them with intensive job training and educational services. Gone were the days when welfare budgets would continue to rise without accountability.

No, these were the days when the conservatives reigned supreme in child support policy. Through the early 1970s, they carefully constructed a new child support program that placed the federal government in a new partnership with the states to pursue fathers for financial resources, rather than to offer services to single-parent mothers. This approach, they reasoned, would provide solid relief for their current budgetary woes, where deficits prompted by exploding welfare costs dominated the election-year debates.

Indeed, the program met with marked initial success. By early 1976, over 11,700 people were employed across the country to enforce support. These employees were in charge of working the over 1.9 million AFDC cases that immediately came onto their books. Of these cases, staffers succeeded in establishing 14,704 paternities and locating 181,504 parents. In addition, the program initially collected $217 million in outstanding support.[48]

Yet there was a steady undercurrent of duress on the system. Women not receiving welfare, or non-AFDC women, were not guaranteed the same rights, benefits, and privileges for child support assistance as AFDC clients. Some states offered them services, while others did not. But the demand for services was very real. By 1981, while the AFDC caseload had climbed to about 5.1 million cases, the non-AFDC child support caseload was catching up. Even with only partial state coverage, the non-AFDC caseload jumped from 159,115 in 1976 to 1.1 million in 1981.[49] Just as the conservatives were getting on their feet in terms of controlling the new field of child support, then, an increasingly vocal client group – non-AFDC mothers – came looking for another set of proactive leaders to advocate on their behalf. They found a new set of policy entrepreneurs in women legislators and women's groups.

---

[48] See the *First Annual Report to Congress*. 1976. Washington, DC: Office of Child Support Enforcement; See also, the *Supplemental Report to the Congress for the Period Ending September 30, 1976*. June 30, 1977. Washington, DC: Office of Child Support Enforcement.

[49] See the *Sixth Annual Report to Congress*. 1981. Washington, DC: Office of Child Support Enforcement.

6

Women Leaders as Challenger Entrepreneurs

The letters were stacked high in her office that January in 1984. Each was different, yet, in many ways, each was the same. It almost did not matter which ones she chose to bring with her and quote as she faced the Senate's Committee on Finance later that month.

I called my Senator to ask for help. His secretary told me that the best thing to do was to sell my house and go on welfare. She said that the Senators get lots of letters from women who can't get their husbands to pay support, and that all they could tell them to do was to keep going through the legal system or just to go on welfare and let the State take care of it. – An Indiana Mother

Because of his lack of support, I have had to borrow money and feed my children out of the food banks. I have tried to go through consumer credit, and they stated they don't know how I have existed this long. – A Washington Mother

My ex-husband is an entertainer in a known group. This group has done extensive travel in the United States, overseas, and has even sung at the White House in Washington for the President. And yet, no one can get him to pay support for his child. – A North Carolina Mother

I have written to our Attorney General, prosecuting attorney, Citizens Complaints, and the judge who has had us in court several times. So far it hasn't done anything. Right now, my ex has arrearages in child support up to $16,000. I don't believe the State would allow this to happen if I was that far behind in taxes; I wouldn't have a home. – A Missouri Mother

I was quite young when my divorce was granted, and I just assumed that when problems with child support payments arose that some legal process would intervene and enforce the original court order. However, my frustration quickly turned into an agonizing obsession. This attitude and indifference of the people in charge of local programs is shocking. Their collective opinions are: "If you are getting anything, feel lucky." Well, I don't. Through all of this procrastination, my son awaits patiently for school clothes, books, supplies, and a chance to enjoy the same privileges as his companions. – An Illinois Mother

Patricia Kelly, president and co-founder of the organization Kids in Need Deserve Equal Rights (KINDER), could have continued reading the letters, but a long line of other women were also waiting to present their cases before Congress and plead for assistance. So she stopped reading the mail piled in front of her and quickly turned to her own story.

For the past four years, Kelly explained, she had been on and off welfare. Her ex-husband, a General Motors employee with a good job, simply refused to pay child support. Within weeks after he left, she had found herself poverty-stricken, and within months, she had applied for and begun receiving welfare benefits. Only recently had she been able to climb out of the ranks of poverty through her remarriage. Summing up her testimony, Kelly made it clear what the new stakes in child support policy were. "The major problem that we have found is that the system bases its whole intent on collecting child support for AFDC-related cases. You know, [non-AFDC] cases don't get any help."[1]

After the decline of the social workers in the 1960s, conservatives emerged to define the child support problem in a completely different way and helped to pass tough new enforcement measures accordingly. Yet, the child support crisis continued unabated. According to the Federal Office of Child Support Enforcement, more than 8.4 million women were raising children without their fathers in 1981. Of these 8.4 million cases, only 5 million had child support orders in place. And of these 5 million, more than 50 percent received only partial payment or no payment at all.[2] Competition to control the public agenda on this issue became fierce once again. The only question that remained was who would take the lead.

The social movements of the 1960s created a new political atmosphere in which previously marginalized populations now demanded access to government. Among these many groups were women, who, although they made up half of the population, still suffered from the multiple problems of wage discrimination, occupational segregation, and sexual harassment,

---

[1] The letters and accounts are taken from "Child Support Enforcement Program Reform Proposals." January 24 and 26, 1984. Hearing before the Committee on Finance, United States Senate. Washington, DC: U.S. Government Printing Office, pp. 144–145.
[2] *Eighth Annual Report to Congress.* 1983. Washington, DC: Office of Child Support Enforcement, p. 2.

among many others. Women organized against these injustices across multiple fronts. Consciousness-raising groups sprang up across the nation with the primary purpose of encouraging women to identify their difficulties not as issues of individual victimization but rather as symptomatic of a greater societal oppression. Street theater groups called public attention to the previously considered "private" problems of rape, incest, and abuse. And other women sought redress in court, suing for contraception rights, abortion rights, employment opportunities, and sexual freedom.[3]

It was not surprising, therefore, that women entering the political arena during the 1970s and 1980s would become the new policy entrepreneurs who sought to redefine the child support issue in an innovative way. Women aimed to challenge the decentralized and localized court-based system of deciding child support cases for non-AFDC families. But like their predecessors, they too had to confront political risk without any guaranteed payoff. And also like their predecessors, they too had to assume the challenge of devising shakeout strategies to compete in the marketplace of ideas.

This chapter proceeds as follows. The first section describes the exact nature of the rent-seeking position outlined by leaders of prominent women's groups and women legislators. As we will see, they sought to redefine the child support problem not as one of welfare cost recovery, but rather as one of welfare prevention. The second section then describes these groups' risk reduction strategies, which were successful in that they were highly cooperative rather than individualized. Women increased their numbers in elective office, formed broad-based coalitions, and created new, overarching groups specifically designed to tackle the nonsupport problem. The third section then turns to the ways in which women's groups and women legislators used the gender gap – a difference in voting patterns between the sexes, which was taken extremely seriously by the American public – as their primary shakeout strategy against their conservative competition. The fourth section describes their victories, and the fifth section concludes.

---

[3] See, for example, *Griswold v. Connecticut*, 381 U.S. 479, 14 L. Ed. 2d. 510, 85 S. Ct. 1678, 1965; *Carey v. Population Services International*, 431 U.S. 678, 52 L. Ed. 2d 675, 97 S. Ct. 2010, 1977; and *Roe v. Wade*, 410 U.S. 113, 35 L. Ed. 2d. 147, 93 S. Ct. 705, 1973, for three important decisions regarding reproductive rights. See *Shultz v. Wheaton Glass Co.*, 398 U.S. 905, 26 L. Ed. 2d 64, 90 S. Ct. 1696, 1970; and *Corning Glass Works v. Brennan*, 417 U.S. 188, 41 L. Ed. 2d 1, 94 S. Ct. 2223, 1974, for two significant cases on equal pay.

DEFINING A RENT-SEEKING POSITION

Up to this point, we have seen two different types of rent-seeking behavior. After the charity workers and local law enforcement laid down the initial components of American child support policy, two other groups entered the debate. From the 1900s to the 1960s, social workers aimed to control the child support agenda by pushing for a new public role in their profession and by emphasizing a service-oriented approach to mothers in need. During the 1970s, the conservatives were able to shift gears and focus attention on fathers of families on welfare. They hoped that this "get tough" approach would endear them to American voters and secure them a place at the political decision-making table in the years to come. During the early 1980s, women legislators and women's groups also formed a new alliance to overtake the child support agenda, albeit from a completely different perspective.

Women leaders wasted no time in laying out what they viewed as the dismal state of the child support system as it existed in the mid-1980s. While during the 1960s social workers had argued that the child support crisis was the product of a lack of economic opportunity for families, and during the late 1970s conservatives argued that it was the result of familial breakdown and welfare dependency, in the 1980s women located the cause in the realm of financial vulnerability. To women leaders hearing from their female constituents, the key factor behind the child support crisis was the government's lack of effort in preventing women from becoming dependent on AFDC in the first place. If women not receiving welfare wanted to receive child support, they had to turn to the courts for help. Yet no one seemed to be studying the impact of this system on the women themselves. In fact, when the previous two groups of entrepreneurs – the social workers and the conservatives – had controlled the agenda, support for non-AFDC women had rarely even been considered.

As an example, Senator Russell B. Long (D-La.), the conservative chairman of the Senate Finance Committee during the mid-1970s when the child support program first began, rejected the idea that the committee should even be contemplating aid to non-AFDC families. Reflecting this outlook, he compared non-AFDC fathers to soldiers who always behave with honesty and integrity.

I know what happens in the upper income families. It is just no problem because when the father leaves, he knows that he is going to be sued, and the mother has enough money to hire lawyers and pay them, and so he is going to be pursued and made to pay, and so he does the decent thing, just like in wartime. A lot of people have been known to volunteer because they are going to be drafted anyway. So, a man might prefer to have a record showing he volunteered, rather than he was drafted into the service. But, in the upper income families, the father knows that he cannot get away without supporting his children and abandoning the children, so he makes arrangements to take care of the mother, and that is all there is to it.

It would seem to me that all we need to do with regard to those situations where the father is well able to pay, is make it clear to them that they cannot escape their obligation, wherever they go; that they are going to be caught and be made to pay, and they will come forward and do their duty, rather than have the record show that somebody had to sue them and had to file criminal proceedings against them, if need be, to make them do their duty. I honestly think that if we pursue this thing vigorously enough, that you will not have to pursue but 1 percent of them to make the other 99 percent comply. And that is the way it ought to be. If the man has a substantial amount of income, you just cannot get away without making a substantial contribution to the children.[4]

In the 1970s, then, most elected officials argued that middle- and upper-income fathers would simply "do the right thing," without the government having to oversee the execution of their financial obligations. The legislative language that established the 1975 child support program reflected this perspective, with the majority of resources directed at fathers of children on welfare. Yet, as women leaders pointed out in the mid-1980s, Senator Long's optimistic predictions about paternal behavior in middle-class families did not come to fruition. Non-AFDC fathers were simply *not* doing the right thing.

The non-AFDC population thus faced an entirely different institutional environment than its AFDC counterpart with respect to the child support problem. In this separate legal framework – the courts – they had a unique set of policy tools at their disposal, which were designed, in theory, to meet their unique needs. Yet the courts, as will be demonstrated, were not adequate to the task at hand.

To complicate matters from the start, each state was unique in its method of deciding child support cases.[5] During the 1970s, the level of court complexity was overwhelming (see Table 6.1). In a state such as Tennessee, over eighty general sessions courts heard divorce/support cases; while in a state such as Louisiana, fifty-three city/parish courts, one family court in East Baton Rouge, and forty-two district courts ruled on

---

4 Chairman Long's testimony is taken from "Child Support and the Work Bonus." 1973. Hearing before the Committee on Finance, United States Senate. Washington, DC: U.S. Government Printing Office, pp. 126–127.
5 For a complete discussion of these systems, see Henry Robert Glick and Kenneth N. Vines. 1973. *State Court Systems.* Englewood Cliffs, NJ: Prentice Hall.

TABLE 6.1. *Structure of the state court systems, circa 1970*

Type of Court	Number of States with This Type of Court	Common Names of These Courts
Supreme Court	All fifty states	Supreme Court, Supreme Judicial Court, Court of Appeals
Intermediate appellate courts	Twenty-three states have one type of this court; three states have two types.	Superior Court, Court of Appeals, Appellate Division of Supreme Court/Superior Court, Superior Court
Trial courts of general jurisdiction	Thirty-eight states have one type of this court; nine states have two types; two states have three types; one state has four types.	Circuit Court, Superior Court, District Court, Court of Common Pleas, Supreme Court
Trial courts of limited jurisdiction	Eight states have one or two types of this court; ten states have three types; twenty states have four or five types; twelve states have six or more.	Probate Court, Justice Court, Police Court, Small Claims Court, City or Town Courts, Juvenile Court, Orphan's Court, Court of Oyer and Terminer, Court of Chancery

Source: Henry Robert Glick and Kenneth N. Vines. 1973. *State Court Systems.* Englewood Cliffs, NJ: Prentice Hall, p. 28.

these types of cases.[6] The confusion was predictable. Without standardized state courts, child support cases flowed in and out of the system in a chaotic way.

One result of this disjointed court organizational scheme was the duplication of child support services. One court would enter a judgment on a case, and then another would do the same without knowledge of the first court's action. Moreover, even if the record showed that another order existed, judges would often take liberties and go about modifying these earlier decisions anyway. Linked to this duplication problem was a similarly frustrating issue – the fragmentation of responsibility that prevented support cases from being processed in an orderly way. According to Marilyn Ray Smith, chief legal counsel of child support enforcement in Massachusetts from 1987 to 2001,

---

[6] *Court Statistics Project, State Court Caseload Statistics, 1995.* 1996. Williamsburg, VA: National Center for State Courts.

Historically, child support programs have suffered from a fragmentation of functions across many agencies within a state, in a complex system where no single authority has control over essential case processing functions.... [T]he district attorney's office is called in when a case needs to be taken to court to establish paternity and to establish, modify, and enforce a support order; the clerk of court collects the child support payments from employers or individual obligors and sends them on to the custodial parent.... Each of these entities may report to a different elected official at the state or county level, perhaps from different political parties, who may have little incentive to cooperate toward a common purpose related to child support enforcement.[7]

Without a single source of accountability, many families were at a loss when a discrepancy occurred in their case account or when a father missed a payment completely. Tracking the path of a single check through this byzantine system proved to be too overwhelming for many single parents, who resigned themselves to accepting nonpayment as a fact of life.

Beyond the problems that afflicted the court system as a whole, individual state judges possessed wide and often arbitrary authority over whether child support should be paid, and if so, at what levels. As it first developed, the guiding philosophy behind this flexibility seemed reasonable enough. Judges were trained professionals, who, by virtue of their education and experience, were considered capable of assessing the merits of each family case separately. This was so because, inevitably, special circumstances would arise: fathers might be in school, with less money available to pay support; children might be spending the majority of time with the mother even though the father had custody, and so on. During the 1950s and 1960s, the conventional wisdom suggested that such special factors should be considered thoroughly before a judge handed down a support decision. Yet, for mothers who relied on a consistent stream of income to feed and clothe their children, this type of judicial discretion spelled financial disaster. Irresponsible judges were simply too numerous to control.

Both the federal government and the states were slow to recognize this problem. Indeed, prior to 1984, only half of the states were offering full or partial enforcement services to non-AFDC families who requested aid in obtaining support. Interestingly, the more services for non-AFDC women the states did manage to offer, the more non-AFDC families began to

---

[7] Marilyn Ray Smith. September 19, 1996. Testimony on "Child Support Enforcement." Hearing before the Subcommittee on Human Resources of the Committee on Ways and Means, United States House of Representatives. Washington, DC: U.S. Government Printing Office, p. 3.

petition the states for help. There was, in effect, a positive feedback process taking place, in which disgruntled parents learned about the availability of services and added their names to the list. The changing composition of the caseload reflected this dynamic. In 1978, approximately 17.1 percent of the total child support caseload was made up of non-AFDC families. By 1984, this number had climbed to 30.3 percent.[8] As families struggled to stay above the poverty line, the demand for services was clearly present. For women leaders, *welfare prevention* became their child support mantra.

RISK-REDUCTION STRATEGIES

Spelling out their position on the child support issue was the easy part of women entrepreneurs' movement to revolutionize the agenda. Before they entered the fray, however, they first had to consider the risks of becoming involved in this particular political battle. Central to their success was one decision that was made quite early. Rather than relying on the magnetism of one star personality to help effect change, women leaders instead embraced a cooperative risk-reduction strategy of building wide-ranging coalitions to attack the child support problem in concert. Key concerns in this risk-reduction plan were building up the low levels of women representatives at all levels of government, and founding and expanding women's organizations on which to rely for aid.

Political Representation

In a representative democracy such as the United States, *who* actually does the representing can have important public policy implications. Women have consistently remained minority players in legislative politics, even though they comprise over 50 percent of the population. This mismatch between their actual numbers in the population and their occupancy rates in legislative bodies extends through all levels of government.

This discrepancy in numbers was especially apparent during the 1970s. As Tables 6.2 and 6.3 demonstrate, in 1976, the mean number of women state legislators was only 12.39, translating into an average of approximately 8 percent of the membership in all state legislatures. By 1979, this number had increased to 15.4, representing slightly over 9 percent of the total membership. Women fared even worse in national politics

---

[8] Statistics calculated from the Federal Office of Child Support Enforcement's *Annual Report to Congress*. Various years. Washington, DC: Office of Child Support Enforcement.

TABLE 6.2. *Women state legislators in the United States, 1976–84*

Year	Mean Number of Women State Legislators	Mean % of Women in All State Legislatures
1976	12.39	8.10
1977	13.94	8.85
1978	14.26	9.11
1979	15.40	9.93
1980	15.48	9.87
1981	18.16	11.59
1982	18.16	11.84
1983	19.84	13.18
1984	19.92	13.19

Source: Center for Woman and Politics (CAWP). Fact sheets, various years. National Information Bank on Women in Public Office, Eagleton Institute of Politics, Rutgers University.

TABLE 6.3. *Women in Congress, 1976–84*

Year	Number of Women in U.S. House of Representatives	Number of Women in U.S. Senate
1976	19	0
1977	18	2
1978	18	2
1979	16	1
1980	16	1
1981	21	2
1982	21	2
1983	22	2
1984	22	2

Source: Center for Woman and Politics (CAWP). Fact sheets, various years. National Information Bank on Women in Public Office, Eagleton Institute of Politics, Rutgers University.

(Table 6.3). In 1976, there were only nineteen women in the House of Representatives, and no female senators. Three years later, the figures remained devastatingly low, with sixteen women in the House and only one in the Senate.

The slow progress of women entering the public arena during the 1970s has received much scholarly attention. Many feminists emerging from the social movement activity of the 1960s argued that while women may have had some initial success in reducing the overt barriers to political participation, other discriminatory practices worked against their becoming equal partners with men in the legislatures. More specifically, women who were interested in the political process still had to manage their dual lives: a public career that demanded a substantial amount of their time, and a private existence that continued to place the balance of familial responsibilities upon them rather than on their husbands. In fact, researchers found that women elected leaders were more likely to delay their political careers until their young children grew older or to refrain from having children altogether, and that they were more likely to be single than their similarly situated male counterparts.[9] By the early 1970s, then, women may have acquired a modicum of legislative representation, but private inequities prevented them from obtaining parity with men in key positions of political power.

The small number of women in politics created more problems than simply an imbalance in representation between the sexes. It also circumscribed the ability of women to make broad changes in the direction of public policy. Instead, women had to devote a substantial part of their time and resources simply to finding their own voice in the legislative arena.

Reflecting these realities, early research on women in public office focused on the "roles" that women legislators assumed in the statehouse, and on whether their roles differed from those of their male counterparts. In many of these studies, researchers found that women were more interested in problem solving than in upward career mobility, were more social service oriented in their outlook, and were more involved in casework than the men.[10] Another study examined different women who ran for office and arrayed them along an ideological spectrum of four types: the housewife-benchwarmer, the traditional civic worker, the women's rights advocate, and the passive women's rights advocate.[11] The main finding

---

[9] See, for example, Sue Carroll. 1989. "The Personal Is Political: The Intersection of Private Lives and Public Roles among Women and Men in Elective and Appointive Office." *Women and Politics* 9: 51–67; Susan Gluck Mezey. 1978. "Does Sex Make a Difference? A Case Study of Women in Politics." *Western Political Quarterly.* 31: 492–501; Ruth Mandel. 1983. *In the Running: The New Woman Candidate.* Boston: Beacon Press; Irene Diamond. 1977. *Sex Roles in the State House.* New Haven, CT: Yale University Press; Debra Dodson. 1997. "Change and Continuity in the Relationship between Private Responsibilities and Public Officeholding: The More Things Change, the More They Stay the Same." *Policy Studies Journal* 25(4): 569–584.

[10] See Jeanne J. Kirkpatrick. 1974. *Political Woman.* New York: Basic Books; Marianne Githens. 1977. "Spectators, Agitators, or Lawmakers: Women in State Legislatures." In *A Portrait of Marginality: The Political Behavior of the American Woman,* ed. Marianne Githens and Jewel L. Prestage. New York: MacKay.

[11] Irene Diamond. 1977. *Sex Roles in the State House.* New Haven, CT: Yale University Press.

was that the *type* of woman who dominated the state legislature, rather than simply the number of women in the statehouse, defined the character of the body overall – that is, whether or not the environment was women-friendly, encouraged women to speak out on the floor, and so on.

In addition, Sue Thomas found in her review of the literature on this issue that women rarely established their own legislative priorities during the 1970s. In other words, although they reported more liberal attitudes in general and recorded more left-leaning roll call votes, women legislators did not carve out their own policy niches when they first entered the legislative arena.[12] For example, an important analysis of elected officials in Hawaii found that although women elected officials mentioned women's issues more often than their male counterparts, their *ranking* of issues by importance was the same as that reported by men (the issues included public policies such as education, transportation, pollution, and housing).[13] Similarly, other researchers found that male and female state legislators tended to rank the same three issues as priorities: planning/development, finance/taxation, and governmental administration.[14] In sum, there was little or no evidence suggesting that women were taking a lead on issues impacting families and children.

While the reasons behind this phenomenon are undoubtedly complex, simply entering into uncharted territory – the male bastion of politics – proved extremely difficult for women. They had to learn the "rules of the game," they had to be accepted by their male colleagues, and they had to prove that they were serious legislators. Moreover, they faced an extraordinary level of discrimination in the statehouse. By their own reports, their male colleagues judged them to be frivolous, unorganized, and unworthy of the public's confidence.[15] They also perceived their placement on certain committees as the product of societally held sex roles rather than reflective of their true areas of expertise.[16]

Things quietly started to change for women representatives during the 1980s. At the beginning of the decade, women comprised only

[12] Sue Thomas. 1994. *How Women Legislate*. New York: Oxford University Press.
[13] Susan Gluck Mezey. 1978. "Support for Women's Rights Policy: Analysis of Local Politicians." *American Politics Quarterly* 6: 485–497.
[14] Marilyn Johnson. 1978. *Profile of Women Holding Office II*. New Brunswick, NJ: Center for the American Woman and Politics.
[15] Emmy Werner. 1968. "Women in State Legislatures." *Western Political Quarterly* 21: 40–50.
[16] Marianne Githens and Jewel L. Prestage. 1979. "Styles and Priorities of Marginalities: Women State Legislators." In *Race, Sex, and Policy Problems*, ed. Marian Lief Palley and Michael Preston. Lexington, MA: Lexington Books.

9.87 percent of the membership of state legislatures. By 1984, this number had increased to 13.19 percent. Women also moved from sixteen to twenty-two members in the House, and from one to two members in the Senate. But behind these small gains was a dramatic shift in attitude. Women became more confident as a group, and thus began pushing their policy priorities with greater vigor than ever before.

Indeed, as more women entered public office, many of the barriers to their legislative influence broke down, and women began to transform policy in the process. The scholarly research strongly supports this changing dynamic in the creation of public law. Using a 1988 survey of legislators across twelve states as well as a series of personal interviews with legislators in six of these states, Sue Thomas found that women began speaking out more in committees, met lobbyists with increased frequency, and exhibited better bargaining skills with their fellow legislators than they had in the past. Most importantly, they became trailblazers of a whole new type of legislation, laws that were directed at improving the lives of women, children, and families. In her analysis of the survey data, Thomas found that women legislators in eight of the twelve states had a higher average priority ranking on issues impacting families and children than did men.[17]

Research by other social scientists confirmed Thomas's findings that women in the 1980s started to make a policy difference in the area of women's and family issues. Michelle Saint-Germain, in her 1989 analysis of bills initiated in the Arizona state legislature from 1969 to 1986, found that women legislators offered more proposals on issues impacting women and children than did their male counterparts.[18] More specifically, as the proportion of women in the state legislatures increased over time, the number of proposals relating to traditional women's issues and feminist issues also rose, along with their enactment rate.

In the area of child support politics specifically, women politicians in Congress also played a primary role in effecting change. Barbara Kennelly, a Democratic representative from Connecticut, immediately took up the issue as her own. Kennelly became the primary sponsor of H.R. 4325, the central bill that passed the House in 1983 to overhaul the child support system.[19] Kennelly argued that her main motivation in

---

[17] Sue Thomas. 1994. *How Women Legislate*. New York: Oxford University Press, p. 75.
[18] Michelle A. Saint-Germain. 1989. "Does Their Difference Make a Difference? The Impact of Women on Public Policy in the Arizona Legislature." *Social Science Quarterly* 70(4): 956–968.
[19] Steven V. Roberts. December 6, 1983. "Political Survival: It's Women and Children First." *The New York Times*, p. B8.

advocating on behalf of reform was the outpouring of citizen complaints she received when she took office in 1982. From these complaints, she concluded that non-AFDC families needed the immediate attention of lawmakers.

Prior to her election to Congress, Kennelly had raised her four children while working on behalf of her husband's political career in the Connecticut Assembly. After a brief stint on the Hartford city council and then in the role of secretary of state, Kennelly ran for and won the congressional seat previously occupied by William Cotter, who died in late 1981. Once in Congress, she immediately impressed then-speaker Tip O'Neill with her issue-oriented drive and persistence. He rewarded her with a seat on the critical Ways and Means Committee, which she then used to her advantage to push Chairman Dan Rostenkowski (D-Ill.) into action on behalf of child support reform. According to Kennelly, she had a special role to fill on the committee. "If women don't do it [push for woman-friendly legislation], who is going to do it? I used to fight that, but now I accept it. You fight for your own."[20]

Joining her in the House as a primary advocate for reform on the opposite side of the political aisle was Marge Roukema (R-N.J.). First elected to Ridgewood's Board of Education in 1970, Roukema ran unsuccessfully for Congress in 1978 before finally winning in 1980. And although she had not planned to come to Congress as an advocate for women's rights, she "came to the conclusion that if people like me didn't take up the agenda for families, no one would. [She] decided to no longer be self conscious about being a woman dealing with women's issues."[21] Roukema recounted how she heard from grandparents in her district who were grateful for the new child support hearings because they were using their hard-earned savings to prevent their grandchildren from relying on welfare. Listening to these painful accounts motivated her to make her initial entrée into the child support arena with dramatic flair. She issued a Father's Day press release in 1983, decrying what she argued was many fathers' complete financial neglect of their children.

In addition to these primary players, other women also fought for child support reform. Pat Schroeder (D-Colo.) became involved in child support in her roles as co-chair of the Congressional Caucus for Women's Issues and chair of the Economic Security Task Force of the Select Committee

---

[20] Ibid.
[21] Robert Cohen. August 25, 1991. "Voting for Constituents: Roukema Bucks GOP 'Line' on Women's, Family Issues." *The Star-Ledger*, Newark, NJ.

on Children, Youth and Families. To Schroeder, extending child support to nonwelfare families was simply part of a larger movement that was then developing to extend to women greater rights in the areas of equal credit, equal pay, and pension sharing.

I became interested because I met so many women struggling to provide for their family because of deadbeat dads. If you buy a car and move to another state, the law doesn't let you avoid payment, so why should it allow you to escape family responsibility?

I did not feel extending enforcement to nonwelfare families was extreme. Most women were one paycheck away from welfare, and collection of child support is a great welfare prevention program.[22]

Crystallizing her motivation to become a champion of change on the issue, Schroeder also noted that "many constituents talked to me about their problems and this motivated me to act."[23] Following her lead, both Paula Hawkins (R-Fla.) and Nancy Kassenbaum (R-Kans.) also became vocal activists on behalf of the issue in the Senate.

Women's Organizations, Coalitions, and Issue-Specific Groups

Not only were women underrepresented in terms of sheer numbers and unable to carve out a legislative niche for themselves in the mid-1970s, they also suffered from a lack of organizational strength that could sustain their efforts on behalf of reform. However, as these barriers were overcome in the legislative arena, so too were they overcome in the organizational arena.

At first, the drive for women's organizational strength proceeded slowly, without major bursts of noteworthy accomplishments. Momentum started with the activism of the 1960s, which gave a voice to many groups that had previously been excluded from the political arena, including women. Before his death, President Kennedy created the President's Commission on the Status of Women, and shortly thereafter, the Citizens' Advisory Council on the Status of Women (CACSW) and a parallel cabinet-level Interdepartmental Committee on the Status of Women (ICSW). By 1964, most states had created their own state-level commissions on the status of women. Composed of politically active women, these

---

[22] Patricia Schroeder. July 18, 2001. Personal correspondence.
[23] Ibid.

commissions came together to produce lengthy reports documenting the prejudice and inequities facing over one-half of the American population in the 1960s.

At the 1966 annual meeting of the state conventions, Betty Friedan, author of the much-publicized book *The Feminine Mystique*, encouraged a small group of women to bolt from the commissions.[24] Frustrated by what she viewed as the lack of action by the government on behalf of Title VII of the Civil Rights Act of 1964 and a lack of responsiveness by the Equal Employment Opportunity Commission (EEOC), Friedan brought together a core of activists and began building the National Organization for Women (NOW). To Friedan, the benefits of such an independent group were obvious. NOW would be unfettered by the regulations of a government agency and thus free to focus almost exclusively on activities designed to further the women's movement.

From the outset, NOW's goals were extremely ambitious. The Bill of Rights laid out at the 1967 national conference explicitly described where the organization's resources would first be dedicated: (1) passage of an equal rights amendment to the constitution, (2) enforcement of a law banning sex discrimination in employment, (3) maternity leave rights in employment and Social Security benefits, (4) child day care centers, (5) equal and unsegregated education, (6) equal job training opportunities and allowances for women in poverty, and (7) the right of women to control their reproductive lives. National, regional, and local NOW chapters would each take on different roles in meeting these goals. Yet for much of the 1970s, financial and organizational concerns slowed the group's forays into legislative politics.

Although it had formed three years earlier, by 1969 national NOW still did not have an office or any paid staff. With approximately 1,500 members and $1,735 in its treasury, NOW struggled to handle the most rudimentary tasks of operation. Regional and local chapters suffered because national NOW had only limited funds for the basic costs of doing business, such as copying, traveling, and telephone usage. These problems were exacerbated when, beginning in 1973, several local chapters began withholding dues from the national organization to express their dissatisfaction with the lack of services offered to them via the Washington office. Although national NOW had dramatically cut expenses in a variety of areas by 1974, such as publishing its newsletter "DO IT NOW" bimonthly instead of monthly and accepting paid advertising for the first

---

[24] Betty Friedan. 1963. *The Feminine Mystique*. New York: Norton.

time, the financial crunch placed an extraordinary amount of stress on the organization as a whole.[25]

Contemporaneously with the beginnings of NOW, Congresswoman Bella Abzug (D-N.Y.) started the National Women's Political Caucus (NWPC) in July 1971. Like NOW, Abzug's organization had ambitious plans. During its initial meeting, NWPC issued a statement of purpose that focused on three primary areas of activity: legislative reform in the direction of equal rights (including passage of the Equal Rights Amendment [ERA], abortion rights, welfare rights, and affordable health care, among many other measures), party reform, and increasing the number of women elected to office. While goal-oriented in its vision, Abzug's group also struggled for years with limited financial resources and a lack of paid staff members.[26]

In addition to these financial problems, there were also disputes surrounding structural organization. Although NOW and the NWPC attempted to invent themselves as quickly as possible in order to get on with the business of actual positive action, other, more radical groups competed for women's attention with the promise of immediate results. Women's liberation groups attracted young activists from the civil rights and antiwar movements who had had a completely different set of experiences. From their work in the Student Non-Violent Coordinating Committee (SNCC) and the Students for a Democratic Society (SDS), these women brought with them specific protest-oriented skills, including waging demonstrations, picketing, taking over bureaucratic offices, and engaging in street theater performances.[27] These women did not want to focus on the minutiae of organization building. Rather, they viewed their primary task as one of consciousness raising, or exposing the everyday forms of oppression that they argued were dominating women's lives.

These difficulties with structure and fracture within the women's movement reflected one important reality at the time: that American women were only beginning to find their political voice. They needed to confront the challenges of monetary support and organizational sustenance before they could mobilize around particular issues. As a result, during the late

---

[25] Maryann Barakso. 2001. "Sustaining Grassroots Activism in the National Organization for Women, 1966–2000." Ph.D. dissertation, Massachusetts Institute of Technology, pp. 110–111.

[26] See Bella Abzug. 1984. *Gender Gap : Bella Abzug's Guide to Political Power for American Women*. Boston: Houghton Mifflin.

[27] For a discussion of how women gained a greater consciousness of their own plight within the black civil rights movement, see Jo Freeman. 1975. *The Politics of Women's Liberation*. New York: McKay, pp. 56–62.

1970s, there were few, if any, national organizations that addressed the child support problem with a single focus. Parents Without Partners became an active lobbying group, but other issues, such as taking care of a separating couple's emotional needs, competed for its time. Moreover, its membership was extremely diverse; the group catered to the concerns of never-married parents, custodial and noncustodial parents, and widows and widowers. The organization therefore did not have the kind of constituency necessary to address the child support problem with a unified vision.

Economic realities, however, soon jolted these broad-based feminist groups into specific forms of organizational mobilization that would later prove pivotal in their work on behalf of child support reform. Drawing upon the gains made by the feminist movement during the 1960s, women all over the country began entering the labor force in greater numbers than ever before. Women were now working not intermittently or when their children reached a certain age, but full-time throughout their adult lives. This behavioral change was dramatic. In 1970, for example, women had a labor force participation rate of only 43 percent. By 1985, this number had risen to 55 percent.[28] But while women were gaining economic power, they were still not guaranteed equal protection under the law.

By the 1980s, this crisis brought about by the disparity between the market realities facing women and the lack of equal status under the Constitution began to infiltrate the political process. In fact, the fight for the ratification of the Equal Rights Amendment played a primary role in bolstering the influence of broad-based women's groups across the country. Begun in 1972 and declared a "state of emergency" in 1978, NOW's ERA campaign mobilized the entire organization to fight on behalf of women's legal standing. National and local chapters pledged to continue drives to stop state rescission efforts, develop new nonviolent protests, and extend the terms of NOW elected officials in order to guarantee continuity of leadership. With the ratification deadline of 1982 looming, official membership reached 225,000. According to Maryann Barakso, these new members provided NOW with the human tools it needed to wage the ERA campaign.

NOW's members gained an enormous amount of experience in creative and cutting-edge techniques for fundraising for the ERA. For example, by 1982 it was capable of raising $1 million dollars per month via direct mail. NOW also

---

[28] These data are from the *Statistical Abstract of the United States*. 1987. Washington, DC: U.S. Government Printing Office.

became sophisticated in its employment of legislative lobbying tactics, in the organization and management of rallies and protests, and in understanding the kinds of influence NOW could wield in electoral contests.[29]

In many ways, the fight for the ERA provided the necessary political training ground for motivated women in their efforts to reshape the legislative process.

In the end, NOW never achieved its goal of passing the ERA. However, when the ratification drive finally came to a close in 1982, NOW and other feminist organizations did not simply withdraw from mainstream electoral politics. Rather, NOW leaders as well as rank-and- file members used the skills they had learned during the ERA battle to transform their policy orientation from one that placed value on persuading elected officials to "do the right thing" for women, to a strategy whereby women themselves would become the key power brokers.

By 1983, feminist groups employed this new strategy to bring women into mainstream political positions. Organizing conferences, rallies, and teaching demonstrations under the slogan "We'll Remember Each November," newly elected NOW President Judy Goldsmith trumpeted the need to harness women's power to enter and win races throughout the country. Looking back on this period, Patricia Ireland, the president of NOW beginning in 1991, wrote that this change represented

a significant shift in NOW's strategy. . . . Instead of just trying to influence those in power, we would now become the people in power. . . . In the six weeks between the defeat of the ERA and the filing deadline for the 1982 elections in Florida, we conducted an urgent search to convince strong feminist women to run for political office. . . . Our strategy worked. Not only did we get more women elected, but we also inspired new campaign workers and women voters by having candidates in whom we could believe with our whole hearts.[30]

By 1984, this new commitment to politics became self-evident when NOW as well as the NWPC endorsed a presidential candidate for the first time.

By the early 1980s, then, broad-based feminist organizations had begun to build cross-associational alliances to move women into office and to

---

[29] Maryann Barakso. 2001. "Sustaining Grassroots Activism in the National Organization for Women, 1966–2000." Ph. D. dissertation, Massachusetts Institute of Technology, pp. 159–160.

[30] Patricia Ireland. 1996. *What Women Want*. New York: Dutton, pp. 135–136.

address the concerns of women and children in the United States. Whereas in the mid-1970s NOW had stood alone as the voice of women in testifying on behalf of child support reform, by the mid-1980s, twenty-eight organizations had formulated a common policy position that they ultimately presented before Congress. These groups included NOW, the American Association of University Women, the Displaced Homemakers Network, the Mexican American Women's National Association, the National Council of Jewish Women, the National Urban League, the National Council of Negro Women, as well as many others. In advocating on behalf of change, their statement was consistent and clear, arguing that "[the scope of the problem necessitates that] state child support enforcement offices handle cases of all families – not just those receiving public assistance."[31]

As national organizations were growing in strength, associations specifically devoted to child support enforcement were also being hatched. As described above, Patricia Kelly's organization, KINDER, was one of many groups that formed at the grassroots level to fight on behalf of child support reform. Interestingly, most of these groups began with a story similar to Kelly's, in that their origins reflected the personal damage wreaked by nonsupport.

In July 1981, for example, Bettianne Welch and Gerald A. Cannizzaro formed a pathbreaking lobbying group, For Our Children's Unpaid Support (FOCUS), in the state of Virginia. Not long before, Welch had been caring for three small children at home when her husband left and moved to New York. With interstate enforcement efforts completely inadequate to compel her husband to support his children, Welch and her friends took to the streets in protest. Within months, she had collected over 5,000 signatures from citizens who were outraged that their tax dollars were being used to support children whose fathers could more than adequately provide for their needs. After the media publicized their activities, FOCUS succeeded in moving an automatic wage assignment bill (which deducted support directly from a father's paycheck) through the state legislature and into law by the end of July 1982. Other goals on the group's agenda included a minimum standard of support that all states would have to implement, the imposition of federal penalties for the willful failure to

---

[31] Ann Kolker. July 14, 1983. Testimony on "Child Support Enforcement Legislation." Hearing before the Subcommittee on Public Assistance and Unemployment Compensation of the Committee on Ways and Means, United States House of Representatives. Washington, DC: U.S. Government Printing Office, p. 130.

pay support, and the creation of a mechanism by which all states could better coordinate their interstate cases.[32]

Another important organization with the same acronym, FOCUS, began when Fran Mattera found herself frustrated by the labyrinth of judicial red tape she needed to cut through in order enlist a judge's assistance to pursue support. Founding For Our Children and Us, Inc., Mattera began her mission by picketing in front of the family courts on Long Island in 1972. Incorporated as a nonprofit agency in 1978, Mattera's organization quickly added paralegals to its staff in order to help women navigate through the complexities of the family court system. These paralegals not only advised women as to their rights regarding financial support, but also offered clients referrals to attorneys and other appropriate law enforcement officials who could help move their cases forward.[33]

Again, like other associations that became active during this period, the Organization for the Enforcement of Child Support (OECS) started as a result of a woman's disappointment with the child support system. Elaine M. Fromm, the president of OECS, described the founding in the following way:

The Organization for the Enforcement of Child Support was founded in 1979 as a result of the many frustrations faced by parents trying to obtain their child support. As individuals, we felt we could get no help and could do nothing to help ourselves, but joined together as a group, we could seek out the problems involved in child support enforcement and also seek solutions to those problems.

I personally have fought the system since 1961 when I was abandoned eight months pregnant and having three babies aged 1, 2, and 3. The struggle to survive was impossible, but worse yet was the struggle to enforce the court-ordered child support of $7 a week per child.

I, like so many others, finally gave up the fight. Now, through this organization, I have my revenge. I wish to avenge my children's plight by doing all possible to rectify the problems for all other children in the nation.[34]

---

[32] Bettianne Welch. July 14, 1983. Testimony on "Child Support Enforcement Legislation." Hearing before the Subcommittee on Public Assistance and Unemployment Compensation of the Committee on Ways and Means, United States House of Representatives. Washington, DC: U.S. Government Printing Office, pp. 118–121.

[33] Fran Mattera. July 14, 1983. Testimony on "Child Support Enforcement Legislation." Hearing before the Subcommittee on Public Assistance and Unemployment Compensation of the Committee on Ways and Means, United States House of Representatives. Washington, DC: U.S. Government Printing Office, pp. 293–301.

[34] Elaine Fromm. July 14, 1983. Testimony on "Child Support Enforcement Legislation." Hearing before the Subcommittee on Public Assistance and Unemployment Compensation of the Committee on Ways and Means, United States House of Representatives. Washington, DC: U.S. Government Printing Office, pp. 293–301.

In its early stages, OECS focused on providing educational services to parents in need. Later, the organization moved to pushing states toward compliance with enforcement laws that were already on the books, and offering information to the executive, legislative, and judicial branches of government on the need for more vigorous support efforts.

Geraldine Jensen had a similar story. After a 1977 divorce, Jensen had moved to Toledo, Ohio, with her two sons, Matthew and Jake. After six months, her husband stopped paying child support. By 1983, Jensen had gone on welfare because her ex-husband refused to provide her with any financial assistance. When the county prosecutor did not do much to re-solve her case – by now, over $12,000 was overdue – she placed a small ad in the local newspaper asking if other women were having the same problem with child support enforcement. The response was overwhelm-ing. Within two weeks, Jenson started the Association for Children for Enforcement of Support (ACES), one of the most active advocacy groups on the issue of child support enforcement today.[35]

In sum, women legislators and women's groups had to face a substantial risk when they entered the political arena to fight for child support reform. In addition to uncertainty, they had to confront the enormous start-up costs of political action, including low levels of representation, outsider political status, and weak women's organizations as sources of support. Yet they, like the social workers and conservatives before them, nonethe-less decided to undertake the tremendous task of policy entrepreneur-ship and attempt to alter the status quo. Their mission was even more overwhelming when we consider *when* they mobilized for political ac-tion. Women leaders initiated their battle for control of the child support agenda during the height of the Reagan presidency.

SHAKEOUT STRATEGIES

Early in 1981, while Ronald Reagan worked in the Oval Office, Robert Carleson, Reagan's former director of the state Department of Social Wel-fare from California, walked through the halls of the Office of Manage-ment and Budget (OMB). He found David Stockman, head of the agency, right where he expected him, laboring over hundreds of reports at his desk. Handing over the president's social welfare plan for the nation, Carleson eyed the young new OMB director and said, "Here is something that

---

[35] For Jensen's complete history, see ⟨http://www.childsupport-ACES.org⟩. Accessed on July 10, 2002.

has already been approved. All you have to do is plug it in. It's like a cassette." After reviewing the plan, Stockman liked what he saw and decided to "plug it in" as soon as possible. By 1982, the government would begin its massive retreat from funding welfare programs, with the first cut aimed at slashing over $35 billion in social spending.[36]

Despite the legacy of Reagan's early reductions in social welfare spending, several programs not only survived but actually expanded to serve new clienteles. This was perhaps most concretely realized in the case of child support enforcement. In an environment generally hostile to the growth of social programs, the federal government agreed to help all women, regardless of welfare status, who requested aid in securing financial payments from their former partners. To comprehend the "why" of this notable exception, it is critical to understand women leaders' search for a key shakeout strategy in this rent-seeking model. They, like the successful entrepreneurs who had come before them, hoped to avoid any semblance of illegitimacy in their tactics – that is, they wanted to focus solely on legitimate means of acquiring power. They found such a weapon in the emergence of the political phenomenon known as the gender gap.

The power of the woman's vote caught Reagan off-guard as he prepared for his 1984 reelection campaign. During the early eighties, political scientists began noticing what they termed "the gender gap," or a pronounced difference in the way men and women viewed important public policy issues. Although feminists had long hoped for the day when women would vote as a bloc (such dreams dated back to the passage of the Nineteenth Amendment), this transformation in collective consciousness never quite took place. For the better part of the early twentieth century, most women, if they were married, voted as their husbands did, and if they were unmarried tended to ally themselves with the voting patterns of similarly situated males.

Why did women fail to vote as a unified bloc? The reasons, of course, are numerous, but a significant factor was clearly the "newness" of their voting right. While men had been voting for years and were thus accustomed to the experience, women had remained at home, tending to domestic matters. They thus had to "learn" to exercise their new citizenship duties, a process that demanded both time and experience. Perhaps more

---

[36] See Edward D. Berkowitz. 1994. *America's Welfare State.* Baltimore: Johns Hopkins University Press, p.141; see also Helene Slessarev. 1988. "Racial Tensions and Institutional Support: Social Programs during a Period of Retrenchment." In *The Politics of Social Policy in the United States,* ed. Margaret Weir, Ann Shola Orloff, and Theda Skocpol. Princeton, NJ: Princeton University Press.

TABLE 6.4. *Gender gap in presidential election years 1980 and 1984, by polling organization*

	ABC/*Wash. Post*		CBS/NYT		NBC	
	Women	Men	Women	Men	Women	Men
1980 Candidate						
Reagan	47%	53%	46%	54%	47%	56%
Carter	42%	35%	45%	37%	45%	36%
Anderson	9%	9%	7%	7%	8%	8%
1984 Candidate						
Reagan	54%	62%	56%	62%	55%	64%
Mondale	46%	38%	44%	37%	45%	36%

Source: The Center for the American Woman and Politics. Fact sheets, various years. Eagleton Institute of Politics, Rutgers University.

important was the natural "letdown" effect that occurred after the passage of the Nineteenth Amendment. For decades, the quest for the vote had occupied the energy of women from all different backgrounds and guided them toward a common end. With the achievement of their goal, women no longer had the same centrifugal force pulling them together. And like men, women had heterogeneous preferences on a variety of policy issues, such as foreign affairs and the trade-offs associated with economic growth. It would take a direct threat to their livelihoods to fuse them together once again.

The country's movement toward conservatism during the late 1970s proved to be such a rallying point around which women could again unite. In fact, 1980 was a watershed election year for women in American politics. For the first time since gaining the suffrage, women voted differently from their male counterparts. In the contest between Jimmy Carter and Ronald Reagan, the CBS/*New York Times* poll reported that women were eight percentage points behind men in voting for Reagan.[37] Moreover, although voters' participation in American politics had been declining for decades, the drop-off was less significant for women than it was for men. Therefore, for the first time in history, women were also *outvoting* their male counterparts.[38] Tables 6.4 and 6.5 summarize these trends.

[37] Carol M. Mueller. 1991. "The Gender Gap and Women's Political Influence." *The Annals of the American Academy* 515: 23–37.

[38] Charles O. Jones. 1985. "Renominating Ronald Reagan: The Complete Politician at Work." In *The American Elections of 1984*, ed. Austin Ranney. Durham, NC: Duke University Press.

TABLE 6.5. *Sex differences in voter turnout: presidential election years from 1964 to 1984*

Presidential Election Year	% of Voting-Age Population Reporting Voting: Female	% of Voting-Age Population Reporting Voting: Male	Number of Voting-Age Population Reporting Voting: Female (in millions)	Number of Voting-Age Population Reporting Voting: Male (in millions)
1964	67%	71.9%	39.2	37.5
1968	66%	69.8%	41	38
1972	62%	64.1%	44.9	40.9
1976	58.8%	59.6%	45.6	41.1
1980	59.4%	59.1%	49.3	43.8
1984	60.8%	59.0%	54.5	47.4

Source: The Center for the American Woman and Politics. Fact sheets, various years. Eagleton Institute of Politics, Rutgers University.

Making matters worse for Reagan, in survey after survey during 1983 women reported being disillusioned with the president. While increasing defense spending, Reagan had advocated the downsizing of many social programs, such as aid to the poor, that most women supported. Because these voting trends first began to emerge during the early 1980s, no one could predict whether the gender gap would grow wider or smaller in the next election. And women's activist groups such as NOW capitalized upon this uncertainty by organizing thousands of new voters and encouraging them to go to the polls.

The initial impetus for NOW's work to mobilize women voters came as the deadline for the states' ratification of the ERA neared. At the time, only four more states were needed, but they were proving to be difficult legislatures to win over. As a result, Eleanor Smeal, president of NOW, began searching for ways in which the political tide against the measure could realistically be turned. In June of 1981, she helped launch the ERA Countdown Campaign in Los Angeles. According to NOW officials, the campaign planned to target six states that had yet to ratify the ERA: Illinois, Florida, Oklahoma, North Carolina, Virginia, and Missouri. Molly Yard and Betsy Dunn, two longtime NOW activists, organized a massive effort to sift through polling data and surveys, which they could then use on behalf of their cause. Pointing out that men and women were voting differently promised to be one key strategy. Indeed, publicizing this differential proved immediately successful, earning NOW articles in such prominent newspapers as the *Miami Herald*, the *Wall Street Journal*, and the *Atlanta Constitution*. By May of 1982, NOW was releasing monthly "gender gap" updates to keep its membership as well as the general public aware of Reagan's declining popularity with women at the polls.[39]

Besides publicizing the gender gap, a second critical strategy employed by women's groups to keep the pressure on Reagan was the Women's Vote Project. Initially composed of thirty-eight core women's groups, the project began with the goal of registering 1.5 million new female voters. The project sought to mobilize women to go to the polls because "women are thinking and voting differently from men on issues including national security, the economy, economic equity and fairness, the environment, education, as well as women's equity issues."[40] As the presidential election neared, the project's original members affiliated themselves with an additional thirty-eight left-leaning groups in an effort to encourage voter registration. Working in local communities through day care centers, job sites, and social service agencies, the project was able to exceed its target registration goal by 300,000 new voters.

Even after the states failed to ratify the ERA in 1982, feminists continued to urge elected officials to better represent "the woman's voice." They threatened Reagan with the gender gap and argued that their potential for electoral retaliation against him was strong. Indeed, pollsters for Reagan grew increasingly concerned about the gap when the economy took a downturn in 1982. Finally prodded into action by women's complaints of high levels of economic duress, Reagan first responded by supporting Sandra Day O'Connor's highly visible nomination to the Supreme Court, as well as by nominating Margaret Heckler and Elizabeth Dole to cabinet positions. The Republican National Committee then announced the formation of its National Women's Coalition, a group of women who would speak on behalf of Reagan during the campaign season. At the Republican National Convention in Dallas, women held placards reading "Women Love Reagan," key women speakers described Reagan's commitment to gender-based equality, and close to half of the delegates were women.[41]

---

[39] Kathy Bonk. 1988. "The Selling of the Gender Gap: The Role of Organized Feminism." In *The Politics of the Gender Gap*, ed. Carol M. Mueller. Newbury Park, CA: Sage Publications.

[40] Johanna S. R. Mendelson. 1988. "The Ballot Box Revolution: The Drive to Register Women." In *The Politics of the Gender Gap*, ed. Carol M. Mueller. Newbury Park, CA: Sage Publications, p. 65.

[41] For an excellent account of Reagan's efforts to curry favor with female voters, see *The National NOW Times*, September/October 1984.

However, these initial efforts did not satisfy most of the activist associations. Women's groups kept pressuring Reagan to move beyond mere token appointments and press events; he had to make a difference for women in the policy arena, such as in the area of child support reform. This was difficult because, in the initial years of his administration, Reagan had vehemently opposed the expansion of the child support program, as it symbolized exactly the kind of government growth he sought to abolish. Was there any way for him, at this stage in his term, to change his position *and* save political face?

Reagan recognized that no matter what position he took, he had to sustain the confidence of one of his strongest groups of supporters – the religious right. As governor of California during the 1970s, Reagan had begun cultivating a conservative coalition that would eventually grow to number in the millions during the 1980s. Groups such as the Moral Majority, the Eagle Forum, and other Christian Coalition organizations began to spread a new theme, a phrase that would become the rallying cry of those on the right for years to come: family values. While different people used the phrase to convey somewhat different ideas, generally speaking, the phrase "family values" came to connote the principles of limited governmental intervention into the lives of citizens, conventional family roles, and adherence to the traditional principles of religiosity.

The prominence of religion in the 1984 campaign was no surprise to Reagan's followers. Providing Christian fundamentalists with access to the While House, Reagan had earned a strong, southern white following. Throughout the election year, Reagan continuously spoke out on behalf of school prayer and the pro-life movement. He even opened a prayer breakfast at the Republican National Convention in Dallas with the observation that "politics and morality are inseparable. And as morality's foundation is religion, religion and politics are necessarily related."[42] While his opponent, Walter Mondale, criticized Reagan for his blurring of the church/state line, key Republican strategists pushed the president to persist in his stump speeches on these issues. In a calculated risk, the Reagan campaigners recognized that social issues in general were of low salience to the average voter, most of whom tended to keep a more vigilant

---

[42] William Schneider. 1985. "The November 6 Vote for President: What Did It Mean?" In *The American Elections of 1984*, ed. Austin Ranney. Durham, NC: Duke University Press, p. 221.

eye on the economy when selecting the next president. On the other hand, for fundamentalist voters, Reagan's positions on these issues were extremely significant. Child support enforcement was one such issue, and in this case Reagan's symbolic embrace of the traditional family could be considered consistent with women's stated economic goals. Reagan therefore needed to utilize the issue strategically in order speak to two audiences: his conservative/religious core and women mobilized by the gender gap.

In selling the expanded program first to the religious right, Reagan argued that an enhanced child support enforcement system, especially for non-AFDC families, would buttress the nuclear family in a variety of ways. Fathers would have to take their ties to their offspring much more seriously than they had in the past. Child support enforcement would also reinforce traditional notions of the family by forcing fathers to face financial consequences if they later chose to abandon their families. And finally, the program would advance religious tenets by discouraging promiscuous sexual behavior. Strong child support enforcement signaled that casual sexual activity could have serious consequences. In its totality, then, Reagan portrayed the larger program – despite the fact that it involved an increase in the size of government – as fundamental to the family restoration goals of the New Right.

After selling this strategy to his conservative followers, Reagan faced a more arduous task – selling the program to women as indicative of his dedication to women's rights. Gender gap politics mandated that he make this commitment clear. To accomplish this task, Reagan first had to locate the voters most receptive to his pitch. Women GOP strategists, hired during the 1984 campaign season, used census-level reports to profile the type of women Republicans had to woo if Reagan were to have any chance at reelection. Supplementing these analyses with a survey of 40,000 women, the Republican pollster Richard Wirthlin decided that it was in the administration's best interest to "divide and conquer" the elusive female constituency. Categorizing the surveyed women by age, marital status, and employment, Wirthlin presented his colleagues with profiles of sixty-four "types" of women, each with its own propensity to vote for Reagan. After collapsing these categories down to eight, Republican strategists made a conscious decision to avoid expending campaign resources on women unlikely to vote for Reagan no matter what his accomplishments were. Instead, they aimed their campaign tactics at the swing female voters, women who were concerned about the economy and issues of fairness.[43] From that point onward, fact sheets from the Republican National Committee highlighted issues that were likely to appeal to these middle-income women, such as increased child care tax credits, the abolition of the widow's tax on estates, and, most importantly for this analysis, child support enforcement.

Within a decade, then, gender gap politics had completely transformed the political rhetoric surrounding the child support enforcement program. To attract women voters and interest groups with the power to mobilize female constituencies, Reagan sold the child support program as women's rights legislation. For example, at a conference luncheon before the Women Business Owners of New York in April 1984, Reagan detailed his plans for helping women business owners to break through the onerous regulations that were preventing them from succeeding in the marketplace. He also sought to demonstrate that he was the champion of the working woman and not the enemy, as many in the press had portrayed him.

Women in the eighties are a diverse majority with varied interests and futures. Some seek to pursue their own careers, some run for political office, some focus on the home and family, and some seek to do all these things. No role is superior to another. What's important is that each woman must have the freedom to choose her path for herself, and I'm committed to just that. The simple truth is I've been frustrated by the perception that's been created about my supposed lack of interest in the welfare of women, and I'm going to take advantage of this opportunity to reveal some things our Administration has been doing and that seem to have been closely guarded secrets until now.[44]

As he remarked that day, legal challenges were only part of his program to ensure economic independence for women. The remainder would come from new federal initiatives, such as equality in pension programs, tax relief, and strengthened *child support enforcement for non-AFDC women as well as AFDC women.*

Two months later, at yet another whirlwind campaign stop, Reagan addressed Republican women officials on the achievements of his administration in the area of helping the average American woman. After citing his female appointments to federal office, Reagan then described the

[43] Carol M. Mueller. 1988. "The Empowerment of Women: Polling and the Women's Voting Bloc." In *The Politics of the Gender Gap*, ed. Carol M. Mueller. Newbury Park, CA: Sage Publications.

[44] From President Ronald Reagan. April 5, 1984. "Remarks at the Conference Luncheon of the Women Business Owners of New York." *Public Papers of the President 1984.* Washington, DC: U.S. Government Printing Office.

amazing upswing in the economy that had taken place upon his election. With unemployment dropping and the range of professions opening to women expanding on a daily basis, Republicans, he stated, were clearly in the vanguard of providing working and middle-class women with opportunities for upward economic mobility. Most importantly, Reagan again spoke to the issue of his support for women as equals.

The GOP commitment to women runs deep. Some people have tried to keep that a secret.... I want to be very clear on this: There's no place in the Republican Party for those who would discriminate against women. And let me say there is no place in the Republican Party for those who would exhibit prejudice against anyone. There's no place in our party for the kind of bigotry and ugly rhetoric that we've been hearing outside our party recently. We have no room for hate here, and we have no place for the haters.[45]

Later in his speech, Reagan promised elected Republican officials that he would improve the economic conditions of women, both through generalized macroeconomic growth and through new laws that would put money in their hands directly, such as child care credits and *child support reform*.

OVERTAKING THE INCUMBENTS

By the mid-1980s, women leaders had designed and executed a clearly defined shakeout strategy. They did not vilify their opponents, nor did they pursue other illegitimate strategies, such as violence, to get their point across. Instead, they publicized the gender gap, or differentials in voting behavior between men and women, which they hoped would persuade others in positions of power to take their arguments seriously. What were, then, the concrete goals for which they were so vigorously fighting?

In brief, when passed, the Child Support Enforcement Amendments of 1984 would require first that the states enact statutes related to the following collection strategies: (1) mandatory income withholding procedures, (2) expedited processes for enforcing support, (3) state income tax interceptions, (4) liens against real property, and (5) reports of support delinquency information to consumer credit agencies. Second, the states would have to use these techniques to pursue interstate cases. Third, and most important for the discussion here, the Child Support Enforcement

---

[45] From President Ronald Reagan. June 29, 1984. "Remarks and a Question-and-Answer Session with Elected Republican Women Officials." *Public Papers of the President 1984*. Washington, DC: U.S. Government Printing Office.

Amendments of 1984 provided that all of the mandatory collection techniques required for AFDC families would have to be used on behalf of non-AFDC families as well.[46] In order to ensure this outcome, incentive payments to the states, which had previously applied only to collection performance based on AFDC cases, were now extended to non-AFDC cases as well.

When Reagan signed the bill into law in August 1984, the impact of the gender gap was clear and strong.

Last year, I proposed that we bolster our Federal-State child support system by mandating effective and proven collection practices. *I believe that we should emphasize service to all children, welfare and non-welfare alike, and improve incentives for state government to get the job done* [my italics]. The Child Support Enforcement Amendments bill contains all these features. . . . This legislation represents a significant break from the tradition of simply throwing tax money at a problem. Instead of creating more dependency on government, we're requiring responsible behavior by our citizens. . . . It will not only make a difference in the lives of our children but for so many women who have been forced through no fault of their own on to welfare rolls due to abandonment. Left with the full load to bear, they often find themselves trapped in a cycle of unhappiness and destitution. . . . There has been much talk of late about the importance of family and traditional values in our society. . . . Programs like this . . . are not only aimed at justice for the children but also at encouraging ethical behavior and bolstering vital social institutions. . . . We hope that by placing the responsibility where it should be, on the parent, people will be encouraged to make moral decisions.[47]

Although he refused to acknowledge women's voting power in an overt way, Reagan's statements at the signing reflected how the gender gap had forced him into developing the policy for, and selling it to, two very different constituencies. Appeasing the right, Reagan took the opportunity of signing the Child Support Enforcement Amendments of 1984 to demonstrate how consistent the new policy was with his traditional perspective on the family. Instead of simply being a welfare cost recovery initiative, the invigorated program would include enforcement measures for both AFDC and non-AFDC families. This was not only the "right" way for children to be supported, Reagan argued, it was the "moral" way. For women voters, Reagan argued, the legislation would ensure increased

---

[46] From the beginning of the child support program in 1975, states could collect support for non-AFDC families. The states were not, however, fully reimbursed for their efforts.

[47] President Ronald Reagan. August 16, 1984. "Remarks on Signing the Child Support Enforcement Amendments of 1984." From the *Public Papers of the President 1984*. Washington, DC: U.S. Government Printing Office.

economic independence. Women would no longer be at the mercy of former partners who neglected their familial responsibilities.

For women leaders, the impact of the gender gap in the passage of the 1984 law was also strong and, in contrast to Reagan's remarks, they specifically named it as the critical political force in moving reform forward. In her comments on the law, Representative Roukema remarked on the upward battle this legislation had faced: "When we put this bill in, men started to use code phrases. They'd say, 'What about due process? Do you assume all men are guilty?' It was another way of saying, 'Don't bother my buddies.'"[48] She also acknowledged that because Reagan had been so adamant about refusing to budge on domestic spending, "gender gap politics [had to have been the factor that] propelled this [child support] legislation."[49]

In addition, Representative Kennelly called attention to the bill's difficult path through the legislative process. "To get the ball rolling was a little difficult. The gender gap has helped us enormously. When we were looking for the hearing [a year ago], this hadn't quite jelled." While confident that the program was helping women on welfare, Kennelly remained steadfast in her insistence that nonwelfare families be granted assistance as well. "These were bright women who had child support orders in their hands and couldn't figure out what had happened. Then the gender gap came along and the election was ahead and things got easier."[50] The shakeout strategy had worked. Remarked Kennelly, "Women, children and family issues are causes of great concern now, and it's not just because of the justice of it, but because of the politics of it. There is a great voting bloc out there, and many of my male colleagues no longer feel they have the luxury of postponing these issues."[51]

CONCLUSIONS

In her final remarks on the 1984 Child Support Enforcement Amendments' passage into law, Representative Kennelly asked an extremely

---

[48] Steven V. Roberts. December 6, 1983. "Political Survival: It's Women and Children First." *The New York Times*, p. B8.
[49] Allan F. Yoder. September 18, 1984. "Women's Issues Boost Roukema." *The Record*, Bergen, New Jersey, p. C1.
[50] Judy Mann. August 10, 1984. "Results." *The Washington Post*, p. C1.
[51] Steven V. Roberts. December 6, 1983. "Political Survival: It's Women and Children First." *The New York Times*, p. B8.

important question that in a tentative way placed women's legislative success in the broader context of risk and shakeout.

There is a definite sensitivity and understanding among women [members of Congress]. We care. A bill like this takes time, it takes staff work. You have to have someone who says this is my priority. If we don't pick a woman's issue to be number one, who will?[52]

There was, undoubtedly, a historic sense of accomplishment that day in August 1984. Women now had a better chance than ever before of recovering the support that they deserved for their families. And only four years later, with the Family Support Act of 1988, Congress provided women with more economic insurance by requiring the mandatory use of financial guidelines in assessing support awards.

Moreover, after Reagan left the presidency, women legislators and women's groups continued to successfully pressure the federal government to tighten enforcement provisions. For example, the Child Support Recovery Act of 1992 imposed a federal criminal penalty on fathers for the willful failure to pay a past-due child support obligation for a child living in another state. The Ted Weiss Child Support Enforcement Act of 1992 amended the Fair Credit Reporting Act to require consumer credit agencies to report all child support delinquencies. Under President Clinton, the Bankruptcy Reform Act of 1994 prevented child support obligations from being discharged in bankruptcy proceedings, and the Full Faith and Credit for Child Support Orders Act required each state to enforce orders issued in other states. Also in 1994, the Small Business Administration Reauthorization and Amendments Act required that all recipients of financial assistance be not more than sixty days delinquent in paying their support, and the Social Security Amendments of 1994 required that state child support agencies improve paternity determinations by a set standard or face federal financial penalties.

In addition, with women continuing to enter public office in greater numbers than ever before, the states also began to pass their own individual laws to help enforce support. Among the many new policies that were launched during this era, revoking drivers' and professional licenses for the nonpayment of support became extremely common. Other states placed themselves on the cutting edge of reform by requiring employers to report all new hires immediately to their state employment agency, using their W-4 forms. Still other states passed versions of the Uniform

[52] Judy Mann. August 10, 1984. "Results." *The Washington Post*, p. C1.

Interstate Family Support Act (UIFSA), which promised enhanced interstate enforcement.

Yet Kennelly's question, "If we don't pick a woman's issue to be number one, who will?," continued to hang in the air as a premonition of the kind of political competition that would be generated on the issue in the future. Women's gains were strong enough to ensure them a seat at the political bargaining table, taking over from their conservative predecessors. Their victory was also strong enough to guarantee them long-term political influence, as evidenced by the flurry of legislative activity that flowed in their direction in the post-1984 years. But other groups clearly had different priorities, some of which were in direct opposition to the policies begun in the early 1980s. In fact, fathers' rights groups were less than a decade away from turning Kennelly's question on its head by asking, "If we don't pick a dad's issue to be number one, who will?"

7

Fathers' Rights Groups as Challenger Entrepreneurs

By the mid-1990s, two types of stories were circulating in the inner circles of the child support community. First, there was the story of Charles Fink, testifying before the New York State Senate in 1996 on a joint custody bill.

I also firmly believe that the *least* important feature a father can give his child is money. And on the subject of child support, I don't believe that a father should be forced to pay if he is being refused visitation. Personally, I paid child support for 5 years while my estranged spouse sporadically denied my visitation. In the summer of 1992, I attempted to pick up my children for summer visitation and was refused. After years of motions to the courts, psychological forensics and over $100,000 in legal fees which left me bankrupt and homeless, I decided to enact my own punishment. I have refused to pay child support for 3 years. I have been thrown in jail, where my life was threatened by hardened criminals. After all of this, if you think taking my driver's or professional licenses will coerce me to pay support without access to my children, you are sadly mistaken. I had a father. He taught me that anything worth having was worth fighting for. He taught me right from wrong. It is wrong to deny a child a father. The only way to get me to pay support will be to let me see my children.[1] [my italics]

Then there was tale of Michael Dodgett in 1998.

Most days you will find Michael Dodgett hanging out in the basement of the James Weldon Johnson Housing Project in East Harlem. Here, Dodgett meets with a caseworker who helps him track down job leads. After his fourth stint in

---

[1] Charles Fink. January 11, 1996. Hearing before the New York State Senate Standing Committee on Families and Children. Member of the National Coalition of Free Men, the Nassau County Family Law Task Force, and director of the Men's Resources Hotline.

state prison for selling crack cocaine, Dodgett now wants to get his life on the right track. For him, this means not only finding better jobs, it means finally being a father to his three-year-old daughter and his daughter on the way. Now, a new twist on an old program will help him with both of his goals. Over the next few months, Dodgett and approximately 300 young fathers like him in New York City, will be encouraged to participate in a new program targeting young fathers on two fronts – assisting them to develop job skills so they can pay child support and teaching them how to be a father.[2]

These men had clearly different accounts of their interactions with the child support system. But underlying these separate accounts were two common themes. First, both men had broken the law. Charles Fink had flagrantly violated the law by willfully withholding child support payments as retribution for what he described as visitation violations by his ex-wife. Michael Dodgett, a convicted drug dealer, had escaped responsibility for supporting his children while in jail and later while he was unemployed. Yet, despite these infractions, both men were now soliciting aid from the government in an effort to transform child support policy. Fink was demanding equal treatment under the law, and Dodgett was pleading for employment programs to help him get back on his feet.

These stories are typical of the ways in which fathers' rights groups have been working to take child support policy in a completely different direction from that taken by their entrepreneurial predecessors. Since the passage of the Personal Responsibility and Work Opportunity Reconciliation Act of 1996 (PRWORA), fathers have become much more vocal about their disappointment with the current policy environment. In many ways, PRWORA represented the culmination of women leaders' efforts to tighten child support provisions after the introduction of full services to non-AFDC mothers in 1984. PRWORA introduced a national directory of new hires to track down delinquents, required states to improve their interstate collection mechanisms, and mandated that all states have procedures in place to revoke driver's and professional licenses when fathers fall behind in their payments. PRWORA even authorized states to deny food stamps to those fathers who fail to support their children.

In response to what they perceive as these draconian measures, fathers have become active protesters against the status quo, taking their

[2] Karrie Donohue. December 10, 1998. "Fathers and Welfare Reform-Investigative Project." Accessed at (http://www.strivecentral.com/media_reports/reports/pff.htm) on August 2, 2001.

grievances to the streets, to their legislators, and to the media.[3] As their efforts have begun only recently, it is difficult at this stage to discern whether or not fathers will replace women legislators and women's groups as the new policy entrepreneurs on the child support issue. We can, however, carefully examine their past as a potential harbinger of their future activities: their rent-seeking position to reduce child support awards (the first section); their risk-reduction strategies in organization building (the second section); and their shakeout methods, which involve moving away from their past anti-woman rhetoric to their current pro-child political rhetoric (the third section). The fourth section describes their level of success so far in overtaking women legislators and organizations as the most important policy entrepreneurs on this issue; and the fifth section concludes.

DEFINING A RENT-SEEKING POSITION

Although fathers' rights groups are numerous and their goals varied, one constant theme has emerged throughout their short history: their central goal has been to modify child support awards, usually in a downward direction. Fathers' rights groups maintain that the country's monomaniacal zeal to catch and punish "deadbeat dads" has produced a child support enforcement system that is inherently inequitable and unjust to fathers. States are pursuing them to the fullest extent of the law, without regard to their capacity, willingness, or desire to pay. According to this perspective, this single-focused mission has forced many men into poverty, or into the underground economy. Fathers have been stalked, and the states have been doing the stalking.

Not only have men been forced into financial ruin because of current child support policy, they also have been forced into emotional ruin. According to David Blankenhorn, the founder and president of the Institute for American Values and a leading fathers' rights advocate,

We respond to the Deadbeat Dad by denying and pretending. If only we could get tough with these guys, that would fix what is broken. Get them to pay. That would help the children. That would relieve the taxpayer. Here, finally, is a family policy we can all agree on.... But this strategy is a fantasy. It is based not on evidence but on wishful thinking.... From the child's perspective, child support

---

[3] For a description of some of their belief systems, see Wade F. Horn, David Blankenhorn, and Mitchell B. Pearlstein, eds. 1999. *The Fatherhood Movement – A Call to Action.* Lanham, MD: Lexington Books.

payments, even if fully paid, do not replace a father's economic provision. More fundamentally, they do not replace a father. [4]

To Blankenhorn and others, for far too long states have reduced fathers to a unidimensional role: that of an economic provider. When fathers are treated as nothing more than open wallets, it is no wonder that they become confused over the proper role they should take in their children's lives. The father–child bond undoubtedly weakens over time, as men perceive themselves as having nothing more to offer their offspring than loose change.

To fathers' rights leaders, most fathers, then, are not "deadbeat dads" but simply men trying to survive economically. But the myth of the "deadbeat dad," they argue, has become so pervasive over the past two decades that all fathers have suffered under the weight of unnecessarily harsh child support laws. In their view, society must acquire a better understanding of their predicament, and states must move to ease their financial burden. They have approached these goals from three primary directions: (1) by encouraging periods of child support "amnesty" and the development of programs aimed at helping low-income fathers to meet their obligations, (2) by focusing on child support guideline reform, and (3) by promoting shared custody arrangements that have the effect of reducing a father's child support bill.

As we have seen from the case of Michael Dodgett, the first goal of fathers' rights groups is to ensure that all fathers who are asked to pay child support can, in fact, meet their obligations. They maintain that the current set of child support award guidelines places them in an economically untenable position. The situation is most extreme when considering the needs of low-income fathers. In these cases, fathers frequently have a difficult time financially caring for themselves, much less taking a proactive, financially responsible position with respect to child rearing. This concept of "capacity to pay" has several important public policy components.

Because the stakes are so high – both financially (for the government) and personally (for the individuals involved) – studies examining the benefits of steady child support for families have proliferated. [5] Much less

---

[4] David Blankenhorn. 1995. *Fatherless America*. New York: Basic Books, p. 127.

[5] Daniel R. Meyer, Judi Bartfeld, Irwin Garfinkel, and Patricia Brown. 1996. "Child Support Reform: Lessons from Wisconsin." *Family Relations* 45(1): 11–18; Philip K. Robins. 1992. "Why Did Child Support Award Levels Decline from 1978 to 1985?" *Journal of Human Resources* 27(2): 362–379; Daniel R. Meyer. 1995. "Supporting Children Born Outside of

research has focused on the states' policy reactions to the needs and circumstances of disadvantaged men. According to Lawrence M. Mead, families with the poorest fathers represent the most difficult cases for the system to address:

> Of all delinquent non-custodial parents, [poor men] are the most disadvantaged. They are the toughest to get to pay because they are the hardest to locate and have the least to lose by not paying. Traditionally, local courts deal with such fathers in a punitive but ineffective manner. Child-support lawyers find them and bring them before family court charged with nonpayment. Judges tell them to get a job and pay, but there is little supervision to see that they do so.[6]

Given the difficulty of even locating these men, can policymakers realistically assume that they will become reliable payers once they are in the child support system?[7]

Recently, various studies have begun exploring exactly these questions. Using data from the 1990 Survey of Income and Program Participation, Ronald Mincy and Elaine J. Sorensen attempted to distinguish between real "deadbeats" and those who truly cannot afford to pay their child support obligations. They divided noncustodial fathers into four groups: able payers, unable payers, able nonpayers, and unable nonpayers. They found that 34 percent of those surveyed were "able nonpayers," that is, fathers who had the resources to pay child support but still refused to pay – the group traditionally targeted by legislators. However, Mincy and Sorensen also categorized 33 percent of their research sample as "unable nonpayers." Given the financial destitution of these fathers, efforts to collect support from this group using traditional methods, they concluded, would continue to be futile.[8]

Marriage: Do Child Support Awards Keep Pace with Changes in Fathers' Incomes?" *Social Science Quarterly* 76(3): 577–593; Donald T. Oellerich, Irwin Garfinkel, and Philip K. Robins. 1991. "Private Child Support: Current and Potential Impacts." *Journal of Sociology and Social Welfare* 18(1): 3–23; Daniel R. Meyer. 1993. "Child Support and Welfare Dynamics: Evidence from Wisconsin." *Demography* 30(1): 45–62; Irwin Garfinkel and Sara S. McLanahan. 1990. "The Effects of the Child Support Provisions of the Family Support Act of 1988 on Child Well-Being." *Population Research and Policy Review* 9(3): 205–234.

[6] Lawrence M. Mead. 1995. "The New Paternalism in Action: Welfare Reform in Wisconsin." Madison: Wisconsin Policy Research Institute, p. 34.

[7] Judi Bartfeld and Daniel R. Meyer. 1994. "Are There Really Deadbeat Dads? The Relationship Between Ability to Pay, Enforcement, and Compliance in Nonmarital Child Support Cases." *Social Service Review* 68(2): 219–235.

[8] Ronald Mincy and Elaine J. Sorensen. 1998. "Deadbeats and Turnips in Child Support Reform." *Journal of Policy Analysis and Management* 17(1): 44–51.

Fathers' life circumstances, however, can change substantially over time. Elizabeth Phillips and Irwin Garfinkel found that although many young fathers have low incomes when their babies are born, their earnings change quite dramatically as their children grow up.[9] Fathers either go back to school or seek promotion opportunities at their current jobs. Pursuing a similar line of inquiry, Judi Bartfeld and Daniel R. Meyer studied the complex question of whether lower absolute awards result in higher levels of compliance among fathers across the income spectrum (the theory being that fathers would perceive their relative burden to be more manageable).[10] For those at the middle and upper income levels, there was no impact. By contrast, they found that lower award levels *did* have a compliance effect on the poorest dads. For these fathers, low awards meant that they could realistically meet their obligations, which evidently raised their level of satisfaction and increased their compliance rates. Several new studies have added the important insight that low-income fathers tend to have the actual means to pay small support awards on a consistent basis.[11] Combining these findings, it may be the case that poorer fathers simply need complete amnesty or lower-than-average obligations at the beginning of their children's lives, or at least until they are in a financial position to dedicate a greater percentage of their income to their offspring.

The second area where fathers' rights groups have been active is in the area of child support guideline reform. Prior to 1984, local judges decided if and when child support should be paid, and if so, at what levels. The 1984 Child Support Enforcement Amendments required that all states adopt numeric guidelines in determining awards, and that they make these awards available to local jurisdictions in their decision making. With the Family Support Act of 1988, the federal government mandated that each state adopt presumptive child support guidelines by the end of 1989. States also were required to review and modify their child support guidelines at least every four years. In general, states currently utilize one

[9] Elizabeth Phillips and Irwin Garfinkel. 1992. "Changes over Time in the Incomes of Nonresident Fathers in Wisconsin." Madison: Institute for Research on Poverty, University of Wisconsin, Paper DP#967–92.

[10] Judi Bartfeld and Daniel R. Meyer. 1994. "Are There Really Deadbeat Dads? The Relationship Between Ability to Pay, Enforcement, and Compliance in Nonmarital Child Support Cases." *Social Service Review* 68(2): 219–235.

[11] Elaine J. Sorensen. 1997. "A National Profile of Nonresident Fathers and Their Ability to Pay Child Support." *Journal of Marriage and the Family* 59(4): 785–797; Cynthia Miller, Irwin Garfinkel, and Sara S. McLanahan. "Child Support in the United States: Can Fathers Afford to Pay More?" *Review of Income and Wealth* 43(3): 261–281.

of four guideline models: the percentage-of-income standard, the income shares model, the Melson formula, or a hybrid formula.[12]

Briefly, the percentage-of-income standard requires that fathers pay a designated percentage of their earnings to their children. The income shares model, on the other hand, is based on the premise that a child should receive the same proportion of a parent's income that would have been paid had the family remained intact. A designated childrearing sum is calculated after the parents' earnings are added together, and the child support award is then pro rated based on each individual parent's income. The Melson formula determines child support awards by first providing for each parent's self-support, and then calculating an assistance amount based on a child's primary needs plus a standard of living adjustment. Lastly, the hybrid formula uses the percentage-of-income standard when a father makes below a designated level of income, and the income shares model when his income exceeds the prespecified level. Currently, Delaware, Hawaii, and Montana use the Melson formula; the District of Columbia and Massachusetts use the hybrid formula; and the remaining states use the percentage-of-income and income shares methods.

Although these guidelines have now been in place for over a decade, fathers' rights groups have been particularly unhappy with the ramifications of their implementation. They have attacked these standards from a variety of angles, perhaps the most important being their per capita treatment of child-related expenses. Simply having a child in the household does not mean, these groups argue, that a child adds a "full person" expense to the family's budget, as current guidelines dictate. Rather, having a child adds a *marginal* cost to acquiring goods and services such as housing, transportation, and utility usage. Child support guidelines need to reflect this reality, these groups maintain, instead of overcharging well-meaning fathers for their children's day-to-day needs. In a secondary line of attack, fathers' rights groups argue that child support guidelines should be based on a father's net income, not his gross income. Current taxation policy completely distorts a person's real earnings, making child support guidelines based on gross earnings an unreliable method of determing childrearing deductions. Nonetheless, the majority of states today rely on gross income figures. In the third and final line of attack, fathers' rights groups question the fairness of child support guidelines that do not address the

---

[12] See Jane C. Venohr and Robert G. Williams. 1999. "The Implementation and Periodic Review of State Child Support Guidelines." *Family Law Quarterly* 33(1): 7–38, for a thorough discussion of these options.

fundamental inequities in the tax code, such as the mother's receipt of the favorable head of household status, child care credits, earned income tax credits, exemptions, and the like.[13]

The third area where fathers' rights groups have attempted to modify child support guidelines relates to shared parenting.[14] Shared parenting is a recent development in custody law. Throughout the early part of the twentieth century, the "tender years" doctrine prevailed, which presumed that in the majority of cases, the mother was the parent best equipped to raise the children. During the 1960s and 1970s, state legislators began to question the gender biases inherent in the tender years doctrine, and thus rewrote the law to include a new, primary caretaker presumption. Under this new policy regime, judges were instructed to award the children to the parent who had been the primary caretaker prior to the family break-up. This practice, lawmakers argued, would provide the children with the greatest stability in their lives during a period of potential turmoil. By the early 1980s, however, states had gradually moved to yet another form of custody. Lawmakers sought to provide judges with a more comprehensive method of deciding where children should reside; determining the primary caretaker would now be only a part of the consideration process. A new, "best interest" of the child standard would prevail. A child's mental and physical health, as well as his or her intellectual and moral needs and the ability of each parent to fulfill these needs, would become significant factors in determining the outcome of these cases.[15]

What were the concrete ramifications of the "best interest" standard? For the most part, children were still almost always awarded to the mother. Judges remained locked into traditional ways of evaluating custody claims, and these practices tended to be reproduced and reified across the fifty states. This intransigence is significant, because during the late 1980s the states were developing their own initial set of child support guidelines. The predominant mode of child custody was sole custody, with the noncustodial parent – usually the father – visiting the child for limited periods. The main concern of these early policymakers was to ensure that fathers supported their children financially to the degree that they were able, mainly to ensure that every mother-headed household remained financially viable.

---

13 Sanford Braver. 1998. *Divorced Dads: Shattering the Myths.* New York: Putnam, pp. 67–68.

14 See Marygold S. Melli. 1999. "Guideline Review: Child Support and Time Sharing by Parents." *Family Law Quarterly* 33(1): 219–234.

15 See Stephanie Barnes. 1999. "Comment: Strengthening the Father-Child Relationship through a Joint Custody Presumption." *Willamette Law Review* 35: 601–628.

During the 1990s, fathers' rights groups argue, joint legal as well as joint physical custody became the more commonplace rules under which to raise children.[16] Joint legal custody refers to shared parental decision making over major issues in the child's life, while joint physical custody implies that the child spends a relatively equal amount of time in both parental households. Currently, twenty-nine states have some version of a joint custody preference on the books. These laws usually take one of three forms: (a) a presumption that joint custody is in the best interests of the child; (b) a stated preference for joint custody by the legislature, but without a strict presumption, so that individual cases are decided by the courts; (c) a presumption that joint custody is in the child's best interest only under the condition that both parents agree.

There are, however, more nuanced forms of custodial parenting as well. Fathers have come to recognize the importance of their spending time with their children, and have done everything in their power to "share parenting" with their former partners. Most fathers' rights groups remain strong proponents of shared parenting arrangements. To these groups, shared parenting provides a variety of benefits to the children, including stronger familial ties, an enhanced emotional support system, and a consistent relationship with both parents. Shared parenting generally involves a child spending more than 20 percent but less than 50 percent of his or her time with the noncustodial parent (anything under the 20 percent threshold is the "ordinary visitation" that typically occurs in most sole custody cases). Fathers would also like to be financially compensated for this increased time spent with their children through reductions in their child support awards.

Child support guidelines, however, have not kept up with these changes. According to fathers' rights groups, child support guidelines continue to assume that the mothers are the primary caretakers of the children. This mindset holds even as fathers claim that they are not only increasingly spending more time with their children but also are becoming more emotionally invested as well. Fathers want their new roles to be taken seriously, and are demanding that the courts and the child support agencies compensate them for the increased time that they are allotting to their children, especially under shared parenting agreements.

RISK-REDUCTION STRATEGIES

Fathers' rights groups, like every other set of entrepreneurs before them, face an extraordinary level of uncertainty in presenting their new ideas to

---

[16] According to the National Center for Health Statistics, about 22 percent of all divorced parents had joint physical custody arrangements for their children in 1997.

the public. One factor that bodes well for these groups is their avoidance of individualized approaches to effecting change. That is, they have not crowned one individual as a spokesperson for their cause and pinned their policy fortunes upon him or her. Instead, in order to diminish the policy uncertainty before them, they have engaged in cooperative risk-reduction strategies, most prominently by building new types of strong, interlinked groups to push their agenda forward.

Organization Building

Over the past decade, the United States has witnessed a massive explosion in the number of fathers' rights groups. They trace their associational roots back to three primary sources of what this analysis calls "male advocacy groups": (1) divorce reformers, (2) men's rights organizations, and (3) religiously oriented groups.

1. Divorce Reform Roots. The first major organizational link to the fathers' rights movement has its roots in the divorce reformers of the 1960s. A group called Divorce Racket Busters, later renamed United States Divorce Reform, was founded in 1960 by Ruben Kidd and George Partis in Sacramento, California. These innovative leaders organized men based on what they perceived to be general ill-treatment by the court system, outrageous alimony settlements, and bias against fathers in divorce cases. Early on, United States Divorce Reform focused on lobbying the state of California to replace divorce courts with family arbitration centers. They argued that arbitration was a much more "humane" system by which to resolve family disputes, especially when compared to the antagonistic judicial system. Although they were not successful in transforming the institutional means by which these cases were decided, as the divorce rate continued to escalate in the late 1960s and early 1970s, groups such as United States Divorce Reform became more prevalent all across the country.

As this movement searched for its intellectual underpinnings, many divorce reformers began to adhere to the philosophy articulated by Charles V. Metz, who in 1968 published *Divorce and Custody for Men.*[17] In this manifesto, Metz argued that men had unreasonably relinquished their authority to women. In all areas of their lives, men were attempting to curry favor with women by doing their bidding. All men needed to do to reclaim their power was to act both independently and authoritatively on matters

---

[17] Charles V. Metz. 1968. *Divorce and Custody for Men.* New York: Doubleday.

related to family life. While Metz's writings were a significant force in articulating the male experience, it was really the leadership of Richard Doyle, author of *The Rape of the Male*, that pushed the movement forward in a more unified direction.[18] To Doyle, men suffered at the hands of women in many more arenas than Metz had described, including criminal justice proceedings, child abuse hearings, paternity determinations, and welfare eligibility screenings. If they were to turn this tide, men needed to systematically collaborate with one another and organize for change.

Pursuant to these goals, Doyle started numerous organizations to further his cause; unfortunately, many failed due to factionalism and leadership in-fighting. For example, the Coalition of American Divorce Reform Elements (CADRE) began in 1971 as an effort to bring together the leaders of the divorce reform movement under one umbrella organization. Initial efforts to organize were aggressive. In fact, three incorporation conventions were held in the Elgin, Illinois area, each attended by the heads of the major divorce reform organizations in the country. As soon as the preliminary meetings were over, however, intense levels of organizational squabbling ensued. Among their many differences, members had opposing operational styles when it came to business planning and attracting outside donors. After CADRE disintegrated, Doyle later formed the Men's Rights Association (MRA) in 1973 along with Ruben Kidd. Unlike CADRE, MRA survives to the present day and has effectively served as an attorney referral service for divorcing men across the United States.

2. Men's Rights Roots. While the aforementioned groups focused primarily on divorce reform, other male advocacy groups – the men's rights groups – flourished with a broader agenda. Three of these early men's rights groups had a particularly strong impact on public discussions regarding the proper roles of men and women in society. One of the most influential, Free Men, was started by Richard Haddad, Dennis Gilbert, Allan Scheib, and Allen Foremen in Columbia, Maryland, in 1977. The impetus for Free Men's birth was Herb Goldberg's book, *The Hazards of Being Male: Surviving the Myth of Masculine Privilege.*[19] In this work, Goldberg methodically argued that society places men in an extremely untenable position. On one hand, society prohibits men from showing

---

[18] Richard Doyle. 1976. *The Rape of the Male.* St Paul, MN: Poor Richard's Press.
[19] Herb Goldberg. 1976. *The Hazards of Being Male: Surviving the Myth of Masculine Privilege.* New York: New American Library.

their emotions, while on the other hand modern culture requires and expects that they will be the primary breadwinners. These pressures force men to conceal their stresses and endure the crises of the workplace alone, without help from their female partners. Men who found Goldberg's arguments convincing quickly formed consciousness-raising groups and generally tried to work with other men's groups in rearticulating the male experience. Later renamed the Coalition of Free Men, this group has served mainly as an educational body on men's rights over the past several decades.

By 1977, Doyle had become active in the organization-building business once again and had formed the second major men's rights group, MEN (Men for Equality NOW) International, or MI. Originally, MI was created to coordinate the efforts of the many men's organizations that were in existence at the time. The rapid proliferation of these groups was a positive development for the movement; however, the lack of coordination had prevented men from obtaining real, concrete improvements in their lives. The major goal for MI at its inception was restoring equal (although not identical) rights for men in many areas of life, including family and employment law.

Like all new organizations, MI struggled to find a unique identity. The group was pulled in a variety of directions, with each membership faction advocating a different set of policy priorities. As an international organization, MI also had to consider the needs and demands of men from all over the globe. The scope of MI's concerns broadened even further when Ken Pangborn replaced Richard Doyle as the leader of the association. Upon taking office, Pangborn began to take on new issues in the men's rights movement, such as defending men against false allegations of rape and child molestation. Currently, MI no longer serves as a membership organization. It does, however, continue to thrive as an association that provides men with referrals to attorneys specializing in divorce cases, expert psychologists, and other educational specialists.

The third and last major men's rights group to be formed during this period, the National Congress of Men (NCM), began in 1980 in Utica, New York. Men from a variety of state-level male advocacy groups decided to create an organization with a wide-ranging scope and mission. The first convention was held in Houston, Texas, in 1981; by 1982, with the completion of the organization's second convention in Detroit, Michigan, members had elected their first president. James Cook of the Joint Custody Association in Los Angeles took the reins of power and attempted to unify the umbrella organization of smaller groups then in place around several key issues. However, like the other organizations developing at the time, NCM suffered from competing pressures. Certain affiliate groups wanted the association to focus on fathers' rights only, while others wanted the organization to work for an equal rights amendment, equality in the draft, increased aid for disabled veterans, and enhanced funding for male health needs.

Partly to address these problems, Jack Kammer, who became president of NCM in the mid-1980s, took the risky step of dissolving the membership of the association in 1986 and transformed it into one of individual affiliation/chapters. Today, the group, known as the National Congress for Fathers and Children (NCFC), continues to address a wide variety of public policy issues impacting men. It also helps men to navigate through the complex system of divorce and custody, including paternity establishment, visitation, and pro se representation in court.

3. Religious Roots. Finally, contemporary fathers' rights groups have emerged from religiously oriented male advocacy groups. One prominent organization has been the Promise Keepers, founded by Bill McCartney and Dave Wardell, two friends who saw the need for the development of a spiritual reawakening among men. Beginning with only a few members in 1990 in Colorado, the Promise Keepers movement quickly blossomed. Its first official conference, held in 1991 at Colorado University's Event Center, brought together 4,200 men. Subsequent conferences, held in 1992 and 1993, both at Colorado University's Folsom Stadium, drew even larger crowds of 22,000 and 50,000 men, respectively.

By 1994, the Promise Keepers had begun a new, comprehensive national campaign. Unified in spirit and driven by a common belief in the power of God to provide direction, the Promise Keepers endeavored to cast as wide a net as possible in attracting new members. By 1996, the organization had held twenty-two conferences that drew an estimated 1.1 million men, and it showed no signs of slowing down in terms of recruitment. Indeed, on October 4, 1997, the Promise Keepers made international headlines by calling for a unified day of prayer on the National Mall in Washington, D.C. Over one million men attended the event under the banner, "Stand in the Gap: A Sacred Assembly of Men."[20]

The core mission of the Promise Keepers is to provide religious guidance to men. The organization promotes men's standing together without

---

[20] Randy Balmer. 1999. "Introduction." In *The Promise Keepers: Essays on Masculinity and Christianity*, ed. Dane S. Claussen. Jefferson, NC: McFarland, p. 4.

fear against a world dominated by sin and mixed messages concerning the role that men should play in family life. In brief, the organization is based upon the realization of seven critical principles: (1) building a personal relationship with Jesus Christ, (2) pursuing close friendships with other men, (3) practicing spiritual, moral, ethical, and sexual purity, (4) building strong marriages, (5) supporting local churches, (6) breaking down walls of race and denomination, and (7) influencing the world for Christ.

With this broad-based mission, Promise Keepers has encouraged men not only to improve their own lives spiritually, but also to hold each other accountable for their actions. This means that each member is responsible for monitoring the behavior of his neighbor, ultimately ensuring that no fathers stray from their families. In general, groups such as the Promise Keepers also encourage marriage wherever and whenever possible in order to strengthen and sustain the traditional family unit. Currently, the Promise Keepers sponsors a radio commentary on over 450 Christian stations nationwide, maintains an active website, and plans stadium-based grassroots conventions.

Other examples of such religiously oriented groups include those associated with the Nation of Islam. On October 16, 1995, under the leadership of the Minister Louis Farrakhan, thousands of African-American men gathered in Washington, D.C., to participate in the Million Man March. Men from all different faiths participated, from Muslim to Christian to African. They came to respond to the important question, "What role do Black men have in contributing to a greater sense of righteousness in their communities?" On the actual day of the event, men prayed, sang, and built new bonds of solidarity with each other. Those who could not participate, such as black women, were encouraged to take part in a "Day of Absence" on which they, too, mobilized in support of black men's commitment to take charge of their lives.

The long-term goals of the March were manifold, and included fostering a sense of economic independence in the African-American community and creating new paths of upward mobility for those already in the workforce. But beyond these immediate economic goals, members of the March were also called together to assume new levels of responsibility in their families – simply put, to become better husbands to their wives and better fathers to their children. Indeed, a fundamental part of the Million Man March pledge was the participants' promise "never to abuse [my] wife by striking her, disrespecting her, for she is the mother of [my] children and the producer of [my] future."[21] Through this commitment, black men were to transform themselves in their children's eyes, supporting them and guiding them to higher levels of spirituality. From this initial organizing rally in Washington, D.C., the men then returned to their own communities to structure local organizations with similar missions.[22]

Fathers Rights Groups: The Present

By the early 1980s, then, three types of organizations came to dominate the male advocacy scene: divorce reformers, men's rights associations, and religiously affiliated groups. From these organizations came the major fathers' rights organizations that participate extensively in the child support debates of today.

For years, male advocacy groups had worked on a variety of issues, of which child support was only one, and a very small one. Divorce reform groups' primary mission was to secure equitable treatment in court, while men's rights associations' core concern was guaranteeing men equal treatment under the law. Finally, religiously affiliated groups' guiding principle was to encourage men to live their lives in concert with the commandments of God.

The gains made by women entrepreneurs during the 1980s and early 1990s in the area of child support, however, forced traditional male advocacy groups to take stock of their past organizational tactics. With the Child Support Enforcement Amendments of 1984, the Family Support Act of 1988, and PRWORA of 1996, men faced a totally new climate with respect to child support policy. No longer were local judges making decisions about their financial futures; instead, they had to confront the full weight and power of the federal government which was enforcing stricter and stricter policies against them. Moreover, with these legislative initiatives, the tide of public opinion was becoming increasingly hostile to their needs and perspectives. Male advocacy groups thus had to retool themselves, giving birth to a variety of fathers' rights groups whose sole focus was to fight for a new wave of child support enforcement reform.

Table 7.1 is a composite listing of the major fathers' rights organizations currently active. The list is composed of twenty-eight organizations,

---

[21] Theodore Walker. 1998. "Can a Million Black Men Be Good News?" *In Black Religion after the Million Man March*, ed. Garth Kasimu Baker-Fletcher. Maryknoll, NY: Orbis Books, p. 17.
[22] Ibid., p. 11.

TABLE 7.1. *Major fathers' rights organizations, 2001*

Organization	Year Founded	Where Founded	Structure	Membership or Other Role
American Coalition for Fathers and Children (ACFC)	1998	Washington, DC	National and state	45,000 members
Americans for Divorce Reform	1997	Arlington, VA	National	30 members
Alliance for Non-Custodial Parents Rights (ANCPR)	1995	Los Angeles, CA	National	4,800 members
Center on Fathering	1995	El Paso, CO	State and local	Referral/info
Children and Fathers Together (CFT)	2000	Plymouth, MA	National	Not available
Children's Rights Council (CRC)	1985	Washington, DC	National and states	Not available
Coalition for the Preservation of Fatherhood (CPF)	1993	Arlington, MA	State and local (in MA)	300 members
Coalition of Parent Support	1992	Bakersfield, CA	State and local (in California)	1,000 members
Dads Against Discrimination	1977	United States	National and state	Not available

(continued)

TABLE 7.1 (continued)

Organization	Year Founded	Where Founded	Structure	Membership or Other Role
Dads Ok	2000	Tulsa, OK	State (in Oklahoma)	30 members
Dads of Tennessee	1995	Johnson City, TN	State and local (in Tennessee)	2,000 members
Divorced Fathers Network	1988	Santa Cruz, CA	State and local (in California)	2,000 members
Domestic Rights Coalition	1988	St. Paul, MN	Mainly Minnesota, Iowa, Wisconsin	Referral/information
Family Research Council	1983	Washington, DC	National	Referral/information
Father on Rights for Custody Equality (FORCE)	1996	Loretto, KY	State and local (in Kentucky)	300 members
Fatherhood Project	1981	New York, NY	National	Referral/information
Fathers and Children's Equality Inc. (FACE)	1978	Philadelphia, PA	Pennsylvania and New Jersey	2500 members
Fathers for Equal Rights	1973	Dallas, TX	State and local (Dallas area)	2,000 members
Father's Rights Association of New York State (FRANYS)	1988	New York	State and local (in New York)	1,000 members

Organization	Year	Location	Scope	Membership
Fathers Rights to Custody (FRTC)	1998	Seattle, WA	National	Referral/information
Men's Defense Association	1972	St. Paul, MN	National	15,000 members
National Center for Fathering	1990	Kansas City, MO	National	Referrals/information
National Coalition of Free Men (NCFM)	1977	Columbia, MD	National and state	Not available
National Congress for Fathers & Children (NCFC)	1981	Houston, TX	National and state	8,000 members
National Fatherhood Initiative (NFI)	1994	Lancaster, PA	National	575 members
Taking Action Against Bias in the System (TABS)	1988	Bellevue, WA	State	Referral/information
United Fathers of America (UFA)	1996	Seattle, WA	Local	Referral/information
Wisconsin Fathers for Children and Families	1987	Madison, WI	State and local	Not available

Note: A "not available" entry under the membership category indicates that the organization does not provide membership numbers to the public.

far fewer than the number compiled by many fathers' rights groups.[23] This discrepancy can be accounted for by the differences in methodology utilized in creating the various types of available lists. First, this analysis included only "active" fathers' rights groups. This means that the organization had to be responsive to inquiries for information as well as currently engaged in fathers' rights–oriented activities. This requirement forced many of the original organizations considered for this list to be dropped, since they were born and then died within a relatively short period of time. Second, this list includes only fathers' rights groups with an American focus. Third, the list incorporates only those groups with an active membership base and/or referral organizations.[24] These decision rules meant that we included only those organizations that maintain a personal interest in reforming public policy, rather than simply providing paid services or emotional support.

As the list indicates, fathers' rights groups vary along a whole host of critical dimensions. Half of the organizations, fourteen out of the twenty-eight, were formed during the 1990s and later. Interestingly, they have not all grown up around the national government epicenter of Washington, D.C. Instead, these groups have emerged from all around the country, from Bakersfield, California, to St. Paul, Minnesota, to Arlington, Massachusetts, to Loretto, Kentucky. They have also taken on a wide array of organizational forms. Approximately 32 percent (nine) have assumed a national structure, meaning that the organization has one central location and attends solely to issues of national scope. The remaining organizations retain either a state, local, or state-local structure. These groups tend to address child support matters first in their own communities, using a more grassroots, activist approach. Finally, they also differ in terms of organizational focus. About half of these organizations are composed of actual members with quotable membership numbers, with the remainder providing information and referral services.

It is important to note that although this list represents a comprehensive compilation of all significant fathers' rights groups in the United States today, these groups do not stand autonomous in their missions. Most of the groups are affiliated with one another and direct their memberships to take advantage of the services offered by other organizations

---

[23] The American Coalition for Fathers and Children, for example, maintained a list including 141 fathers' rights organizations as of April 20, 2001.

[24] This meant that we excluded internet chat groups, online support groups, private companies specializing in custody and child support, publishing houses, magazines, and individually maintained websites. This list was compiled in the spring of 2001.

that specialize in a different set of potentially helpful activities. Moreover, the membership of these organizations is extremely fluid. Cross-group membership is common, as highly motivated participants elect to affiliate themselves with multiple organizations. Taken as a whole, then, these organizations epitomize the concept of a cooperative rather than an individualized approach to risk reduction. No one organization has come to dominate the others, and they all remain highly interdependent in their pursuit of the collective goal of child support reform.

SHAKEOUT STRATEGIES

One of the most interesting features distinguishing the current entrepreneurs who are attempting to control the child support agenda is the evolution of their shakeout strategies over time. Social workers, conservatives, and women leaders each immediately selected a legitimate means to shake out their competition. Social workers infiltrated successive presidential administrations, conservatives stressed the importance of automatic programs, and women leaders used the gender gap in order to emerge as the new victorious entrepreneurs. But male advocacy groups – the precursors to the fathers' rights groups – were not as successful in selecting legitimate shakeout strategies. Before transforming themselves into the fathers' rights groups of today, these organizations utilized illegitimate tactics designed to demonize the current holders of power: members of the opposite sex.

By the mid-1980s, as we have seen, male advocacy organizations took on a variety of forms, from those pressing for divorce reform, to men's rights associations, to those with religious affiliations. Their areas of expertise and concern varied as well, as they actively voiced their opinions on topics such as men's reproductive rights, women's role in the military, and what they perceived to be unfair hiring quotas that worked in favor of women. In order to deliver their message, most of these groups took on an extremely adversarial tone. In their view, women were often the enemy, and in order to secure male rights, they felt they had to paint as stark a picture of their opponent as possible.

Before giving birth to the fathers' rights groups of the 1990s, then, many male advocacy groups represented themselves as unabashedly anti-woman. Their campaigns to reduce child support awards were multifaceted, but they generally revolved around three critical tactics: (1) the sexual degradation of women, (2) the portrayal of all women as "gold diggers," and (3) the suggestion that all women are financially irresponsible.

One of the earliest strategies male advocacy groups employed in their attempts to reduce their child support obligations was to cast women in the role of "sexual tease," or manipulative and thus unworthy of financial assistance. These groups argued that women used and abused their sexuality in two ways, thereby trapping men into paying unreasonable levels of child support. First, women were promiscuous, which resulted in an excessive number of babies born out of wedlock. In this view, the sexual revolution had gone too far, with women now expecting men to assume all of the responsibility for birth control. When men "trusted" women to be practicing birth control and they subsequently became pregnant, these groups argued, could anyone blame the too-trusting fathers from running away from these unexpected outcomes?

Male advocacy groups highlighted these insidious sexual games in their testimony before Congress during the mid-1980s. Ken Pangborn, of Men International, emphatically articulated this viewpoint to the Senate Committee on Finance in 1984 when he wrote,

Our society is in the midst of a cultural revolution, and the feminist movement has bombarded our society with demands for sexual liberation of the female. This special interest regards as a basic right, the right of a woman to freely engage in sexual activity. . . . Our society also dictates that the entire question of reproduction is solely vested in the hands of the woman. Reproductive rights is a question where the feminist special interest has been quite clear that the male is completely without voice or legal standing. . . . We are only beginning to pay attention to some harsh realities in our society. We are beginning to see an openness about women choosing to become pregnant as a means of economic livelihood. There are those who deny this, but accounts of women who boldly admit to such an intent, and claim such as a "right" are becoming more frequent in the media.[25]

Beyond the significant problem of women "trapping" men into child support by not properly using birth control, there was also the issue of women having affairs once they were married. Again, according to Pangborn in his written testimony to the Senate Finance Committee,

We are in an age of unrestrained sexual conduct. Adultery is running high. Are you aware of the number of legally married women that become pregnant as the result of her adultery and bring another man's child into a legal marriage? This legal concept that all children born to a married woman are her husband's might seem like a nice legal exercise, but when it comes to maintaining and continuing a marriage relationship it's for the pits, few adulterous wives are fooling their husbands, and these marriages shortly break up. In my seventeen years of work with separated and divorced men I can confirm that the number of adulterous

---

[25] Ken Pangborn. 1984. Testimony on "Child Support Enforcement Program Reform Proposals." Hearing before the Committee on Finance, United States Senate, p. 268.

women is high. American fathers should be given the legal right to challenge every child born to his wife.[26]

To groups like Men International, men needed protection from Congress in the form of a clearly delineated fathers' bill of rights in order to prevent such entrapment. Child support awards should also reflect this skepticism about women's "inherent" promiscuous nature.

Women were also portrayed as sexual manipulators in the courts. Male advocacy groups accused their former partners of having sexual relationships not only with their attorneys, but also with presiding judges in order to influence child support decisions in their favor. In this view, the entire judicial system was stacked against men. According to Ken Pangborn, again in his written testimony before the United States Senate Committee on Finance,

> I would like to paint a glowing picture of a socio-legal system that functions perfectly, one that hums like fine tuned machinery. I'd like to paint the picture of a utopian democracy. I'd like to say that the "night court" sessions of female litigants with the Judges don't exist. I would like to suggest that sex between female divorce litigants and their lawyers never happens. I would like to say all of these things, but I would be lying if I did. A few years ago the Oregon Bar Association elevated the sexual exploitation of female clients to a Bar sacrament, ruling that this was not unethical. The sexual services provided by the female litigant provides her with almost limitless legal assistance at no charge. Perhaps someday female lawyers will begin providing similar arrangements for male litigants. In short, the ruling of the Oregon Bar simply confirms to most men their worst suspicions, that being that the Courthouse is in reality a "whorehouse."[27]

Pangborn and others thus painted a picture of a judicial system that was rife with sexual corruption. Not only could women entrap men into paying for children they never wanted in the first place, they could also have sexual relations with judges and attorneys, thereby securing favorable outcomes in court. Since courts were basically "whorehouses," Congress needed to step in and protect the interests of men.

The second area in which male advocacy groups demonized women was in their role as "gold diggers." To these groups, women did not want child support so that their offspring could lead better lives and enjoy a higher standard of living. Instead, women demanded outrageous sums of child support so that they themselves could live extravagantly. Danny Piper, founder of HELP – Help Encourage Loving Parents – in Burke, Virginia, articulated this theme before the Senate Finance Committee. In

[26] Ibid., p. 270.
[27] Ibid., p. 279.

his written testimony, he cited the 1981 United States Supreme Court case *McCarty v. McCarty*, which involved a divorcing couple and the question of whether a man's retirement pay should be equally divided between a former husband and wife.[28] After the Supreme Court ruled against this division, Congress passed the Uniform Services Former Spouses Protection Act in 1982, which effectively reversed this judicial action and made retirement pay once again available for contestation.

I know that dollars are the bottom line here and many pressure groups will overwhelm you with THEIR statistics. We need to keep these in perspective by considering motivations. For example, in the greatly publicized *McCarty v. McCarty* case, why did no one question the lack of child support for the three children? When Mrs. McCarty left Colonel McCarty, he got the three children and she received 77 percent of his retirement pay, why doesn't she pay any child support? Where was your concern for children? Do only men have that responsibility?[29]

Pangborn, of Men International, echoed a similar theme when he vividly described an example of this "gold digger abuse" in his written testimony before the Senate Committee on Finance:

This is a story of a Wisconsin Dentist [named Richard], relatively successful with five clinics in operation. When he could no longer deal with his wife's spending habits and ugly disposition, his nerves shattered, he filed for divorce and went into the hospital. The property division was simple, as they usually are for men. His wife got custody of the children, was there ever any doubt, she also was awarded the couple's $250,000 five bedroom, 5 bathroom home complete with an Olympic size swimming pool. Oddly, she was also awarded the five dental clinics. In less than 3 months, she managed to alienate the employees of the clinics and the staff quit en-masse. She was initially awarded $1000 a month in child support, but with the failure of her clinics, the judge decided this would just not be enough to keep her in the style to which she had become accustomed. . . . Richard, now back in dentistry, still does not earn gross what he is ordered to pay in child support.[30]

To Piper and Pangborn, the story of most divorces was a familiar one. It was the man who worked hard, paid the bills, and planned his life with great care. When the marriage did not work out, it was the woman who, armed with her stealthy attorney, tried to seize as many marital assets as possible in order to maintain and in most cases enhance her lifestyle. Only

[28] *McCarty v. McCarty*, 453 U.S. 210, 69 L. Ed. 2d 589, 101 S. Ct. 2728, 1981.
[29] Danny Piper. 1984. Testimony on "Child Support Enforcement Program Reform Proposals." Hearing before the Committee on Finance, United States Senate, pp. 314–315.
[30] Ken Pangborn. 1984. Testimony on "Child Support Enforcement Program Reform Proposals." Hearing before the Committee on Finance, United States Senate, p. 277.

legislative intervention could put a stop to these injustices and assess child support awards in a responsible, not extravagant manner.

The third and final technique used by these early male advocacy groups to achieve their goal of lower child support payments was to suggest that most women are financially irresponsible. One consistent claim was that all women "believe that money grows on trees" and thus could not be trusted to disburse their child support dollars effectively. In his written testimony before the Senate, George Doppler, of the male advocacy group the George Doppler Effort in Pennsylvania, voiced such concerns over women's demands that men simply be moneymakers to the exclusion of any other role.

Now tell us how an American father is going to pay a fixed amount for child support, wife support, alimony, medical bills, and he is never, never expected to have a financial setback, plus there are additional expenses in a broken home to maintain a relationship with one's children, plus there are now two living places that must be provided. How do you divide up a net take home pay of $280? And this is a national average. Many bring home less. Fathers are expected to do the impossible. Women think a man has some kind of magic chute and all he has to do is pull the cord and more money falls from the sky.[31]

Other male advocacy groups made more specific accusations concerning women and their irresponsibility when it came to financial matters. The key problem, according to these groups, was that women were not required under current law to account for how they spent their child support payments. Mothers could easily misuse and abuse child support funds by failing to pay the appropriate bills on time, not buying the children necessary goods, such as food and clothing, or by redirecting the money toward their own needs. In order to correct these problems, according to James Cook, president of the National Congress of Men, all fifty states should

[r]equire, as a prerequisite for participation in the federal program, that the same power of subpoena, investigation, and examination of records to ascertain the income of a non-custodial support-paying parent also be utilized, including penalties, to require that a custodial parent provide a verifiable accounting of support expenditures by both parents.[32]

---

[31] George Doppler. 1984. Testimony on "Child Support Enforcement Program Reform Proposals." Hearing before the Committee on Finance, United States Senate, pp. 440–441.

[32] James Cook. 1984. Testimony on "Child Support Enforcement Program Reform Proposals." Hearing before the Committee on Finance, United States Senate, p. 307.

Although legislators never went so far as to request financial statements from mothers, these early male advocacy groups had formulated a
stinging argument. They had vigorously called into question every
mother's capacity to manage her household budget.

During the early 1980s, then, male advocacy groups took on the child
support issue and attempted to modify policy using a variety of anti-
woman tactics. Not only did they question the sexual morality of women
who subsequently "ensnared" men into paying child support, they also
accused women of being gold diggers and/or financially irresponsible.
These strategies were clearly successful in grabbing headlines and increasing membership in these groups across the country. However, they failed
to secure their primary policy objective of reducing child support awards.
Members of Congress as well as the mainstream media generally viewed
their claims with disdain and outrage, especially when they attempted
to superimpose on women hurtful and inaccurate stereotypes that had
only recently been overcome by the feminist movement of the 1960s and
1970s. Their shakeout strategy of stereotyping an entire class of people
was thus perceived as completely illegitimate.

These early actions taken by male advocacy groups were not, however,
totally in vain. During the early 1990s, fathers' rights groups were born,
many hatched from these same male advocacy groups of the early 1980s.
By the time these fathers' rights groups gained political momentum, they
had learned effective lobbying skills from the mistakes of their predecessors. Their primary shakeout strategy would be to cast the current set
of policy incumbents – women's groups and women legislators – not as
the enemy but as a set of potential allies. Their new mission would be
one not of employing fiery antifeminist rhetoric, but rather of challenging
women and all Americans to place the needs of the children involved in a
separation or divorce first, before all other priorities.

The first item on this rhetorical shakeout strategy agenda was to create
new organizations with memorable names implying sole dedication to the
cause of saving children from the ill effects of parental breakups. They
drew upon the same membership as the earlier male advocacy groups and
shared many of the same goals, but distinguished themselves by placing
the word "children" in their titles. They hoped that this change would
signal that they were, indeed, a new type of male advocacy group, one
that could hopefully attain support from both sexes. The transformation
of the National Congress of Men (NCM), originally formed in 1981,
perhaps best illustrates this dynamic. During the 1980s and 1990s, NCM
switched names twice to reflect its new identity. During the years 1986–95,

the organization was known as the National Congress for Men and Children (NCMC), and from 1995 onward, it has been called the National Congress for Fathers and Children (NCFC). The father-child relationship has been placed center-stage in the organization's public persona.

The second major shakeout strategy was to emphasize father-child contacts and not just mother-child contacts as critical components of familial health. In the past, researchers had pointed to a variety of factors that inhibited the timely payment of child support, including fathers' lack of involvement with their children from infancy. In fact, researchers showed that this emotional and physical distance could have serious long-term consequences. Children from single-parent families frequently lagged behind their two-parent counterparts in many areas, including academic performance, mental health, and rates of juvenile delinquency.[33] The ramifications of single parenthood for children were even worse when the ages of the parents were taken into account. Childhood developmental outcomes for the offspring of teen parents were abysmally low.[34]

Fathers' rights groups immediately seized upon these findings to try to give themselves added legitimacy at the expense of the present holders of power, women leaders and women legislators. The major father's rights groups have prioritized these emotional roles and made them the centerpiece of their organizational identities. The Children's Rights Council, for example, states that it primarily

works to assure a child the frequent, meaningful and continuing contact with two parents and extended family the child would normally have during a marriage.

[33] See, for example, Sara S. McLanahan and Karen Booth. 1989. "Mother Only Families: Problems, Prospects, and Politics." *Journal of Marriage and the Family* 51(3): 557–580; Sara S. McLanahan and Larry Bumpass. 1988. "Intergenerational Consequences of Family Disruption." *American Journal of Sociology* 94(1): 130–152; Sheila F. Krein and Andrea H. Beller. 1988. "Educational Attainment of Children from Single-parent Families: Differences by Exposure, Gender, and Race." *Demography* 25(2): 221–234; Frank F. Furstenberg, Jr. 1980. "Burdens and Benefits: The Impact of Early Childbearing on the Family." *Journal of Social Issues* 36(1): 64–87.

[34] See Frank F. Furstenberg, Jr. 1990. "Divorce and the American Family." *Annual Review of Sociology* 16: 379–403; Catherine S. Chilman. 1980. "Social and Psychological Research concerning Adolescent Childbearing: 1970–1980." *Journal of Marriage and the Family* 42(4): 793–806; Arline T. Geronimus and Sanders Korenman. 1992. "The Socioeconomic Consequences of Teen Childbearing Reconsidered." *Quarterly Journal of Economics* 107(4): 1187–1214; Douglas M. Teti and Michael E. Lamb. 1989. "Socioeconomic and Marital Outcomes of Adolescent Marriage, Adolescent Childbirth, and Their Co-occurrence." *Journal of Marriage and the Family* 51(1): 203–212; Deborah Rhode. 1994. "Adolescent Pregnancy and Public Policy." *Political Science Quarterly* 108(4): 635–669.

[We] work to strengthen families through education, favoring family formation and family preservation. Unlike many other organizations with some of the same concerns, CRC is genderless; we are not a women's group nor a men's group. Rather, we advocate what we believe to be in the best interests of children including the Children's Bill of Rights.[35]

Similarly, the National Congress for Fathers and Children (NCFC) maintains that

[its mission] is to serve as a national organization, to assist state and local efforts, compatible with our goal of assisting parents who desire to remain actively involved in the lives of their children, regardless of marital status. We desire to provide a forum to coordinate local efforts, to impact national initiatives, and to bring national attention to local concerns of our affiliated groups, chapters and members.[36]

The important point to note about both of these mission statements is their focus on the rights of children, not of fathers or mothers. This rhetorical shakeout strategy has put all opponents of these fathers' groups, including the incumbent women's groups, in a defensive position. Who, after all, would take umbrage at the idea of children needing fathers in their lives in order to sustain their personal well-being?

OVERTAKING THE INCUMBENTS?

With the growing number of single-parent families in the 1970s and 1980s, the potential strength of fathers' rights groups took on added importance. Presidents Ronald Reagan and George H. W. Bush both described the downfall of the American family as one of the worst crises facing the country, and advocates for fathers scrambled for ways to counteract this trend. But were fathers' rights groups able to achieve the three components of their rent-seeking position – attending to the needs of low-income fathers, modifying child support guidelines to produce overall lower awards, and implementing shared custody arrangements that adjust awards downward?

First, consider the government's response to low-income fathers. Policymakers first responded to these groups' demands by arguing that there was an important and as yet untapped way of engaging young dads from birth. *State social service agencies* could encourage paternal contact in a

[35] Accessed at ⟨www.gocrc.org⟩ on May 8, 2001.
[36] Accessed at ⟨www.ncfc.net/mission⟩ on May 8, 2001.

variety of ways. In June 1995, President Clinton initiated action in this direction by instructing all federal agencies, via a memorandum, to help strengthen the role of fathers in families. The U.S. Department of Health and Human Services (DHHS), in response to Clinton's memorandum, immediately issued a plan of guiding principles:

Because families are diverse, so too are the roles of fathers and mothers. While the importance of the role of the mother and mothering in the family has received a great deal of study and attention, this is less true of the father and fathering within the family. It is clear that the role of the father is not limited to that of an economic provider.... We want to encourage and support the many roles that men can and do play in the lives of their own children and other children they care for.[37]

To support these diverse roles, DHHS policymakers laid out five beliefs that would thematically link their programs together in the upcoming years. These included the following: (1) all fathers can be important contributors to the well-being of their children; (2) parents are partners in raising their children, even when they do not live in the same household; (3) the roles fathers play in families are diverse and related to cultural and community norms; (4) men should receive the education and support necessary to prepare them for the responsibility of parenthood; and (5) the government can encourage and promote fathers' involvement through its programs and through its own workforce policies.[38]

While many states have pursued their own projects for low-income fathers, the most important cross-state program has been the Parents' Fair Share Demonstration (PFS), which used an experimental design for quality evaluation purposes. Implemented in 1992, PFS focused on low-income fathers in the following seven cities: Los Angeles, California; Jacksonville, Florida; Springfield, Massachusetts; Trenton, New Jersey; Dayton, Ohio; Grand Rapids, Michigan; and Memphis, Tennessee. The program offered nonpaying or delinquent noncustodial fathers several types of opportunities: enhanced contact with local child support enforcement personnel, peer-group meetings for similarly situated noncustodial fathers, and mediation services for fathers facing conflicts with custodial parents. The centerpiece of the program, however, was job training. Across a number

---

[37] "Fathering: The Man and the Family: The Department of Health and Human Services – Response to President Clinton's June 16 Memorandum to Strengthen the Role of Fathers in Families." October 16, 1995. Memo produced by the U.S. Department of Health and Human Services, Washington, DC, p. 1.

[38] Ibid., p. 2.

of sites, noncustodial parents worked part-time while acquiring skills that would be useful in the ever-changing economy. Agency directors established contacts with local businesses to ensure that workers ultimately had a good chance at long-term, stable employment. Additionally, "job club" activities helped fathers to polish their résumés and to present themselves effectively in interviews.

With the demonstration projects now complete, several studies have provided early insight into PFS's strengths and weaknesses. In one interim report, the Manpower Research and Development Corporation (MRDC) presented some of these mixed results. Although fathers enrolled in the program paid greater amounts of child support than did fathers in the control group, their employment prospects and earnings did not improve. MDRC found that the various partners in the program – such as the child support agencies, community-based organizations, and job-training teams – differed over the need for immediate job placement, and thus differed over both short- and long-term employment strategies. In the future, resolution of these tensions across partnerships such as PFS might prove to be a significant factor in improving fathers' earnings over the long-run.[39]

In addition to providing job training for low-income fathers, states have taken a much more active approach to addressing the problem of arrears, or back child support payments that have accumulated over time. Fathers can accrue child support arrearages for a variety of reasons, including inaccurate payment records, the establishment of an overdue obligation upon a recent recognition of paternity, or simply nonpayment. Over time, these arrearages can mount to such a level that they simply become unpayable by the noncustodial parent. Recognizing that such debts can become overwhelming to the fathers, several states have begun "arrearage amnesty" programs. Iowa's Satisfaction Support Program, for example, bases its arrearage forgiveness amounts on how well a father maintains his current track record in paying support. If a father successfully pays for six months, then 15 percent of his arrears is forgiven; if he pays for twelve consecutive months, then 35 percent of his arrears is forgiven. At the end of a twenty-four-month period, a father can receive amnesty for 80 percent of his past-due support payments. Other states, such as Maryland and Minnesota, base their arrearage forgiveness amounts

---

[39] Fred Doolittle, Virginia Knox, Cynthia Miller, and Sharon Rowser. 1998. *Building Opportunities, Enforcing Obligations: Implementation and Interim Impacts of Parents' Fair Share.* New York: Manpower Development Research Corporation.

upon the fathers' successful completion of a prespecified fatherhood program.[40]

While fathers' rights groups have been relatively successful in encouraging the federal and state-level governments to consider the needs of low-income fathers, their success in influencing modifications to state child support guidelines has been much more modest. The four basic standards remain: the percentage-of-income formula, the income shares model, the Melson formula, and the hybrid formula. Only four states have changed models since 1989. Montana switched from an income shares model to the Melson formula; West Virginia did the opposite. Wyoming and North Carolina moved from a percentage-of-income model to the income shares approach.[41]

The main areas of debate over the guidelines, however, remain unresolved. Only twenty-nine states have moved toward updating their cost schedules related to estimating the expenses associated with raising a child.[42] These modifications have been incorporated into these states' income shares and Melson formulas. In terms of fathers' rights groups' influence over the use of net versus gross income as a resource base for calculating support, twenty-nine states plus the District of Columbia continue to use gross income as their standard.[43]

One recent movement in this debate that has had the backing of many fathers' rights groups, most notably the Children's Rights Council, is the development of a new "cost-shares" guideline for determining support. The income shares guidelines, which are now utilized in many states, use economic estimation techniques based upon adult consumption patterns in order to approximate child care costs. The cost-shares approach, on the other hand, employs actual child cost data from the U.S. Department of Agriculture and the U.S. Department of the Interior. Allocation of costs is also slightly different than in the income shares model. Parents must split their childrearing costs based on income, after retaining a self-preserve fund for themselves. The cost-shares guidelines also require that the differential tax treatment of custodial and noncustodial parents as well as parenting time be factored into this child support formula. While

[40] Paula Roberts. 2001. "An Ounce of Prevention and a Pound of Cure: Developing State Policy on the Payment of Child Support Arrears by Low Income Parents." Center for Law and Social Policy, Washington, DC.

[41] Jane C. Venohr and Robert G. Williams. 1999. "The Implementation and Periodic Review of State Child Support Guidelines." *Family Law Quarterly* 33(1): 26–27.

[42] Ibid., p. 27.

[43] Ibid., p. 19.

the movement for the cost-shares approach is still in its infancy, several state lawmakers are taking the new methodology seriously; the Georgia legislature, for example, considered such a transformative bill during the summer of 2001.[44]

Finally, consider the third component of fathers' rights groups' rent-seeking position: implementing shared parenting laws as a means of reducing child support payments. There is, in general, a growing evolution of state law in this area. Many states have moved to modify child support awards when a child spends a "substantial" amount of time with the noncustodial parent. Each state, of course, defines "substantial" in a different way, but most jurisdictions consider at least 25 percent of a child's time spent with the noncustodial parent to be an actionable cause for a downward support adjustment. This is also known as the threshold "trigger" for modifications in child support awards.

There are a variety of ways in which support awards can be modified, from simple mechanisms to the more complex. Nineteen states approach the issue using a "deviation" system. Generally, this means that judges adhere to the established guideline award schedule unless one parent requests compensation for shared parenting. Judges can consider such requests and require compensation, but they must document their reasons for "deviating" from the guidelines in their decisions. As a rule, the judicial system in these states tends to discourage these types of exceptions.

Most nondeviation states where shared parenting is compensated as a matter of routine, such as Alaska, use a cross-credit approach. This means that a hypothetical support order is calculated for each parent based on his or her income level, and then each parent is credited accordingly with the amount of time he or she spends with the child. Other states, such as Wisconsin, compensate noncustodial parents for the costs associated with child rearing based on the number of overnights the child spends with each parent – the per diem approach. Still other states make allowances for time spent with the noncustodial parent based on particular cost categories (allowing certain costs to be compensated but not others), and a handful of states use a mathematical adjustment or formula to compensate noncustodial parents. Only a few states have refused to address the issue at all in their statutes. Table 7.2 summarizes these trends.

Overall, then, fathers' rights groups have had mixed success in achieving their goals. Programs serving low-income fathers have proliferated,

---

[44] House Bill 672 was sponsored by Rep. Earl Ehrhart (R-Powder Springs) and co-sponsored by Rep. Ben Allen (D-Augusta) during the 2001 legislative session.

TABLE 7.2. *Shared parenting trends, 2000*

State	Approach	Type	Time Threshold
Alabama	Deviation		
Alaska	Formula	Cross-credit	30%
Arizona	Formula	Cost category	
Arkansas	Deviation		
California	Formula	Adjustment	20%
Colorado	Formula	Cross-credit	25%
Connecticut	Deviation		
Delaware	Formula	Cross-credit	50%
District of Columbia	Formula	Cross-credit	40%
Florida	Deviation		
Georgia	Deviation		
Hawaii	Formula	Per diem	27%
Idaho	Formula	Cross-credit	35%
Illinois	Not addressed		
Indiana	Deviation		
Iowa	Not addressed		
Kansas	Formula	Cross-credit	50%
Kentucky	Not addressed		
Louisiana	Deviation		
Maine	Deviation		
Maryland	Formula	Cross-credit	35%
Massachusetts	Deviation		
Michigan	Formula	Adjustment	35%
Minnesota	Not addressed		
Mississippi	Deviation		
Missouri	Formula	Cost category	30%
Montana	Formula	Per diem	30%
Nebraska	Formula	Cross-credit	
Nevada	Deviation		
New Hampshire	Deviation		
New Jersey	Formula	Cost category	28%
New Mexico	Formula	Cross-credit	30%
New York	Not addressed		
North Carolina	Formula	Cross-credit	34%
North Dakota	Not Addressed		
Ohio	Deviation		
Oklahoma	Formula	Cross-credit	30%
Oregon	Formula	Cross-credit	35%
Pennsylvania	Not addressed		
Rhode Island	Deviation		
South Carolina	Deviation		
South Dakota	Deviation		

(continued)

TABLE 7.2. *(continued)*

State	Approach	Type	Time Threshold
Tennessee	Deviation		
Texas	Deviation		
Utah	Formula	Cross-credit	25%
Vermont	Formula	Cross-credit	30%
Virginia	Formula	Cross-credit	25%
Washington	Deviation		
West Virginia	Formula	Cross-credit	30%
Wisconsin	Formula	Per diem	30%
Wyoming	Formula	Cross-credit	40%

Source: The National Conference of State Legislatures, Child Support Project fact sheets compiled in April 2000.

with most policymakers in agreement that fathers' employment prospects must be improved if society is to hold them accountable for financially supporting their children. On the other hand, fathers' rights groups are still struggling to achieve award guideline modifications and credit for shared parenting. These two battlegrounds promise to be the most contested in the years to come.

CONCLUSIONS

Has the fathers' rights movement been successful in overtaking the incumbent set of policy entrepreneurs – women's groups and women legislators? This is the critical question upon which the current trajectory of political entrepreneurship will turn.

Clearly, fathers' rights groups have become increasingly vocal champions of their proper place in the child support debate. Practically, this has meant that, over time, members of Congress have actively sought out their opinions and advice on most proposed changes to the child support enforcement program. This is not a trivial development. During the late 1970s and early 1980s, not a single fathers' rights group was solicited for its views regarding reform. Now, from the late 1990s through the twenty-first century, fathers' rights groups are routinely consulted and encouraged to testify at committee hearings.

Substantively, fathers' rights groups have also made their mark. They have placed the critical issue of the capacity of low-income fathers to actually pay their ordered support on the national agenda. As we have seen, the issue has become a significant part of the public policy debate on legislative reform. The federal government is now pouring millions of dollars into demonstration projects designed to discover exactly how society should help fathers to meet their support obligations.

Yet, despite these gains, it is not clear that fathers' rights groups have completely overtaken their predecessors as controllers of child support policy. The federal government has not ordered the states to modify their guidelines, nor have the states been instructed to reduce the level of child support awards overall in exchange for shared parenting. The Fathers Count Act, the major fathers' rights initiative that passed in the House during 1999, but not in the Senate, is an example of this mixed success.

On November 10, 1999, the House passed the Fathers Count Act of 1999 by a vote of 328 to 93. Supported by numerous conservative organizations, and endorsed by then vice president Al Gore, the measure aimed to provide $155 million to organizations that support marriage and opportunities for low-income men to acquire jobs. Women's groups, however, were able to effectively question the necessity of these expenditures, arguing that over 80 percent of men who owe child support are not impoverished and thus not in need of such subsidies. Moreover, women's groups claimed that the bill had no protections for women who were victims of domestic violence. Under this legislation, women would be encouraged to marry their partners no matter what their past history of abuse might be. Using these arguments, women leaders were able to prevent the bill from coming up for a vote in the Senate the following year.

Yet, despite these defeats, fathers' rights groups show no signs of slowing down in their campaign to transform the entire nature of the child support system. Father's Day, for example, has taken on new meaning, as a variety of fathers' rights organizations are now using the occasion to march on Washington to gather support for their agenda. Moreover, in the spring of 2001, the American Coalition for Fathers and Children (ACFC) organized a nationwide protest against the family court system entitled "Building Bridges to Our Children." They brought together hundreds of men at family courts across the country to demand that they be considered more than "just a paycheck" in the child support system. And the Children's Rights Council held its Thirteenth Annual Conference in May 2001, with workshops on promoting shared custody, reducing parental alienation, and rethinking child support guidelines. Clearly, as the strength of these initiatives demonstrates, an active battle over who will control the next round of entrepreneurship is still under way.

8

Innovation and the Vibrancy of American Entrepreneurship

In the final analysis, how can we understand the process of policy change over the long run? One fact is certain. The path toward new public policy in the area of child support enforcement did *not* take rapid turns and twists over the last two centuries. Rather than being characterized by hairpin turns, the road was, at most, bumpy. Different sets of policy leaders were able to wrest control of the agenda at different points in time, producing change in sometimes surprising directions. But because their entrepreneurial activity reflected the core components of debate that Americans expect when it comes to political change, what could have been hostile takeovers instead became methodical transfers of power.

What we have seen is that new directions in policy are not cataclysmic events in the American political system. When a state legislature passes a new law creating term limits for elected officials and sends it to the governor for approval, the earth does not shake beneath us. When Congress establishes an innovative legislative approach to environmental waste management and the president agrees, the world does not come to an end. When the Supreme Court reverses itself over the death penalty, we all still get up the next day and go about our business.

The point is that while each of these events is newsworthy, the American public does not regard them with complete surprise. Change is inherent in our political system. We all know that one day we will face a new set of elected leaders, with perhaps different policy preferences than those of the past. We also know that the particular constellation of interest groups that currently holds sway will ultimately evolve, both in scope and composition. And we also sense that we, ourselves, might change our minds over the direction of specific public policies in the years to come.

And yet, while Americans may be accepting of change, it must be change pursued in a certain way. In the case of child support enforcement, for example, not everyone who has desired change has been able to effect change. The classic example is the propagation of the Child Support Assurance System (CSAS), a policy that was developed at the Institute for Research on Poverty (IRP) at the University of Wisconsin during the late 1970s. There, a team of researchers led by Irwin Garfinkel and aided by scholars all over the country, including Judith Cassetty, Harold Watts, and Isabel Sawhill, proposed a new system for ensuring that children receive a steady stream of child support payments.[1] In brief, the CSAS had three major components: (1) child support award guidelines that every judge had to follow, (2) child support withholding from paychecks, and (3) an assured benefit. Provisions (1) and (2) were relatively uncontroversial and later became part of national child support legislation with the passage of the Family Support Act of 1988. The assured benefit, however, ran into many more political difficulties.

The basic premise of the assured benefit was that no child should be without financial support owing to the absence of a father. It would be available to all families, rich or poor, where the father was absent. For those fathers who could afford to pay child support, there would be no assured benefit. But for all fathers whose private contributions were under a certain threshold, the assured benefit would kick in, filling in the gap between their private support and a certain guaranteed minimum provided by the government. For those fathers who were either unwilling or unable to pay support, the full assured benefit would automatically be delivered to the family. This benefit would count as taxable income for the resident parent and would continue until the child turned nineteen. For parents receiving public assistance, the assured benefit would be reduced dollar for dollar; however, the assured benefit would never be reduced for any income earned by the custodial parent. By the early 1990s, Garfinkel and his colleagues were proposing an assured benefit worth from $2,000 to $2,500 per child per year.

Despite the innovativeness of this idea, the assured benefit never became a fundamental part of child support policy. To understand why, one merely has to review the lessons for successful policy innovation contained in this book. First, consider the *who* of policy entrepreneurship. Political

---

[1] See Irwin Garfinkel. 1992. *Assuring Child Support.* New York: Russell Sage Foundation; Irwin Garfinkel, Sara S. McLanahan, and Philip K. Robins, eds. 1992. *Child Support Assurance.* Washington, DC: The Urban Institute Press.

science and economics have clearly brought us far in understanding entrepreneurs, albeit from vastly different perspectives. As a starting point, students of politics have frequently stressed the importance of defining the characteristics of potential innovators. Successful entrepreneurs must be constantly alert to new opportunities to affect the policy process. Because opportunities to take over as the new policy leaders in a particular issue realm are so rare, looking out for these moments becomes a full-time job. Entrepreneurs must also be persistent; while their friends and colleagues may be distracted by a wide variety of activities, the successful entrepreneur must be single-minded in the pursuit of a clearly defined goal. Finally, successful entrepreneurs must be skilled at using rhetorical ingenuity. Since there are so many competitors who wish to take over a particular issue area, hopeful policy leaders must be able to frame the issue in a way that is advantageous to themselves at the expense of their competitors.

In reflecting upon these ideas, one broad expansion of the potential set of innovative actors is imperative. Based on the characteristics delineated here, entrepreneurs can be much more than isolated individuals working on behalf of policy change. Rather, the evidence presented here suggests that there are important reasons to cast a wider definitional net. Policy innovators can include individuals, but can also include groups, professional organizations, legislative blocs of power, and social movements, among other combinations. In fact, we can better conceptualize these groups of entrepreneurs as *entrepreneurial movements*. All that matters is that the entrepreneurs exhibit the traits that are necessary for success.

Second, consider the *why* of policy entrepreneurship. We have suggested that the literature on rent seeking is especially informative in articulating the spark behind the entrepreneurial motivation. Like their counterparts in the economy seeking a competitive edge, policy entrepreneurs aim to gain a privileged position in government in order to further their own ends, needs, and position vis-à-vis others with competing visions for a better society. In order to accomplish this goal, they present their proposals in the marketplace of ideas and advocate on their behalf, hoping that their vision will top everyone else's. In the game of entrepreneurial politics, this is the quintessential war of words, where the value of freedom of speech is played out in the democratic arena every day.

Third, consider the *how* of policy entrepreneurship. As the discipline of economics has pointed out, risk taking is a fundamental component of executing change. Risk taking means that not only must entrepreneurs tolerate uncertainty reasonably well in their pursuits, they must also be willing to fund the important start-up costs in mounting this challenge. To reduce risk, entrepreneurs should avoid acting alone. Instead, successful entrepreneurs will decrease their risk by building solid organizations of like-minded individuals committed to the same cause. The key is getting as many people involved in the process as possible. And while some might join in the excitement of the moment, the value of political participation is what sustains this action over the long run.

In addition to risk taking, entrepreneurs must be willing and able to execute an effective shakeout strategy, thereby dislodging the current holders of the reins of power in order to replace them in their leadership roles. But entrepreneurs must use only legitimate shakeout strategies; that is, they can use only techniques that are commonly accepted by the American public. These include media exposés of their opponents, changing institutional rules in order to benefit themselves at the expense of their foes, altering the terms of the debate, and so forth. Those entrepreneurs who operate outside these boundaries – by advocating and/or using force, fraud, or deception to eliminate their competition – do nothing but set themselves up for innovation failure.

So why did the assured benefit fail to become a critical component of child support policy? The advocates of reform – or the *who* of policy entrepreneurship – were alert, persistent, and used rhetorical ingenuity. There is no doubt that advocates of this approach lobbied state and national leaders whenever and wherever possible to present their ideas. Indeed, from 1980 onward, they were able to convince state legislators in both Wisconsin and New York to pilot test their program.[2] They also cast the assured benefit as a fundamental component of reducing child poverty, a clever use of rhetorical ingenuity because the public, to the extent that it favors doing anything about poverty, favors measures that protect the very young and the very old first.

In addition, their rent-seeking position – the *why* of entrepreneurship – was also clear: they wanted fathers to continue to pay private support wherever possible, but also demanded that the government intervene if and when the private system failed. As academics, they could also claim the moral high ground in making their arguments; that is, their rent-seeking position did not seem selfish, at least on its surface. They did not

---

[2] See, for example, Irwin Garfinkel. June 30 and July 1, 1992. Testimony on "Downey-Hyde Child Support Enforcement and Assurance Proposal." Hearing before the Subcommittee on Human Resources of the Committee on Ways and Means, United States House of Representatives.

want anything *personally* from a shift in policy. They simply wanted to improve the lives of children across the country.

The real failure lies in the *how* of policy entrepreneurship. Advocates of the assured benefit were never able to mount a cooperative risk-reduction strategy. Designers of the policy at the Institute for Research on Poverty at the University of Wisconsin never built a comprehensive organizational infrastructure to push their idea forward. In 1984, for example, Congress granted Wisconsin permission to seek a waiver for a pilot test of the assured benefit as long as the drafters of the proposed policy could show that it did not harm children. However, between 1984 and 1986, there was a gubnatorial election, one that replaced Democratic Governor Anthony Earl with Republican Tommy Thompson. Thompson, initially a foe of the measure because he feared it would increase welfare costs, later compromised on the pilot project issue. However, partly as a result of his administration's worries and delays, local county officials became mobilized against the project. Indeed, by 1990, only four counties were able to test the assured benefit – the issue was, in effect, politically dead. Advocates of the assured benefit, most of them located in academic centers scattered across the country, were never able to persuade a large and committed body of politicians and bureaucrats to run wholeheartedly forward with their ideas.

Advocates of the assured benefit also never devised an effective means of "shaking out" their competition. Recall that the assured benefit was proposed during a period when conservatives and then women leaders were the prominent policymakers on the issue. In order to properly shake out these adversaries, they had to render their opponents immobilized or at least weakened through some type of legitimate political strategy. Yet the leaders of this new approach to child support were academics, not politicians. They therefore tended to focus on the merit of their ideas in the purest sense, as simply "better" than the ideas that were currently being played out in the policy realm. They paid much less attention to strategies that could dislodge the incumbents in power, and partly because of this oversight, their ideas were never able to get off the ground.

There are lessons to be learned from this failure for those who want to change public policy not only in the area of child support enforcement, but in other areas as well. Ideas are clearly important. Without a good idea, nobody will begin to pay attention. But ideas are not the only things that matter in effecting change. Policy entrepreneurship is a full-time pursuit, necessitating full-time efforts to move ideas forward. It is a full frontal mission without any room for mistakes, false steps, or a lack of planning.

In the end, strategy matters just as much as the ideas themselves, for without strategy, ideas simply sit forever incubating, regardless of where they were hatched.

THE CURRENT CLIMATE FOR CHILD SUPPORT INNOVATION

On June 7, 2001, President George W. Bush left the White House and traveled the short distance to the Hyatt Regency Hotel on Capitol Hill. Flanked on one side by Secretary of Health and Human Services Tommy Thompson and on the other by Senator Evan Bayh (D-Ind.), Senator Thomas Carper (D-Del.), and Representative J.C. Watts (R-Okla.), President Bush addressed the over 500 men and women attending the National Fatherhood Initiative's Fourth Annual National Summit. He began his speech without delay.

The fatherhood movement is diverse, but it is united by one belief: Fathers have a unique and irreplaceable role in the lives of children. For our children and for our nation, nothing is more important than this initiative.

Nearly every man who has a child wants to be a good father. I truly believe that. It's a natural longing of the human heart to care for and cherish your child. But this longing must find concrete expression. Raising a child requires sacrifice, effort, time and presence. And there is a wide gap between our best intentions and the reality of today's society.[3]

The core of Bush's fatherhood plan presented there brought together many of his own personal domestic priorities into one overarching theme: the promotion of the traditional family unit. On that day, he announced that his administration would simultaneously promote two fundamental goals. First, the states would be encouraged to pursue increased flexibility through their TANF programs in order to foster father-friendly families. Second, the federal government would provide community and faith-based initiatives with $64 million in fiscal year 2002 to offer job training, parenting, and marital skills programs to certain targeted populations. On top of this amount, the federal government would funnel over $300 million to the states over the next five years to fund programs that help keep families together.

Bush described his plans before the National Fatherhood Initiative (NFI), an organization begun by Dr. Wade Horn, a clinical child psychologist, in 1994. Horn started the NFI with the primary goal of increasing

---

[3] These are President George W. Bush's comments to the National Fatherhood Initiative. Accessed at <http://www.fatherhood.org/presidentbush.htm> on July 31, 2001.

fathers' involvement in their children's lives. Over its short life, the NFI has pursued three interlinked policy strategies. First, the organization conducts wide-ranging public education campaigns to encourage fathers to become more responsible parents. Second, the NFI has become actively involved with states and localities to promote the principles of strong fatherhood within families. Toward this end and under the leadership of Horn, the NFI has worked closely with the National Governors Association and state-level social service agencies to strengthen the emotional bonds between fathers and their children. Finally, the organization publishes educational materials that are distributed to local communities and fathers in need of a more structured way to approach their paternal role.

That Bush presented his proposals first before the NFI, and only later before the nation, was no accident. The ties that bound the president to the NFI were the product of a working relationship that had begun while Bush was still governor of Texas during the late 1990s. Impressed by the work of the organization, then-governor Bush announced one of the first statewide fatherhood programs in the country – the Texas Fatherhood Initiative (TFI) – in December 1999. Receiving a two-year seed grant from the governor's office, the TFI developed a series of programs to bring attention to the nature and complexity of the fatherlessness problem in the state. These programs included establishing community-based fatherhood programs across the state and starting the Texas Fatherhood Resource Center, which continues to offer referrals, educational materials, and technical assistance to those groups committed to helping fathers build new relationships with their children.

But Bush's decision to announce his administration's plans before the NFI and the nature of the proposals themselves were much more than a tribute to ideas that he had embraced while still in Texas; they were also indicative of the new wave of child support policy that is currently on the horizon. By the very nature of Bush's brief comments, it was clear that fathers' rights groups had started to make a strong impact on the policy agenda. On that June day, Bush chose *not* to decry the millions of dollars that were outstanding in owed child support, nor did he hold up "deadbeat dads" as emblematic of society's worst problems. Instead, on that day, Bush was entirely sympathetic to the plight of fathers attempting to make a difference in their children's lives. To Bush, all fathers clearly *wanted* to contribute to their children's well-being. The problem, as articulated in the president's approach to the issue, was that (1) men did not know how to be good fathers, and (2) men needed the resources that the federal government could provide in teaching them how to be effective parents.

Yet, as soon as the president offered fathers a sympathetic ear, the battle over the child support agenda reached a new, feverish pitch. Women leaders, still trying to hold on to the title of the Incumbent Entrepreneurs, came out with fighting words against the president's proposals. They first attacked Wade Horn, who, in addition to being president of the NFI, had recently been nominated by Bush to the position of assistant secretary of family support at the Department of Health and Human Services. Horn was on record in a variety of publications as believing that many public benefits, such as TANF and Head Start, should first be allocated to stable, two-parent families rather than to single-parent families. There should be, in his words, a prioritizing of different family types as they queued up for aid. This misguided system, women leaders argued, would place single-parent families – usually mother-headed families – in severe financial distress. They would now rank second to the traditional family unit in their quest to secure the resources they need to support their children.

More odious to the women leaders than the nomination and later confirmation of Wade Horn to a high-level administration position was the content of Bush's ideas on child support policy. Of these, the new TANF initiatives sounded a particularly piercing alarm. Their concerns originated in the formal language of the 1996 law, which laid out four family formation goals: (1) "to provide assistance to needy families so that children may be cared for in their own homes or in the homes of relatives"; (2) "to end dependence of needy parents on government benefits by promoting job preparation, work and marriage"; (3) "to prevent and reduce the incidence of out-of-wedlock pregnancies and establish annual numerical goals for preventing and reducing the incidence of these pregnancies"; and (4) "to encourage the formation and maintenance of two-parent families."[4] In order to achieve these goals, the federal government has offered "incentive payments" to the states based on the percentage point increase they report in the number of children living with married parents.

By 2002, states had responded to these incentives in a variety of ways. Some had targeted a broad-based population in their efforts. Virginia's Partners in Prevention program, for example, uses TANF monies in local

---

[4] Language from the Personal Responsibility and Work Opportunity Reconciliation Act of 1996, P.L. 104–193, Title 1, Part A, Section 401.

community groups to emphasize that marriage is the context in which all children should be born. Other proposals aim to reward women currently on welfare with cash bonuses if they marry the father of their children. Mississippi, North Dakota, and Oklahoma have endeavored to encourage marriage by disregarding all income of the new spouse in calculating benefits during a post-wedding period of between three and six months. West Virginia allows a $100 marriage incentive payment to any family that includes a married couple. Still other states, such as Arizona and Oklahoma, have used large grants under the TANF program to sponsor pro-marriage initiatives, including public awareness campaigns and outreach to young parents.

Not surprisingly, women leaders have adamantly opposed these initiatives, arguing that they are simply a repackaging of the failed Fathers Count Act of 1999, which they had so adamantly opposed.[5] Not a single American woman, they argue, should have to marry her way out of poverty. Marriage is a highly personal issue, and should not be driven by purely economic calculations. Moreover, to the extent that the government should be involved in women's lives at all, legislators should focus on issues such as raising the minimum wage, providing affordable child care, ending sex discrimination in pay, and decreasing occupational segregation. These measures would enable women to be economically self-sufficient on their own, without having to rely on a man for financial support. These alternative types of financial assistance would also help support all types of families, and not penalize some families based on their male-female composition.

Women leaders argue that these marriage incentive plans also ignore the harsh realities already facing many women on welfare. Women often leave relationships and turn to welfare because of emotional or physical abuse. Several studies have documented these patterns of maltreatment among welfare recipients. In one survey of over 700 welfare clients in Massachusetts, for example, over 19.5 percent reported some type of

---

[5] See, for example, the websites of the National Organization for Women <www.now.org>, the National Women's Law Center <www.nwlc.org>, and the Feminist Majority <www.feminist.org>, which all posted information on this issue in July 2001. Also see testimony from Jacqueline Payne, Martha Davis, Yolanda Wu, and Sherry Lewant. May 22, 2001. "Statement of the NOW Legal Defense Fund." Hearing before the Subcommittee on Human Resources of the Committee on Ways and Means, United States House of Representatives; Joan Entacher. June 28, 2001. "Welfare and Marriage Issues." Hearing before the Subcommittee on Human Resources of the Committee on Ways and Means, United States House of Representatives. Both hearings accessed at <http://thomas.loc.gov> on August 2, 2001.

domestic violence. Similarly, in another survey of over 800 recipients in New Jersey, 14.6 percent reported being victimized by domestic abuse.[6] Marriage incentive plans would do nothing but force these abusive relationships back together again, placing the women involved in grave danger.

Another part of Bush's proposals that strikes fear in women leaders is the particular way in which the money would be targeted toward fathers. On one level, there is simply the question of resource allocation. Single mothers clearly need more help in making ends meet than men, who, for the most part, do not shoulder as much of the childrearing responsibilities in contemporary American families. Equally incendiary for women leaders is the designation of groups that will be in charge of distributing these funds. If most fathers' rights groups become eligible, then fringe groups that still advocate a strong antiwoman agenda would receive financial assistance. For example, the Fathers' Rights Coalition, an organization that distributes pamphlets to fathers on the most effective ways to reduce and avoid their child support payments, could soon be in charge of distributing millions of dollars in federal assistance.

From all of this activity, it is clear that right now, there are no winners in the child support debate. Women leaders and fathers' rights groups continue to argue their case, each aiming to outmaneuver the other. And so without final resolution the struggle goes on, as does the cycle of political entrepreneurship.

THE TRANSFORMATION PROCESS AND THE VIBRANCY OF AMERICAN ENTREPRENEURSHIP

As this book has demonstrated, entrepreneurial policymaking has been alive and active in one critical area of public policy: child support enforcement. Rather than taking a single snapshot view of the problem, we have pursued a long-range analysis. Tracking this issue over time has been important because by so doing, we have completely revolutionized our understanding of the entrepreneurial process.

Traditional views of policy innovators have portrayed them as one-time players in the political arena. In other words, social scientists have

---

[6] Both surveys are reported in Jody Raphaeland and Richard M. Tolman. April 1997. *Trapped by Poverty /Trapped by Abuse: New Evidence Documenting the Relationship Between Welfare and Domestic Violence*. Chicago and Ann Arbor: Project for Research on Welfare, Work, and Domestic Violence.

argued that a single set of entrepreneurs lies in wait with a novel way of approaching a particular public policy problem. When a politically opportune moment to act finally arrives, these policy leaders quickly attach their preferred solution to the problem and then exit from the political arena. Their work, in effect, is done. Unless the political climate dramatically shifts, no other group is expected to address this problem again.

While this might be an adequate conceptualization of how "easy" public policy problems are solved, the model does significantly worse at elucidating how long-standing social problems are attacked by policy entrepreneurs. A simple example demonstrates this dynamic. For years, environmentalists lobbied state and city governments to implement newspaper and bottle recycling programs. Although local officials were initially resistant, they finally instituted such programs. Environmental activists, satisfied with these results, moved on to other, more pressing issues. Barring any new movement toward recycling retrenchment, environmentalists, in effect, left the political stage on that issue for good. This is, by one definition, an "easy" problem. It is clearly delimited and thus amenable to a carefully specified solution proposed by a single group of political actors.

The case of child support enforcement has showed us that entrepreneurial politics can be much more complex. Social problems often must receive the attention of multiple sets of policy entrepreneurs before an adequate dent is made in the lives of the people at issue. More specifically, with the rise in the number of single-parent families throughout the nineteenth, twentieth, and early twenty-first centuries, more and more children have been subject to the ill effects of financial instability. In these new, usually fatherless homes, children face not only lower incomes, but also an increased chance of experiencing a whole host of negative outcomes, including juvenile delinquency, teenage pregnancy, and drug addiction. To transform this tide after the charity workers and local law enforcement began the development of child support policy, four successive waves of entrepreneurs have lined up in this policy arena, each with a unique mission and approach to transforming the policy agenda.

From the 1900s to the 1960s, social workers were the primary advocates on behalf of the poor and, in particular, female-headed families. When many of their ideas, such as community action programs and grassroots economic organization, failed to achieve their expected results, conservatives moved in to fill this leadership vacuum during the mid-1970s. These conservatives argued that in order to improve the lives of young families on welfare, fathers must be held accountable. Rather than allowing the federal and state-level governments to provide for these families, fathers must step in and reimburse the public coffers for the expenditures already paid out on behalf of their offspring. These conservatives thus introduced the early, founding philosophy of the child support enforcement program, which targeted collection efforts at fathers of children on AFDC. However, because the number of low-income female-headed households continued to escalate, a new set of policy leaders – women legislators and women's organizations – argued that child support enforcement should take on a second mission. Rather than simply reimbursing the federal and state governments for welfare expenditures, child support establishment services should be extended to nonwelfare mothers as well, thus preventing them from having to rely on the public purse in the first place. The latest entrepreneurial contenders to enter the arena have been fathers' rights groups. While their goals are varied, they remain concerned with ensuring that low-income fathers can meet their support goals, modifying state award guidelines, and acquiring compensation for time spent with their children beyond ordinary visitation.

What will the future bring in terms of innovation in the child support arena? The literature on policy analysis suggests two possibilities – in the terms laid out by Frank R. Baumgartner and Bryan D. Jones, either a *negative feedback cycle or a positive feedback cycle*.[7] Under the negative feedback view of the world, the political system can be viewed as largely homeostatic. As Baumgartner and Jones explain, policy dynamics often function as a self-regulating system. Whenever there is some type of pressure on the system, counterpressure emerges to stabilize all political players. Policy is therefore relatively constrained – each political actor is always assessing how far he or she can alter the status quo without incurring the fairly predictable counterattacks that are always on the horizon.

In one of the most-cited perspectives using the negative feedback model, David Truman in his classic *The Governmental Process* argued that policy change can, in fact, be somewhat predictable.[8] Each cycle of policy change derives from the hard work of groups that aim to move their particular agenda forward. In this "disturbance theory," groups that are successful can alter the policy landscape by pushing forth new ideas that run directly counter to past practice. Yet with each success, there is a rebound effect. Groups that achieve their goals must often confront powerful countermobilization efforts by those who oppose their goals. There is, in a

[7] Frank R. Baumgartner and Bryan D. Jones. 2002. *Policy Dynamics*. Chicago: University of Chicago Press.

[8] David Truman. 1951. *The Governmental Process*. New York: Knopf.

sense, frequently an overextension effect created by the policy "winners." Opponents can be expected with some degree of certainty to roll back some of the recently implemented changes in the next wave of policy battles.

Yet this book demonstrates that policy change is not as predictable as Truman would expect. Instead, elements of Baumgartner and Jones's *positive feedback cycle* are clearly apparent. In the positive feedback policy world, change is much more erratic. Rather than the political system operating as a self-correcting, fairly contained body of pressures and counter-pressures, public policy in the positive feedback paradigm is fluid. Dramatic breaks with past initiatives can occur under this regime, because there are no built-in barricades to success. Rather, there are numerous dynamics in place that can, in a sense, "prime the pump" for a series of rapidly different policy regimes.

One of the most important of these dynamics is attention shifting. As human beings, we are necessarily limited in the amount of information we can process on a given issue at a given time. Issues are complex, and more significantly, the world around us is complex. It is virtually impossible to understand every single point related to every single public policy issue that enters the political domain. To make sense of this multidimensional world, then, we must rely on the information that is filtered to us by highly motivated actors who crave policy change. Those entrepreneurs who can attract enough attention that their worldview rises above the din of the activists around them can succeed in bringing about a tidal wave of new policy reforms.

It is thus *not* the case that each group that ultimately "wins" in the policy arena creates an environment of excess, which is then rolled back by the next group of leaders in this area. Instead, what we have witnessed with child support enforcement is that each group contesting public policy represents a *separate* stream of activism. More specifically, these groups are pursuing their own rent-seeking agenda, at times without any reference to past gains by their opponents. These are groups that are forward-looking in their vision, and not necessarily looking for ways to undo the past. And, as we have seen, many have succeeded in sponsoring sea changes in public policy.

This again brings us to the question of what child support policy will look like in the future. This all depends on the actions of the entrepreneurial leaders of tomorrow. It is possible that we will see the resurfacing of past political players, such as the social workers, as they craft new, service-oriented ways to approach the problem. It is also possible that we will witness the emergence of new entrepreneurial groups who promise to take the issue in a completely different direction. Psychiatrists could organize around the issue, arguing that monetary support has some type of impact, as yet undisclosed, on a child's mental health. Mothers' groups could organize in direct opposition to the fathers' groups that are now flourishing across the country. And with increasing numbers of older Americans taking care of their children's children, grandparents might spearhead their own movement for reform. Like every other cycle of entrepreneurship, this one is just waiting to unfold.

Index